AWOL ON THE
APPALACHIAN TRAIL

DAVID MILLER

PUBLISHED BY:

amazon encore

Published by AmazonEncore
P.O. Box 400818
Las Vegas, NV 89140

ISBN-13: 9781935597193
ISBN-10: 1935597191

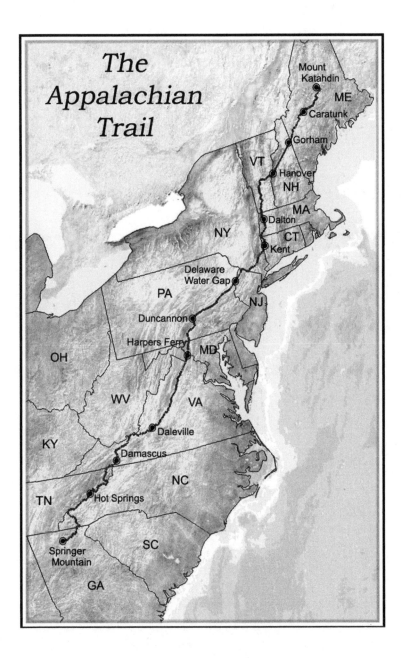

The Appalachian Trail

Mount Katahdin

ME

Caratunk

Gorham

VT

Hanover

NH

MA

Dalton

CT

NY

Kent

Delaware Water Gap

PA

NJ

Duncannon

Harpers Ferry

MD

OH

WV

VA

Daleville

KY

Damascus

NC

TN

Hot Springs

Springer Mountain

SC

GA

Contents

Introduction

In the spring of 2003, a few thousand people strapped on backpacks and headed out into the mountains of north Georgia. Their destination: Maine, over two thousand miles away. Eighty percent of them didn't make it.

The path they follow is called the Appalachian Trail, commonly referred to as the AT. It starts on the summit of Springer Mountain in Georgia and ends on top of Mount Katahdin in Maine.

Imagine drifting in a hot air balloon over the wooded hills of the Appalachian Mountain range, on a course that parallels the northeasterly slant of the eastern seacoast, low enough to peer down between the trees. You'll see a well-worn trail threading its way through trees, over rocks, over mountains, and down valleys. The AT doesn't skirt the mountaintops. Instead it takes a punitive path over every peak it can find. Few stretches of the trail form a straight line. In places, the trail curves wildly, seemingly with will, to buck off the hikers or ramp them over yet another hill. All this bobbing and weaving adds mileage. On foot the distance from Springer to Katahdin is 2,172 miles. Your balloon ride would be only thirteen hundred miles with significantly reduced risk of snakebite.

The trail passes through fourteen states. The mountains of Georgia and North Carolina are steep and densely wooded, immediately challenging hikers' resolve. The Great Smoky Mountains National Park, on the border of North Carolina and Tennessee, has more varieties of trees than there are in all of Europe. Virginia is less physically demanding than the first three states. Hikers celebrate upon reaching the town of Damascus, then move into Grayson Highlands, with open grassy ranges and wild ponies. By the middle of Virginia, hikers have walked off the enthusiasm they had at the start of their journey, and the end is still nowhere in sight. One quarter of the AT is in Virginia. The ten miles of trail in West Virginia are notable for passing through the headquarters of the Appalachian Trail Conference in Harpers Ferry.[1] This is the emotional halfway point.

In western Maryland the trail clips through Civil War battlefields. Pennsylvania and New Jersey are infamous for rocks. Hikers have days in which they hardly ever touch soil. The AT in New York finds a corridor of woods between the mainland and Long Island. The cultured New England states of Connecticut, Massachusetts, and Vermont contrast with the haggard look of hikers who have endured months on the trail. The White Mountain National Forest in New Hampshire is one of the most scenic and hazardous sections of the trail. Sixteen miles of the trail are above tree line. The trail finishes fittingly with the longest ascent on the AT, a five-mile climb to the summit of Mount Katahdin in Maine.

The Appalachian Trail was conceived by Benton MacKaye in 1921. He envisioned an outdoor recreation area that city dwellers would use on weekends and vacations. For the most

---

1   The name was changed in 2005 to Appalachian Trail Conservancy. For a wealth of data about the AT, visit www.AppalachianTrail.org.

part, that is what the AT has become. The majority of people who set foot on the trail return to their homes at night.

What Benton MacKaye did not anticipate was anyone touched with the desire to walk continuously from end to end. No one did until 1948, when World War II veteran Earl Shaffer lugged his army rucksack from Georgia to Maine. Shaffer's accomplishment came to be known as a "thru-hike," and everyone who does the feat is called a "thru-hiker." This story is about the year I became one of them.

A thru-hike is an extended nomadic camping trip. Follow the path through the woods all day. Stop, set up camp, eat, and sleep. Get up, pack your things, and start walking again. At times the AT is steep enough to require hauling yourself up with your hands, but you won't need climbing skills or equipment. You carry your house (tent), your bed (sleeping bag), your stove, your food, and everything else you need until the next opportunity to resupply. If you need it, you have to carry it.

AT backpackers carry enough food to last three to five days. The food needs to be lightweight and durable. "Cooking" is adding hot water to something light and durable to make it edible. Hikers cherish the opportunity to eat real food. Opportunities come when the trail crosses a road within walking or hitching distance of a town. Hikers fill their bellies, clean up, and sometimes get medical care. They restock their packs with store-bought supplies, or supplies they've arranged to have mailed and held for them at post offices. Drinking water comes primarily from streams and springs along the trail. Most hikers will treat the water chemically or with a filter.

The towns know the hikers are coming, and hikers know every one of these towns: Hot Springs, North Carolina;

Damascus, Virginia; Harpers Ferry, West Virginia; Duncannon, Pennsylvania; and Hanover, New Hampshire. Trail towns and the people who live near the trail are an integral part of the AT hiking experience.

Every hundred yards or so a tree or rock will be painted with a vertical bar of white—a "white blaze"—six inches tall and two inches wide, marking the AT. Hikers do get lost, but it is not common. More frequently, a hiker will take a break and resume hiking in the wrong direction, sometimes for miles. When you have a monumental number of miles to travel, repeating even a single mile is disheartening.

The typical thru-hike takes six months with an average of twelve miles walked per day. Hikers must reach Katahdin by October 15 when the park containing the mountain closes for the winter, so they usually start in March or April. Most thru-hikers go it alone. About three out of four hikers are men, but the percentage of women is increasing. The majority of thru-hikers have recently graduated or retired.

None of my peers could concisely articulate why they were doing a thru-hike. Most were motivated by a convergence of reasons. The time was right, they liked being outdoors, they were tired of their job (or their employer was tired of them), they wanted to lose weight, they had friends hiking, or they were inspired by another person's thru-hiking experience. The outdoor experience gives you a chance to get away from it all, have time for introspection, and to go many days in a row wearing the same unlaundered clothes on your unwashed body.

The exertion of carrying a pack up and down mountains day after day is incredibly fatiguing. You get hungry, you get rained on, your feet blister, and your legs ache. While hiking, you experience hardship, deprivation, drudgery, and pain, and the cooking stinks. The similarities to marriage don't end there. Some people love it, and many are committed to seeing it through.

Thru-hikers love to tell how steep the trail is and how much it rained because the difficulty of the endeavor is also part of the appeal. Many of the most gratifying experiences in life are those that are the most demanding. Seemingly in contradiction to the low probability of a successful thru-hike is the fact that anyone can thru-hike. A six-year-old has done it, and many grandmothers have done it. The trail was completed by Orient, a guide dog, and his master, Bill Irwin, who thru-hiked in 1990.

Back in late April of 2003, I wrote this brief description of myself before starting my hike:

I am 41 years old, and I've worked since getting out of college as a computer programmer. I'm in decent shape for a person who's been holed up in an office for so long. I'm married and have three little girls. Our fifteenth wedding anniversary will pass in my absence. Nothing is wrong with my life. My family is outstanding. I have what most people would consider to be a decent job. I'm not unhappy, and I'm not hiking to escape from anything. My life is precariously normal. I've been told that taking this trip at this time in my life is irresponsible, a charge I won't contest. Maybe doing it later in life would make more sense. But my father had bypass surgery and my mom is fighting cancer. My opinion of "later" is jaded.

I'm headed for Maine.

Jessie's Letter

April 24 2003

It is 3:10 P.M. on a Thursday, and my too little sisters my parents and I are geting redy for one of the bigest days of our LIVES my dad is going to hike the Afalation Trail! Now you might be thinching, So what? But, So What? is for people who don't know what the Afalation Trail actuley is. So let me put it to you this way, it's a Big trail. Still not imprest? Maybe you need more details. The Afalation trail is 2172 miles long from Gordia to Maine. Well thats all for now, By!

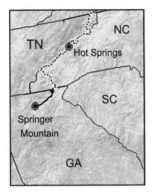

1
Springer Mountain to Hiawassee

My journey started with a walk that had my heart pounding and my legs burning. Sweat drenched my shirt and got in my eyes. Thirty minutes and I hadn't gone anywhere. That was a year ago on a treadmill after being turned down for a leave of absence to hike the Appalachian Trail. I was determined to hike in a year, even if it meant going AWOL.

For over a year of training on a treadmill, I never got blisters, never went uphill so steeply I could touch the ground ahead of me, and never got rained on. All of these things beset me within days of starting my hike.

Computer programming was the job from which I walked away. My last assignment put me in the dark corner of a little-used building. On a good day, two or three people would pass by my desk. Other programmers seemed content to plug themselves into their machines—attached to the keyboard by their fingers—for nine hours a day. When a programmer had an issue, he would get on the phone to another programmer two cubes away. I could hear both ends of the conversation. They could have heard each other without the phone. I felt out of place. I struggled to stay awake, propped my eyes open with cups of coffee, and fantasized about winning the lottery.

If I had been given a leave of absence the first time I asked, it might have tempered my enthusiasm. Getting turned down solidified my resolve. I pondered the future. Would I continue reporting to a cube until retirement, with a few vacation days sprinkled in? After putting in ten years with my current employer, I would start earning three weeks of vacation a year. Yippee!

This is how it's "done" in middle-class America. Shouldn't I be thankful that life is as comfortable as it is? Most people are devastated if they lose their jobs. At the beginning of April in 2003, I broke the news to my boss. He said, "If you need to have a midlife crisis, couldn't you just buy a Corvette?" I appreciated him for putting me at ease with his humor. I even considered taking "Corvette" for a trail name. He was supportive and did all he could to get me a leave. It just wasn't part of corporate policy.

As I tell my story, I will speak of other inspirations for my hike. In doing so I am not contradicting myself. My job dissatisfaction was just one factor in my decision to hike the AT. Most thru-hikers, when asked, will offer up a single motivation. In part it is the reason currently dominating his thoughts, in part it is the type of answer that is expected, and in part it is the type of answer that is easiest to give. It is not that simple. The reasons for a thru-hike are less tangible than many other big decisions in life. And the reasons evolve. Toward the end, possibly the most sustaining rationale to finish a thru-hike is the fact that you have started one.

I chose to start late—April 25—to avoid the winter, although many nights during my first month on the trail were chilly for my native Floridian blood, dipping into the thirties. I planned to finish quickly, also to avoid cold weather, and to minimize time away from my family (my wife, Juli, and our three daughters). A "quick" thru-hike is four months or less. The typical AT thru-hike takes over five months.

❀ ❀ ❀

My family drives with me to the start of the trail at Amicalola Falls, and we stay in the wonderful rustic resort located there. I leave my wife and kids in the room and head up the infamously rigorous eight-mile approach trail in a misty morning rain. To my surprise, the hike is not challenging. I feel fresh, and the exertion is overwhelmed by my excitement. New growth on the forest floor, coupled with the dampness, gives the trail a tropical feel. I use the timer on my camera to get a photo of myself walking out into the fog on the trail as it slices through a field of one-foot-tall umbrella-shaped plants.

Resisting the urge to burst down the trail, I focus on self-preservation. I've heard a thru-hike will take five million steps, and I naively reason that I can land softly on every one and keep making painless steps all the way to Katahdin.

On top of Springer Mountain I pick out a small rock, intending to deliver it to Mount Katahdin in Maine. There is a log book, with forty-five thru-hikers signed in on March 1, but today I make the first entry. I've walked the approach trail without seeing anyone.

I pass my first white blaze.[2] On the way down from Springer, I feel a twitch on the outside of my right knee. I lift my foot and shake it, trying to loosen the feeling of contracted thigh muscles. The feeling is still there, faint and foreboding. Nine-tenths of a mile down from the top of Springer, my family waits for me at Big Stamp Gap. I return with them for another night in the lodge. Tomorrow they will return me to the gap, where we will say our goodbyes, and I'll start my hike in earnest.

Back at the lodge, we walk tourist trails near the top of Amicalola Falls. My knee has stiffened, and on every downward step I feel an unmistakable, undeniable twinge of pain. Worry and guilt cast a shadow over the last night with my family. This knee problem could be the end of my hike. I should've done more to prepare myself. I think of all the people that I've told about my adventure. I quit my job. I promised to write updates for my hometown newspaper. I feel foolish. I'll be one of the statistics, one of the hikers that other hikers half-mock for quitting before getting out of Georgia. Juli agrees to delay her trip home until I've passed my first bailout point.

Juli and the girls return me to Big Stamp Gap. My girls are beautiful. Every night I go to their rooms to look at them sleeping. I walk away from them now with plans for them to visit me only once on the trail. It will be the longest I've been separated from them, and it is incredibly difficult. I feel a knot forming in my throat, and tears drop on the trail. I hope no other hiker sees me.

---

2   The Appalachian Trail is marked by stripes of white approximately six inches tall and two inches wide, usually painted on trees at eye level. In the absence of trees, blazes are painted on rocks or signposts. Ideally, the blazes are spaced such that the next white blaze is visible from the current one.

The trail is picturesque, moderate, and varied. There are pines, rhododendrons, stream crossings, and just a few rocky areas. It is all a novelty to me. I try to put into words all that I see. I take pictures of everything. I stop to photograph mica glittering at my feet, unusually formed trees, and the trail submerged by a diverted stream. I pass the day quickly, my senses overloaded with the sights, smells, and sounds of the trail, my head swimming with emotion.

Peter, the first thru-hiker I meet, sits on the side of the trail. He's young, thin, pale, and quiet. I guess he is just out of college, probably from a northern state. We talk little. We are both tentative about socializing, and besides, I feel certain I will meet up with him again soon enough.

I come upon the short side trail to Gooch Gap Shelter sooner than I expect. I've caught up with section hikers looking at Wingfoot, the same guidebook that I have, also questioning if the structure one hundred yards away is really what we think it is.[3] I can see the shelter looks full. Gear is hung from the roof, and I can hear the indistinct hum of conversation. I'm not ready to walk into a shelter full of hikers. I want more time alone to get comfortable with my new world.

Further on, I check out another rickety shelter. This must be the old Gooch Gap Shelter that is to be disassembled. Sleeping bags cover the floor, but there are no hikers in them; they must be getting water. Happy to have missed them, I hike on. At Gooch Gap there is a gravel road crossing and a camping area full of noisy Boy Scouts and their irritated leaders. My day is getting long—much longer than

---

3   Dan "Wingfoot" Bruce, *The Thru-Hiker's Handbook* (Conyers, GA: Center for Appalachian Trail Studies, 2003). Thru-hikers most often refer to it as "Wingfoot" instead of by title. Mr. Bruce has since retired. For a contemporary guidebook, visit: www.theATguide.com.

expected—and now the trail is headed uphill. I was supposed to be coddling my knee. Is that an ache I feel?

On the shoulder of Ramrock Mountain, I finally find
an inviting campsite. I am efficient at getting my tarp up
and dinner made. Using Wingfoot, I figure I've walked 17.6
miles my first full day on the trail, with a late (10:30) start
and a worrisome knee. I'm not ready to berate myself for
the long day. It just happened. Walking longer than intended would become routine for me on the AT. If there was a
full shelter, an imperfect campsite, or an undesirable crowd,
my solution was always to keep walking. The lack of knee
pain is inexplicable good fortune. But I'm still not out of the
woods, figuratively and literally.

I am on my way—really doing it—hiking the Appalachian Trail. My equipment all has the fresh, crisp, clean look
and the new vinyl smell it had in the sporting goods store. I
am still clean, shaven, and relatively unworn. The air is crisp
and clear, branches are barren, and the forest is budding
with the newness of spring. All is in harmony.

Near midnight I wake to relieve myself. I stumble out to
a perfectly clear night. There are more stars than sky, beam-
ing through the leafless branches. I am thrilled to be in this
place, my adventure under way.

❊ ❊ ❊

I walk in a T-shirt and shorts. The mountaintops are
brown with leafless trees, but the valleys are green, and
green is spreading uphill. Wildflowers decorate the trail.
Just beyond a road crossing, I see a khaki-clad couple
fingering plants at the side of the trail: just what I was looking for. "Do you know these wildflowers?"

First night on the trail.

"A little." They're up for the challenge.

"What is this?" I say, pointing to a plant draped with rust-colored flowers.

"Columbine," they answer in unison.

"Back a ways I saw a waxy yellow flower with five petals."

"Buttercup." They're good at this.

I point to a violet flower at my feet and state, "These are everywhere," implying another question.

"Those are violets," they say with a bit of condescension.

"What is that umbrella-shaped…"

"Mayapple," they answer before I've asked.

Now I'm trying to trip them up. "There is a light blue flower with yellow on the tips of three petals."

"Crested dwarf iris" is the answer, with a tone that taunts. "Is that all you got?"

I tried learning my wildflowers from books. The pictures are sterile and out of context. What I see on the trail is a small percentage of all that exists. Now that I see them, learning is easy and permanent.

On the way up Blood Mountain, there are many people strolling along without packs. A parking lot is thirty minutes away. Teens in Skechers and jeans give me curious looks. I'm sure when I get out of earshot they ask each other, "Why is that dumbass carrying a backpack?" An old Civilian Conservation Corps stone building on the summit still serves as a shelter. Many people are scattered around the rocky summit, none of them encumbered by a backpack. The smell of marijuana and sounds of a foreign language emanate from the shelter. The building is occupied by a handful of young Europeans in goth attire with more piercings than I can count.

Blood Mountain Shelter.

A number of trails radiate from the hut. This is common near landmarks. Most of the trails only go as far as needed to relieve oneself in relative privacy; others lead to views. I guess that the trail going most steeply downward is the AT headed north. More teens are coming up the trail. Seeking confirmation and chancing ridicule, I ask, "Is this the AT?"

"I dunno," one replies. "What's the AT?"

These interactions have me feeling awkward. The steep, rocky descent makes matters worse. I feel a jolt of pain down the outside of my right knee. I struggle where carefree day hikers buzz up and down this trail that they can't even identify. One of the drug-addled Europeans passes me, jogging in Doc Martens.

I desperately want to be off this mountain. I can see the road below, and I'm scanning for the store I know to be there. As I do this, I step on a root and feel my foot turn nearly ninety degrees. I can feel my weight supported by the outside of my foot before I make a stumbling burst forward to right myself. No damage done. I chide myself for what may have happened in that moment of carelessness, but I also take confidence from the incident, noting that my ankle could stand up to the abuse.

Neels Gap is the first milestone of my thru-hike. The trail passes a store selling gear, food, bunk spaces, and showers. Hikers resupply, rest, or, many times, go home. About one thousand thru-hikers have come through, a low number this late in the year. I share the bunkroom with four other aspiring thru-hikers. Jean had all her food taken by a bear on her first night out. Orone came from Israel to hike the AT. All of them have been here a day or more nursing wounds. All acknowledge that they are unlikely to reach Maine and are rescoping their plans. It dawns on me that I've not seen Peter.

Gear is the topic of conversation. Oohs and aahs are elicited by a sleeping bag that is six ounces lighter than anyone else's. The outfitter has helped the hiker "Smiling Joe" reduce his pack weight from fifty to thirty-five pounds by selling him twelve hundred dollars worth of new equipment. They covet my thirty-three-pound backpack. I think it weighs too much. I've sacrificed to keep the weight down. I carry two cook pots that also serve as bowl and cup. A spoon is my only utensil. Mitch sifts through his pack. He tells us he came to the trail with little advanced planning, and it shows. He has a full spool of parachute cord, a family-size bottle of ibuprofen, and a full-sized tube of toothpaste. Two extra pairs of underwear! I've saved myself the hassle of changing out of dirty underwear by not bringing any. I have a child-sized toothbrush and travel-sized toothpaste that is only half full. Anyone who has done any amount of preparation knows to shave those ounces.

At one end of the bunkroom there are two overflowing cardboard boxes containing all sorts of stuff like what we see Mitch tossing from his pack: clothes, packets of oatmeal, fuel bottles, forks, socks, matches, books, Boy Scout kitchenware sets. These are called "hiker boxes," receptacles of unwanted gear, free for the taking. They are at every hostel along the trail. A hiker could come here with an empty pack and leave completely equipped.

Mitch keeps a bulky set of syringes, explaining that he is allergic to bee stings, and instructs us on how to inject him if we find him convulsing on the side of the trail. I say, "You better hope we don't find you napping."

Knee pain is commonplace. Mitch, fresh out of college, is laid up due to his knees. This makes me feel less old. Orone describes pain in both knees similar to what I've been experiencing.[4] It's agreed that we all dread downhill more than uphill. Orone shares with us the knee preservation pointers he has heard, one of which is to walk backwards when going downhill. The day hikers are going to love seeing me do that.

---

4   Iliotibial band friction syndrome: The iliotibial band is a tendon that runs along the outside of the thigh, connected to the hip and shin. The tendon glides across the outer surface of the knee joint when the knee bends. On days when the knee is flexed more often than normal, the friction between the band and the joint causes inflammation. Stretching helps, but the real solution is prevention.

I head out alone in the morning. On Cowrock Mountain, the trail breaks from the trees, exposing a grand overlook. I sit for more than an hour writing notes, relishing the experience. I am intrigued by the unknown—not only what lies ahead on the trail, but life beyond and how the journey might make it different.

Twelve miles into my day I reach Low Gap Shelter but don't plan on stopping. A hiker is here sleeping, with no sleeping bag, still with his shoes on. As I go about my business of getting water and a snack, I hear him stir.

"Got any Advil?" are his first groggy words.

"How many do you need?"

"Four."

I hand him four, and he takes them all with a swig of water. He looks like a seasoned hiker with long hair and a shabby beard, and he introduces himself as Ziggy. "Ziggy" is a trail name, an alias used by the majority of thru-hikers. It fits with the sense of escapism we have out here. While many hikers give themselves a name, some risk being named by other people. There are hikers on the trail named "Mudbutt," "Slow Poke," and "Fat Man," so I've preemptively named myself "Awol," a reference to my job situation.

Initially I was uncomfortable using a trail name, but I've coached myself into this thru-hiker persona. I'm here; I'm going to act like a thru-hiker until I become one. I tell him, "I'm Awol."

"Your knees bothering you?" I ask.

"No, I thru-ed in 2000 and never had any problem with my knees. But I wrecked my ankles. I'm only going as far as Damascus this year."

As I hike away from the shelter, the phrase "wrecked my ankles" keeps running through my head. It worries me to see this hiker with an ailment years after his thru-hike. I thought that once my knee toughened up, I'd be waltzing down this trail. Permanent damage was not part of the deal. On cue, my right knee starts acting up again. The trail has turned rocky, and I get a jolt of pain with every uneven step. Over the course of a few miles, my gait slows from an occasional limp down to a crawl, like a car running out of oil. I have to make my leading downhill step with my ailing right leg. Then I can drag my left leg forward no further than my right. It is slow going, and dark concern over the future of my thru-hike creeps back into my thoughts.

Tents are set up around Blue Mountain Shelter when I arrive after 7:00 p.m. Shelters are spaced non-uniformly five to fifteen miles apart. Minimally, they have three walls, a roof, and a wood floor that serves as a sleeping platform. Shelters hold six to twelve hikers and at least as many mice.

To my surprise, Ziggy shows up shortly after I do. Advil worked. In a display of yet another thru-hiker mannerism, Ziggy goes straight for the spiral-bound notebook that serves as a shelter register. He reads an entry in which a hiker warns that mice got into his food bag. Scanning the ridgepole of the shelter, I see a handful of short strings dangling with a short stick tied to the end. These are for hanging food bags. Empty tuna fish cans are tied to the ropes. A hole is poked in the center of the can, and it is suspended between the ceiling and the stick. Ostensibly, the can poses an obstacle to a mouse trying to climb down the rope. Mice don't give up so easily. They will make running leaps from the rafters and try to latch on. They know a food bag when they see one. The hiker who wrote in the register speculates that the mice of this shelter escaped from a lab where they were used to test performance supplements.

I've built a mental list of hikers ahead of me by reading the registers. Hikers who use prominent signatures or tidbits of artwork to identify themselves stand out the most. "The Cardinal" ends every missive with a sketch of the bird; "Green Turtle" uses a stamp with green ink to imprint a comical turtle; "Wolverine" scratches his signature with multiple strokes, in all caps. The name, and the way it is signed, summons an image of a rugged, macho character, like his namesake in the *X-Men* movies. From his entry I learn that he stayed here last night.

The ambition of my early hiking is evident by my catching up to names I've read in the registers. I plan to reach Hiawassee tomorrow on my fourth day since finishing the approach trail. It is more typical of hikers to take over a week. It's unwise of me to be putting in these miles with a sore knee, but I can't deny taking pride in gaining a day on Wolverine. Hugh Jackman is on the trail, and I'm running him down!

Another hiker enters the shelter. "Just Art, no trail name."

"How far are you going, Art?"

"As far as I can go," he says, adding, "It's been rough," to explain his tentative answer.

We share tales of woe, eventually putting Art at ease. We joke about the conversational dance that takes place at this early stage. We've been humbled by the trail, and it sounds too bold to say our intent is to thru-hike. We hedge by saying we have our sights set on the next town, or that we are simply "headed north." We know to give each other wiggle room by asking "Where are you headed?" rather than putting them on the spot with "Are you thru-hiking?"

Ziggy is cowboy camping (sleeping under the stars) and the others are tenting, leaving me alone in the shelter to fend off the mice. The lead mouse is out before I'm asleep. We make a deal. I show him where my food is hanging and say, "If you can get to it, then have at it. Otherwise, don't chew through anything that doesn't have food in it, stay off my face, and don't shit on my gear."

I hope they don't get my meager rations. Obsessing over pack weight, I've carried just enough food for breakfast and a midday snack. I go to sleep hungry and cold. Hiawassee is eighteen miles away.

I'm talking to my wife on the phone. We're making plans to meet for lunch, as we might do during our workdays. I suggest we make it somewhere where we can get pizza. Then I wake up. The realization that this plan won't happen is depressing. It won't happen today; it won't even be next week. When I tell Juli of this dream, I'll take care to attribute a greater share of my disappointment to not seeing her than not eating pizza.

It takes me an hour and twenty minutes to get on the trail. I have to take a long walk to get water, cook breakfast, and pack. Everything takes a long time. There are six straps to adjust and two buckles to snap every time I put on my pack. My backpack has a single large compartment that loads from the top, so when I want something I have to unload until I find what I'm after.

Fog burns away by the time I reach the peak of Tray Mountain. On this clear day I look north toward the Great Smoky Mountains National Park. I know the Smokies will be a challenge. The highest point on the trail is Clingmans Dome in the middle of the park. Then, it's downhill to Virginia, and people have told me Virginia is a cakewalk. I'll learn soon enough that "easy" trail beyond the Smoky Mountains is as much a fantasy as my dream lunch with pizza...uh, I mean Juli, but for now I've convinced myself all will be well once I get through the Smokies.

I leave Tray Mountain Shelter at 1:00 with ten miles to go. I've eaten the remainder of my food. I've been hiking roughly two miles per hour. Downhill is slower due to my sore knee. I need to get to Hiawassee by 6:00 p.m., the check-in deadline at Blueberry Patch Hostel, where my mail drop is waiting.[5] I have little margin, so I decide to push for a while. I down a couple of Advil and "open it up" for the first time this trip. In the next hour I cover 3.5 miles. Another 1.5 miles and I am out of water, since I skipped all the side trails leading to streams. Five miles to go, and I'm running out of steam. Half the strands of muscle in my legs have taken the rest of the day off, leaving the other half to do all the work. My throat is dry. Less than a mile to go, a widening stream parallels the trail. It is nearing 6:00, but I can handle the thirst no longer. There is a five-foot drop down an embankment to the stream. Hurriedly I drop my pack and camera case, which I have clipped over the belt of my pack. The camera starts rolling down the embankment, headed for the stream. I lunge for it and miss. It stops on its own in the nook of a tree root.

I have to be more careful. I'm already paranoid about losing or breaking gear. Every time I resume hiking after a rest, I stop a few steps down the trail and look back for anything I may have left behind. There's nothing in my pack that I don't need.

Finally, I'm at the road leading to Hiawassee, with ten minutes to spare. Only a few cars pass before I have a ride. My first hitch: no problem. As it turns out, the Blueberry

---

5   "Mail drop" is a box of supplies, mostly food, mailed ahead to post offices. Hotels, hostels, and outfitters also hold mail as a courtesy to hikers.

Patch is closed for the night anyway. The owners are sick. Fortunately my ride waited and took me eight more miles to the center of Hiawassee. I stay at Holiday Inn Express, a huge contrast to the rest of my day.

I shower and walk across the street to Dan's All-You-Can-Eat Buffet. AYCE: the thru-hiker's favorite acronym. I anticipate meeting other thru-hikers. A young man and woman making their first pass at the food bar look like they might be hikers. The man is no bigger than the woman, and his hiking boots look too big for his spindly legs. I stop by their table on one of my many trips to the buffet. "Are you on the trail?" I ask.

"I'm Wolverine, and this is…" Her name fails to register because I'm thinking to myself, "You're Wolverine? The macho man I've been (unilaterally) competing against is just a kid?" Then I notice the hat. It's blue with a maize *M*, the hat of the Michigan Wolverines.

I had written my journal entries and e-mailed them home before dinner; now I call home knowing Juli will have read them. Juli edits my daily journal entries before posting them on the Internet.[6] On the phone, we speak about my entries, her reaction to them, and parts she would like to clarify. After we review the entries, Juli asks, "How's your knee?"

"Okay, I guess," I answer, trying to find the right words to describe my outlook. "It's not worse. It only hurts part of the time."

"Gary called, and he has already seen your first two journal entries. He saw what you wrote about your knee. He wants to make sure you are okay; he has to turn in your

---

6   The superb Web site www.TrailJournals.com hosts Internet journals for hikers of all major trails.

notice on Monday." Gary, my immediate supervisor, has gone out on a limb for me, allowing me to use the week of vacation time that I had remaining during the start of my hike. That gave me an opportunity to return to work within the first week if I changed my mind or got injured. I could go back, and it would be as if I just took a few days off. My vacation days have run out. Come Monday, Gary will have to turn in my letter of resignation to our human resources department.

"Should I tell Gary you are not coming back?"

"Yes."

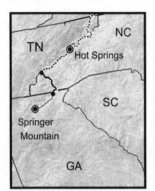

2
Hiawassee to Fontana Dam

I wake up with a sore left thigh, probably because my left leg has been compensating for my sore right knee. In no hurry to get going, I lounge around the room picking through my gear and mail drop. I've concluded I don't need maps, and my seven-ounce guidebook weighs too damn much. I cut the pages from the binding, divide them into four sections, and mail three of the sections home to be mailed back as I need them.

Hiawassee is a compact and attractive town. It's an easy walk to the library and post office. I hitch a ride from Paul, a college student at Young Harris, who turns his car back toward town after dropping me off. He drove ten miles out here just to help me. I don't get on the trail until 12:20 p.m. Because of my ailments, I will take an extra day to reach my next planned stop, the Nantahala Outdoor Center, but an extra day of food is heavy and takes up all of my pack space. It's a catch-22; going slower means struggling with more weight.

The trail climbs from the road, as it always does, and rises steadily to the Georgia/North Carolina border. A twisted, sprawling tree has a simple wood sign reading "GA/NC." One state behind me, thirteen to go. Normally, this would be a cause for celebration, but it is starting to rain. I continue, hardly breaking stride.

I wonder how they will write my obituary as I walk in the lightning and rain on this ridge. How will they find me? With my shoes blown off in the woods? These are some of the less wonderful thoughts I've had walking the AT. I thought I was near the top at the border, but the trail kept going up. The trail and my hopes play tricks on me. I want to believe that I see the top just ahead. The trail leads up the highest mound in sight. When I get there, the trail makes a turn, ever so slight, and reveals more uphill path, even steeper than before. I slip on slimy, muddy rocks. I lean forward and grab rocks, tree branches, tree roots, anything to maintain my uphill progress. The trail levels out, even dips downward, but then goes back up. I'm angered by the brief reprieve. It's not worth the gumption lost on false hope. I want it to just go up until I get "there." I don't even know where "there" is. "There" is a nameless peak somewhere on this trail that I will reach and then head reliably downhill for as long as I've spent climbing up. Never mind that I'll just start the process over again. Hey, what if the trail was just level for a while? There's a novel idea. This has been the most difficult, disheartening climb so far.

I've been playing a game with my rain jacket. The cold rain is no match for the heat that I am generating, so I get completely wet from sweat anyway. I loosen my shoulder straps so I can worm out of the sleeves of the sauna suit one arm at a time while walking and without taking my pack off. It takes a few minutes, but I'm covering ground. About the time I finish, the rain picks up again, and I have to wiggle back in, still walking. I must've done this eight times.

Three men are in Muskrat Creek Shelter ahead of me. Two of them look out from the dripping edges of the roof, grinning in recognition of what I have been through. They've been through it, too, and know how good it feels to finish a day like this one. I meet a hiker named Crossroads, who is as much my contemporary as anyone I'll meet on the trail. He is just a few years younger than I am, and we walk at roughly the same pace, so we will see more of each other on this trail. Crossroads left his job in midcareer, but unlike me, he was granted a leave of absence. His employer wants him to move up to a position with more responsibilities. Crossroads finagled time off, saying he needs the time to decide. "Crossroads" is an apt moniker. He wants to finish the trail, but doesn't think he has enough time to do so. He is not enthused about the new position, or even going back to the same job. He gives lip service to skipping parts of the trail, but at heart he is a "purist." More about that term tomorrow.

A young hiker from Tennessee joins the conversation. The only other hiker staying the night is an older gentleman already in his sleeping bag. He has on headphones and speaks not a word for the remaining hours of daylight while the rest of us talk, cook dinner, and spread out our gear. I know he is not asleep because he pulls his hands out of his bag a few times to tune his radio.

I woke up at 2:02, 3:15, 5:08, 6:30, and more times when I didn't check my watch. That's how sleep has been for me, caused by a combination of soreness, sleeping on hard surfaces, and odd (but typical) shelter noises. One of those noises must have been the headphones guy packing, because he is gone. One of the aches is the bunion on my left foot.

Five years ago I had surgery to fix a bunion on my right foot. Recovery from foot surgery is painful and lengthy.

I had hoped that I'd never have to do it again. I take my sock off and see that the bunion is grotesquely swollen. It looks as if half a golf ball has been implanted under my skin on the "knuckle" of my big toe. It is such a captivating deformity that I sit there staring as thoughts race through my head. I need to get new shoes. Where's the next town? Is there an outfitter? A doctor? My foot doesn't hurt that badly; maybe it will get better. Why kid myself? This will just get worse. I should get off the trail, go home, and have another bunion surgery. Maybe I can try the trail again in a few years. With this sense of finality, I stuff my swollen foot back into my shoe and head north.

Oddly, I feel as strong as I ever have on the trail. The rain has stopped, and the terrain is better. My foot feels more numb than painful. Before long I catch up to the older gentleman, sitting on the wet rocks that line the trail, looking over his map. He introduces himself as Russ. He makes no apology for being unsocial last night, and seems polite and only slightly reserved.

Pointing to his map, he says, "You see this big loop here? Well, that's the AT. It goes around here to hit Standing Indian [Mountain] and Albert Mountain. I can take the Kimsey Creek Trail and cut all that off. I can't make it to Maine any other way." Using this shortcut, he could walk less than six miles to rejoin the AT. That point would be about nineteen miles if he were to follow the white blazes. And two mountains could be avoided. Standing Indian is the highest mountain south of the Smokies, and Albert Mountain is famously steep.

The Kimsey Creek Trail, like most other side trails, is marked with blue paint blazes. What Russ is proposing is dubbed "blue-blazing," and it is heresy in the minds of many thru-hikers, but he had announced his plan unapologetically. There is contention over what it means to be a "thru-hiker." A "purist" is a backpacker who believes a thru-hike is traveling every inch of the AT in one direction, carrying your pack every step of the way. Others will say they are thru-hiking even though they take blue blazes to shorten the distance, avoid obstacles, or to explore a more interesting route. There is a tedious abundance of customs and opinions about how to thru-hike. Conversations about the purity of a thru-hike will last the duration of my hike, and of course come to no conclusion. Everyone does his own walk, guided by conscience or by expediency.

The Appalachian Trail Conference (ATC) is the organization with primary responsibility for the trail. The ATC issues "2000-miler" certificates to "any hiker who reports he or she walked the entire length of the Appalachian Trail." The certificates are awarded on the honor system. The ATC does not differentiate between hikers who hike the trail in one trip, or piece it together over a number of years. Their minimal 2000-miler policy states that blue-blazing is acceptable in emergency conditions. The trail can be hiked in any direction, in any sequence, with or without a backpack. The important point exposed in my current conversation with Russ is that the topic is touchy. Russ snapped out his plan as a preemptive strike against any purist preaching I might be inclined to offer. Even in trying to stay neutral, conversing about plans can be misconstrued as making judgments.

A snake crosses the trail right as I pass, somehow slithering between my feet without getting trampled. He freezes, so I look him over but cannot identify him. And I thought I knew them all. The trail tunnels through patches of rhododendron; otherwise, visibility is good. Most deciduous trees are still leafless, and some of the evergreens are dead. Standing Indian Mountain has a nice, long, steady grade with switchbacks. Even though it is the highest mountain so far, the ascent is easy. At one switchback, I can see Crossroads up ahead, flying up the trail. He must have been taking a break as I pulled close.

The climb up Albert Mountain is steeper than anything to this point, but relatively short. I actually enjoy the hand-over-hand climbs. I stand at the fire tower atop the mountain and look out over the mountainscape. My visit is cut short when I see rain clouds rolling in at a startling pace. I throw my pack on and hustle down to Big Spring Shelter. A man is in front of the shelter, topless, with his pants down around his knees. He's taking a sponge bath, and I guess he wasn't expecting company. "I'm going down to the stream," I say, giving him a few minutes to dress and me a few minutes to decide if I want to stay here. A derelict tent is set up next to the shelter; it looks like it's been here for months. The shelter is a wood structure with a metal roof and an ample overhang in front.

The hiker is also from Florida, and he's out doing a section of the trail. It is easy enough to assess that he is harmless. He knows some of the thru-hikers on the trail this season from their Internet journals. It is windy and storming overnight, but I have a great night's sleep. My Big Agnes sleeping pad is working out well and is the envy of everyone else in the shelters. I still have to turn every so often. I have a side-back-side rotation. I've also learned that tucking my knees higher while on my side takes pressure off my hip bone.

It is a beautiful morning, cloudless but cold. I've finished one hundred miles of the trail. The bunion on my left foot is not hurting, and fears of having to quit no longer loom over me. My plans for the day are uncertain. One shelter is too close (twelve miles) and the next is too far (twenty-five miles). It looks like rain again today, so I'd like to avoid sleeping in my tarp. At Winding Stair Gap, the trail crosses a well-traveled road, and a hiker named Fujiboots jumps out of the bed of a pickup, having hitched in and out of the town of Franklin, North Carolina. The weather is clearing, so I continue on, even taking off my shirt to get some sun.

The weather quickly deteriorates, and it's raining within an hour of my leaving the gap. This storm is even more frightening than the last. The wind howls like a jet engine. I've never been in the woods with winds like this; I don't know what to expect. Is this what a twister sounds like? I look around for somewhere I might hide. There are no caves. I wonder if I should hang on to the biggest tree around so I don't get sucked away by the wind. The rain is coming down heavy and cold, blowing into my face and leaking into the neck of my rain jacket. Rain has destroyed the guidebook pages I am keeping in my pocket, but I know I should be within a mile of Siler Bald Shelter. Lightning flashes. I feel vulnerable. I wish the shelter was here.

Conventional wisdom says I shouldn't be near the top of a hill in a lightning storm, but there is not much I can do about it. I've been on a rolling ridge walk for more than a mile. I cannot backtrack and get down with any speed. If I was to bushwhack, I would have to go so far from the trail I'd probably get lost. My best option, or the option that is as good as any other, is to push forward and hope that I don't get struck dead by lightning. I feel powerless to mitigate the risk. There is no way to be careful on top of a ridge in a lightning storm. Is hiking the trail an acceptable risk?

Finally, I fork off onto the side trail leading to Siler Bald Shelter. The rain is so hard it hurts my exposed hands and bounces off the ground. It's hail! No wonder it hurts. I go a few hundred yards and still see no shelter. In my advance planning for the hike, I rarely planned on going to shelters that were far from the trail. But this is an unplanned stop. I wish I had taken the time to read the sign back at the fork in the trail. I'm seeing no blue blazes that should mark the route. Tentatively I backtrack a dozen steps, considering going back to the fork and making sure I'm on the right path. Damn! It's cold. I don't have time for this. I wheel around again and continue down the unmarked path.

Fortunately, it is the right path. Two hikers are in the shelter already. Two hours later, I finally stop shivering enough to write in my journal. Half of the shelter opening is covered with clear plastic to keep out the cold. It's not the half where I'm sleeping. The plastic is peppered with a colony of gnats, who get excited by our cooking. Kahota (from Florida) shares orange slices, Fujiboots (from Maine) gives me a bagel, and I eat my freeze-dried meal for two. I also eat Kahota's leftover scalloped potatoes. Then I go to bed hungry.

Morning is my time for doubting. It is cold, and I have to coerce my sore, swollen feet into my shoes. I plan to walk slowly, thinking it will be a sort of rest while moving. I have a pleasant walk through a field of wildflowers, seeing wonderful samples of Dutchman's britches and purple trillium. I spot a luna moth camouflaged in the leaves.

The condition of the trail in North Carolina has been great. Maintainers were just here, and I see sawdust where they cleared blow-downs. There is a fire tower on Wayah Bald made of stone. It is an earthy building that blends well with the woods. From atop the tower, Albert Mountain is visible. It looks further than just two days away. I look at the woods between there and where I am and try to imagine the path and myself passing along it.

Luna moth.

I weave past three weekend hikers who are heckling each other about being unfit. The trailing hiker is a big guy, clearly walking in pain. He is probably the star of their softball team, but his size is no asset here. I sit out a ninety-minute rain shower at Cold Springs Shelter. The three weekend hikers come in during the rainstorm, shed their dripping ponchos, and trade their wet boots for sandals.

"Damn!" one of them exclaims to the big guy. "Look at your heel." The entire back side of his white sock is red with blood.

"Yeah, I know," he responds casually.

"If I were you, I'd throw those boots in the fire and walk outta here barefooted."

There is always some solace in seeing someone with a condition worse than your own. But he only has another half day to walk. I have over two thousand miles to go. I eat dinner and move on for a pleasant walk late in the day to Wesser Bald Shelter. A couple calling themselves "the Bears" are regaling the rest of the hikers in this full shelter with tales of the trail ahead. They are the first southbound thru-hikers we have seen.[7] One bit of disappointing news: their hike is nearly over and they haven't seen a bear. I wonder if I'll get to see any.

Crossroads is here ahead of me. It is the first time I've seen him since Standing Indian Mountain. The other hikers refer to him as if he is an überhiker. Obviously, he has told them his start date, April 25, same as mine. I say nothing of my own schedule, so as not to diminish the über status he is enjoying.

I am up at 6:30, packed, peed, and on the trail by 7:00 for my earliest start yet. My routine has been to get going between 7:00 and 8:30 and finish between 6:00 and 7:30 p.m., unless it's raining or I'm hitting a resupply point. It now takes me about forty-five minutes to eat and pack in the morning. I expected to be faster.

I intended to take a short break at Nantahala Outdoor Center (NOC) and move on, but my knee is bugging me on the six-mile rocky downhill hike, so I am staying put. NOC is a large complex built along the Nantahala River. There is a restaurant, snack bar, motel rooms, bunkhouses, and an outfitter. The outfitter caters to kayakers and backpackers, and they have held a mail drop for me.

---

7   Northbound and southbound hikers are most likely to meet in New England. The Bears are on an atypical, long hike started in the summer of 2002. They hiked through winter and are finishing in spring.

Up to now, I have been sleeping inside two summer sleeping bags, but they are not keeping me warm. Also, I am still struggling with volume. When I have a new food supply, I can barely cram it all in my pack. I send home the two summer bags and buy a twenty-five-degree down sleeping bag. Crocs are rubber cloglike shoes that are running rampant on the trail this year. Everyone is trading in their sandals because Crocs weigh about a pound less. I buy a pair. I buy new gaiters and a rain jacket that is supposed to be more breathable. I feel guilty about the expense. In my prehike preparations, I bought and tried two backpacks, three tents, three rain jackets, two sleeping bags, and more shoes than I can recall. Now I'm under way and still buying equipment. Gear on the trail is like equipment on the golf course; everyone's looking for better results through technology.

I hang around the center watching kayakers and soaking my feet in the freezing water. It is a beautiful, sunny afternoon, yet I'm content to spend it here instead of hiking. I do laundry, shower (must've been in for twenty minutes), eat voraciously, and use my PocketMail to send and receive e-mail.[8] By now, most of my friends have seen my online journal entries or read my first article in the newspaper. I get a handful of e-mails responding to what they have read. Their feedback is incredibly uplifting:

David, The highlight of my day is reading your journal. The article in Sunday's paper was terrific, very well written. We all think of you often and I find myself sitting in my office thinking of you out on the trail. I am not sure which is worse, having a mouse shit on my gear or dealing with [a situation at work]. I guess I would take the mouse. Hang in there and stay strong.

---

8   PocketMail is a device similar to a PDA. I would compose journal entries or letters on the trail and send them when I reached a phone, via an acoustic coupler.

I wake to the sound of thunder and rain on the tin roof of the NOC bunkhouse. I hit the trail about 10:30 after abandoning the fantasy that the rain would go away. The walk from NOC is the longest continuous uphill so far, going from 1,723 feet to 4,750 feet in six miles. The downside of dropping into towns is the climb out. The trail is a stream. Rain comes down in a heavy, continuous barrage. My defenses—a hooded rain jacket, gaiters, and Gore-Tex pants and shoes—only hold for about two hours. My shirt, pants, and socks are all wet.

I feel strong, even with a load bulging with six days of food. The half-day rest did me good. Thunderless lightning illuminates the sky. These flashes don't alarm me; I don't even know if they present a threat. I walk nonstop for three and a half hours to get to Sassafras Gap Shelter. In some ways, this weather is conducive to such a march. There is nowhere to stop, not much can be seen, and walking is the only way to stay warm.

This is a wonderfully large shelter with two levels of bunks, a large covered area in front, and clerestory windows. Two hikers are already here. They've been holed up since last night, having better sense than to venture out in the rain. Four more soaked hikers drag in after me. Most everyone I'm seeing on the trail is a thru-hiker.

The rain continues and shows no signs of letting up. I get chills once I stop walking, so I have some hot food and jump into my sleeping bag with wet clothes, testing the theory that body heat dries them out.

At 8:00 a.m., it's been raining for more than twenty-four hours. Sleeping in wet clothes is good for the clothes but bad for the sleeping bag. My brand-new down bag kept me warm, but it is now dank and smelly. Walking in the rain is doable, but my wet feet will get more blisters (I now have three blisters on each foot), and even with a rain cover my pack slowly absorbs water from the space between me and the pack. I have to be careful to keep my sleeping bag dry. I'm going to wait for the rain to stop.

I spend much of my rainy day talking with Mike, a robust, round-faced, bearded technical writer from Minnesota. He has a technical approach to thru-hiking as well. He has studied the trail guides and maps and can recite the elevation gain and loss that we will face in the Smokies. He knows the pros and cons to all the equipment choices. His soft-spoken demeanor reminds me of football announcer Merlin Olson, and he has wizardly acumen. I think he should have the trail name "Merlin," but I am inhibited about telling him so.

Due to my rain-shortened walk yesterday, I will abandon my plan to travel six days without resupplying. I set my sights on Fontana Dam, two days away. I need to move on at least nine miles to the next shelter to make that happen, but it is well past noon and it is still raining. Mike bemoans being "stuck" for another night, since he doesn't have the speed to move on so late in the day.

At 2:30 the rain stops. I pack and make a break for it. Running scared that rain could start again, I do the nine-mile stretch to Brown Fork Gap Shelter in four hours. This late-day burst saves me from losing another day on my schedule, and puts me in good position to head into the Smokies. I'm happy, opportunistic, and lucky to make it here. Pulling off a move like this gives me confidence. I suspect I won't see Mike again, so I leave a note in the shelter register, suggesting the trail name "Merlin." I hope he sees it.[9]

---

9   "Merlin" was the only trail name I ever suggested. I received a note from Mike late in my hike that read in part: *"Congratulations on your imminent completion of your through-hike! I made it about 600 miles before stopping. Actually, I went up north and climbed Katahdin and was ready to start the 100-Mile Wilderness southbound (flip-flopping) when I decided I didn't trust one of my knees for such a long stretch with a lot of food, so I stopped for the year...Rain and Shine read your suggestion in the Brown Fork Shelter log, that I use 'Merlin' as my trail name, and I liked it (a lot, actually), so 'Merlin' it is."*

I lay in my sleeping bag reading by headlamp. A section hiker is at the other end of the shelter, and a mouse crawls over the foot of his sleeping bag and crosses the sleeping platform diagonally toward me. He peers into my headlamp for a moment and then scurries past, behind my head. Hours later, after I am asleep, I wake to the sound of celebratory whoops coming from the trail, and look out to see the flicker of headlamps. I see the silhouette of two small bodies outside, whispering to each other in a foreign language. One head is hairless; the other has short curly hair. I can't tell if they are women or boys, and won't know until morning. They slip inside and go to sleep.

The hikers are Snail and Patience, women from Israel. They came all the way from NOC yesterday, undeterred by the rain. I am impressed. A storm began last night after their arrival, and it is still lingering. I am once again waiting for a break in the rain before leaving the shelter. Snail and Patience don't wait. They don ponchos and go. When the rain is down to a drizzle, I'm determined to break out of this jungle. I'm less bothered by the rain since I'll make it to town (Fontana Village) and have a chance to dry. Also, I feel a little shown up by the women. Foggy trail and the cacophony of birds add to the rainforest effect. On the trail there are a number of appliance-sized boulder fields where I can hear the roar of unseen streams underneath.

My hiking day is spent leap-frogging Snail and Patience. Like many hiking partners, they hike separately at their own pace and meet up at landmarks. I catch up with Snail first. She gets her name from being the slower of the two, although both of them are young women fresh out of the Israeli army, and both hike more strongly than most other thru-hikers. I learn that they have an unusual plan for hiking the trail. They started their hike by walking the section of trail in Pennsylvania, reasoning that they would "get their trail legs" while hiking the flattest state. Then they hitched down to Georgia and headed north. When they reach Pennsylvania, they'll skip ahead to New Jersey and continue north to Katahdin.

I catch up with sarcastically dubbed Patience while she is waiting restively for Snail. She gives me some miniature Hershey bars, but I cannot find any food with which I can reciprocate since she is a kosher vegetarian.

Fontana Dam is the highest dam east of the Mississippi. I can see the dam through the trees a few miles away, and it looks like I'm only minutes from it. It makes for a long, frustrating descent when my goal seems to keep moving away from me. I am as grungy as I've been on the trail. Getting rained on daily, sweating in rain gear, wet shoes, and mud everywhere make for a potent mix.

Fontana Village is a hamlet two miles from the dam, which once housed the builders of the dam. As a tremendous courtesy to hikers, a phone is located at the dam, where I call and get a shuttle into town. I stay at a nice hotel in the village, at a dirt-cheap thru-hiker rate. Rain is forecast, so I plan to take a zero day tomorrow.[10]

---

10   A "zero" is a day in which a thru-hiker does not hike. Hikers will use it as a noun or verb: "Yesterday was a zero" or "I'll zero tomorrow." I used the term "nero" for a day in which I walked only a few miles.

3
Fontana Dam
to Hot Springs

I have entered the third state on the trail without leaving the second. The AT defines the North Carolina/Tennessee border in the Smokies. There are nine peaks over six thousand feet, including Clingmans Dome (6,643 feet), the highest point on the AT. The hike up from Fontana Dam is grueling as it ascends twenty-eight hundred feet from the dam to the ridge of the Great Smoky Mountains. This is the fourth time I've climbed this section.

My first two trips up this trail were made on consecutive days twenty-three years ago. My father, my brother, a friend, and I set out to hike the length of the Appalachian Trail in the Smokies starting from Fontana Dam. My dad was roughly the same age as I am now. A few miles into the hike, my dad started falling back. All of us were tired; it was a rough uphill climb. Later I began backtracking to see if he was still coming. He encouraged me to push on. I went ahead to catch up with the other two and convinced them to come back to check on him.

This time it was obvious that he was more than just tired. The workload went beyond what his heart could handle. It turned into a long day getting him down and to a hospital, and we spent a sleepless night sitting up in our car at a rest stop. The next day we headed back up the trail. Dad wouldn't have it any other way.

He improved and took a flight back home before we finished our hike. But he had sustained damage to his heart that would eventually lead to early retirement and open-heart surgery.

I've had doubts about my ability to thru-hike, but thankfully my heart is not a problem. My challenges have been knee pain, blisters, and a swollen bunion, but for the moment these problems are manageable. Thru-hiking is more demanding than I had imagined. In spite of the difficulties, this is where I want to be.

❁ ❁ ❁

The morning weather radar shows clearing skies, a fact I can confirm by looking out of the window. Without hesitation, I ditch my plan for a zero day in Fontana Village, pack my things, and hop a shuttle back to the trail. I'm barreling into the Great Smoky Mountains under clear blue skies.

Ridgerunner Roger "Manysleeps" is on the trail about a half mile up from Fontana Dam. Ridgerunners are ATC employees and volunteers who oversee the trail. Roger has manned his post from 7:00 a.m. to 5:00 p.m. every day of the hiking season, counting thru-hikers. I'm northbound thru-hiker number 927. He tells me that the dropout rate for thru-hikers has consistently been 50 percent before finishing the Smokies. Ninety percent of the trail is still ahead.

There is a crowd of thru-hikers headed up from the dam, at least six from Fontana Village and eight more from Fontana Dam Shelter. It is an exciting, fresh start with so many hikers heading out from the same point. I walk across Fontana Dam with Crossroads. He comments on all the young people, and how he is the old man in the crowd at the age of thirty-five. His assumption that he is older is an ego boost. I want to put on some miles today because I fear that the first couple of shelters will fill up. Last night and this morning I ate AYCE meals at the inn. Dinner was the only time in my life that I was purposefully gluttonous. I believe it paid off, and I hike energetically all day. I feel excitement in passing other hikers. One by one they fall back. I make good miles despite gaining three thousand feet in elevation, getting a late start, and stopping with two hours of daylight remaining. Snail and Patience are the only other hikers from the crowd to make it this far. We stay at Spence Field Shelter, beautifully set among an orchard of flowering Sarvis trees that rain white petals down on the grassy terrain.

Right from the start of my second day in the Smokies, the trail goes into a number of PUDs (pointless ups and downs), some of them very steep. This lasts until Derrick Knob. My knee is holding up better, and as a result I hike faster and wear out more quickly. The trail has few blazes in the Smokies. Many times I walk hundreds of yards without seeing a white blaze. Anxiety over getting lost adds to my weariness.

I peter out near dumpy Double Springs Shelter. Recent rains have swamped the grounds, and puddles extend all the way into the shelter floor. Black flies (biting, gnatlike bugs) swarm the area. I take a long break, eat, and have a dose of Vitamin I.[11] Feeling better, and inspired by clear weather, I march up Clingmans Dome. Once above fifty-six hundred feet, the trail buries itself in a spruce-fir forest with the look and smell of a Christmas tree lot. The dome is capped by a tower with a long ramping spiral walkway. From the observation deck, I can see that all of the larger firs have been killed.[12] I have to drag myself up and over one more mountain to reach the shelter. This was a hard day of hiking. Mount Collins Shelter is in good condition, having an excellent privy and bear cables.[13]

❀ ❀ ❀

I am fond of this shelter due to my previous visits here. This shelter is easily accessible from the road leading up to Clingmans Dome. In 2001 my family and I took an impromptu short vacation in and around the Smokies. One day we parked on the access road and hiked in to Mount Collins Shelter. I wanted to show the kids a bit of the trail and let them see a shelter. While we ate lunch, a former thru-hiker showed up.

He had done the trail after he retired. He returned to walk a section of the trail and to place a plaque in honor of a hiker who passed away at a shelter north of here. The unfortunate hiker had a heart attack during the night, and they found him dead in the morning. He also told us more upbeat stories from the trail. On the first day of his hike, he met a retired woman who was also attempting to thru-hike. She didn't even know how to set up her tent, so he helped

---

11   "Vitamin I" is a trail term for ibuprofen.
12   The balsam woolly adelgid is responsible for fir devastation. See http://www.nps.gov/ grsm/pphtml/subenvironmentalfactors28.html.
13   Bear cables: A horizontal steel cable is strung between trees, supporting a vertical cable by a pulley. Hikers attach their food bags and pulley them up to a height of about fifteen feet. Bears can't reach the food from the ground or by climbing a tree.

her, thinking she wouldn't be on the trail for long. They hiked together all the way to Katahdin.

This planted the seed for doing a thru-hike. I had imagined that only young people did this sort of thing, but speaking with this man made me consider the possibility of thru-hiking with Juli when we retire. I immersed myself in books, magazines, the Internet, anything I could read about hiking. The more I read, the more interested I became.

A few months later, I was peppering Juli with stories I had read about the trail. This was just weeks after I had shared with her my interest in an AT thru-hike being a potential retirement activity, and I was revealing to her that reading had changed my attitude. I was completely uncertain of her reaction, so I said with a tone of jest, "Maybe I should go by myself. Maybe I should go now."

Her reply was immediate: "Maybe you should."

I was just testing the waters, and I surprised myself with the wave of enthusiasm I got from Juli's go-for-it response. All of a sudden, hiking the AT went from a crazy whim to a real possibility. And I wasn't intimidated by the possibility. When the path is clear to pursue a fledgling goal, the path is also clear for deeper insight into your desires. Sometimes the reality of it is less romantic than the fantasy, and you get cold feet. Not this time. The inner me was elated, screaming, "Hell yeah, let's go!" Outwardly, I tried to give Juli the impression that my question was hypothetical. But I knew she was not indulging me with a flippant response. She was serious and supportive, and she knew that the answer she just gave was a commitment.

❊ ❊ ❊

I hit Newfound Gap midmorning on a Saturday. This is where U.S. 441 crosses the mountains, and there is a major parking area. Tourists stop for pictures at the overlook or take a day hike. I am shamelessly setting myself up for venerated trail magic. "Trail magic" is a broadly used term covering any form of serendipity encountered on the trail. Hikers believe that good karma exists in the hiking community, which manifests itself in the form of assistance when the hiker is in need: a hitch from the middle of nowhere, lost equipment turning up, and, most coveted of all, hot food or cold drinks offered at road crossings.

Most often, trail magic comes from previous thru-hikers or family members following current thru-hikers. When you encounter tourists unfamiliar with the needs of thru-hikers, you have to wheedle your way into their coolers. This fine art of giving karma a little push is called Yogi-ing.[14] Sometimes the trick is to look pathetic without looking scary.

Or you can engage in conversation about the trail:

"Walked all the way from Georgia…

"…Haven't seen a bear yet…

"…No, I don't carry a gun…

"…I'm headed for Maine…

"…About five months."

If they don't catch on and break open the cooler, subtlety goes out the window: "Yeah, I get pretty tired of eatin' nothin' but raisins. Tried to catch me a squirrel last night…"

The problem is, I'm terrible at Yogi-ing. Best I can do is linger to increase my odds of being seen by the right person. I splash-bathe over the bathroom sink and set up to cook in a high-traffic area between the men's and women's bathrooms. I take out my tiny stove to boil water for oatmeal, trying to look none too happy about eating it. No success. Plenty of tourists around, but only one diffident couple speaks to me.

---

14   Another trail term, taken from the cartoon bear with a fondness for picnic food.

"Thru-hiking?" the man asks.

"Yep."

That's the whole conversation, verbatim. He gives a grinning glance back to his wife, as if to say, "I told you we'd see one of them here trying to beg for food. Isn't this fun to blow him off?"

The section just north of Newfound Gap is austere. The ridge is sharper, more open. At times there is enough sun exposure to make me uncomfortably hot. The terrain is rocky, and evergreens are the dominant trees. The weather is clear, and I am treated to excellent views from Charlie's Bunion, a rocky feature four miles up from the gap. I'm headed for Tricorner Knob Shelter, which will make for the third long day in a row on my sprint through the Smokies. I am tiring from the effort, and again I feel knee pain.

Charlie's Bunion, Great Smoky Mountains National Park.

Of more urgent concern is the gastric percolation that I am experiencing. While all of the woods are potentially a rest stop, thick forest growth prevents me from getting off the path. When there is a clearing, there is a steep drop-off. I can wait no longer and crash through the foliage. Hurdling fallen branches is a true test of my continence. I'm forced to make four more stops like this before reaching the shelter, sputtering like a near empty bottle of mustard. I'm worried that I may have picked up the dreaded Giardia bug, and I think back through my stops at springs to get water. I have used a water filter or water treatment chemicals every time I have refilled my water bottles, but I may have been careless enough to get a residue of untreated water on my bottle.[15] Could I get sick from a tiny residue of bad water? My supply of toilet paper is exhausted after the second stop. Then I recycle my Georgia guidebook pages. Next I move on to rocks—the smoothest, cleanest ones I find. They're not as bad as they sound.

After a restful night's sleep in the crowded Tricorner Knob Shelter, I head out into a windy, gloomy morning with an irrational fear of a tree falling on me. With the recent storms, there are blow-downs all over. I have heard but not seen trees falling. It rains for over two hours. In the midst of the storm, I come to another shelter and go in for a reprieve from the downpour. Another hiker and a ridgerunner named Ron are in the shelter. They've stayed the night and are getting ready to brave the rain. The hiker is decked out in a hooded rain poncho and high gaiters. He makes an unceremonious exit from the shelter, making it clear that there is no love lost between them. Ron makes a "Wall Street" comment about the hiker, who is attempting to thru-

---

15   I would maintain the habit of treating water for the duration of my hike. I used either a pump-filtering device called First Need or drops called Aqua Mira.

hike, so that becomes his name.[16] I also tell Ron of my fears about falling trees. He reassures me by telling me I am much more likely to get struck by lightning. For good measure, he tells me the story of two hikers who were killed some years ago when lightning struck a shelter.

By the time I reach the next shelter, the rain has stopped. A hiker is out front having lunch. I introduce myself, and he answers with disdain, "You just met me at the last shelter."

It is Wall Street, but I failed to recognize him without his poncho. We have a curt conversation while I eat my lunch. I look over the shelter register and see an entry from the Cardinal, with the familiar bird sketch. This entry is longer than most, because it is his last entry. The Cardinal explains that he is grateful for all that he has learned about himself, but will be stopping now, with 234 miles on his boots.

"I haven't seen your name in any of the shelter registers," I mention to Wall Street.

"I don't sign them," he retorts. "I don't see any reason why I should."

Instead of a privy, there is a PRIVY AREA sign to one side of the shelter. It is a minefield of soft spots where droppings of previous shelter denizens are buried in shallow holes.

Beyond the shelter I am on a nice downhill stroll. My stomach is more settled, and I am certain that I suffered only garden-variety diarrhea. I'm relishing the success of making it through the Smokies. Not long ago I viewed this park as the first test of my hike; a test that I've now passed. I feel an itch on the back of my right heel.

North of the Smoky Mountains National Park, there is a confusing road walk on segments of three different roads to get hikers over the Pigeon River and under Interstate 40. Each time I have to guess when to change roads and which

16   "Ron" and "Wall Street" were not their real or trail names.

way to go, since there are sparse markings. Over the entire length of the trail, I spent more time searching for my way on roads than I did in the woods. On the last leg of the road walk, I take a turn down a gravel road away from the trail, headed for Standing Bear Hostel. Wall Street is stomping down the road toward me, cursing the lack of marking. He had made an unintended trip down to the hostel only to find he is off the trail. I'm happy that he won't be staying and not unhappy that he is astray.

On the trail, "hostel" is a generic term for any inexpensive or free lodging. This could mean bunkrooms at a private residence, outfitter, or church, or steerage-class accommodations at a hotel or bed and breakfast.

The Standing Bear Hostel is a wedge of land with a stream running through it and an assortment of structures. One building is the home of Curtis and Maria, the owners. Curtis started this hostel. He's proud of his handiwork and gives me a tour. He's built bunks in what used to be a garage. He built a bunkroom on top of a bridge over the stream. There are outdoor showers, an outhouse, and a fire pit. There is a small shelter with laundry machines, a phone, and a laptop computer for Internet access (it's not working). He has converted a tool shed into a storeroom where he sells an assortment of trail foods.

This is Curtis's job, but clearly he also likes the company of hikers. Tonight he takes a drive to pick up pizzas for me and Matt, the only hikers staying. I choose to sleep in the bunkhouse on the bridge for the unique (and cold) opportunity to sleep over a babbling stream.

The itch that I felt on the back of my heel yesterday is now a blister the size of an almond. I can hardly believe that such a large blister could form when all I felt was an itch.

I pop the blister with a needle, drain clear fluid, and put a bandage over it. I've seen blisters come and go already, and I figure my feet get tougher with every callus. They are of no concern.

The day is perfect for hiking. It is clear and cold enough to wear fleece when I'm not moving and a T-shirt while hiking. I hardly break a sweat. The trail here has a lot of variety and is nicely graded. For miles there are fields of white and pink trillium, mayapples, and purple wildflowers. There are two grassy balds, pine forests, blooming mountain laurel, rhododendron tunnels, and many stream crossings. Set loose, a child would run down the paths, scramble up the rocks, lie on the earth. Grown-ups more often let their minds do the running, scrambling, and lying, but the emotion is shared. It feels good to be here.

The wind is blowing strong all day and is especially noticeable when going over the larger bald, Max Patch. I stumble across it, fighting the wind like a drunk trying to hold a straight line.

The trail across Max Patch Bald.

Walnut Mountain Shelter is a ratty old shelter with a platform that would comfortably fit five or, uncomfortably, fit six. I am number six. Usually I would pass on a crowded shelter, but it is late in the day and I am ready to stop. I try to evaluate the group. Wall Street is snuggled into his bag at one end of the shelter, looking miserable and asking for cold medicine. "Hello, Awol," he says feebly. His hello is sincere. I recognize friendliness buried under his brusque persona. I am glad that I stayed cordial with him when I had considered him off-putting.

The other four men are obviously familiar with one another. One of them I take for a day hiker. He has rag-tag gear and a car-camping-sized stove. He introduces himself as Steve O., and says he intends to thru-hike. I am immediately uneasy about Steve O.—not because I have any special powers of perception, but because he would make most people uneasy. He has a hard-living look to him, with leathery skin and worn, yellow teeth. He has an odor that stands out even among thru-hikers. I make my dinner on a log in front of the shelter, minimally unloading my gear. This is a nonverbal way of showing that I'd like to stay. They catch on and start talking amongst themselves about making room for me in the shelter. Three of them crowd to one end, leaving a half-body-width space next to Steve O. Now it is clear to me that they know him, but are not "with" him. Steve O. isn't budging, so there won't be room for me. I pack up and move on.

One of the guys says he heard a radio weatherman forecasting temperatures down to twenty-five degrees in the mountains tonight. It is obvious he feels badly about me moving on from the shelter late on a cold night. The wind makes it seem colder. It tries to blow my tarp away as I try to stake it down. I have found a place to camp a mile from Walnut Mountain Shelter, just off the trail on a cozy bed of pine needles. I sleep warmly in my down mummy bag with the hood string drawn tight, to the sound of my tarp flapping in the wind. I leave only a two-inch circle open around my nose.

I've slept in shelters more often than I have slept under my tarp, and I will continue to do so. But I sleep better in the solitude of my tarp and wake rested, content, and feeling self-sufficient. I put away my gear, sit down to eat, and notice a rabbit chewing leaves just fifteen feet away, not bothered by the noise I made packing. We eat our breakfast together.

Magic Rat, one of the friendlier guys from Walnut Mountain Shelter, catches up while I am trying to take a photo of myself using a timer on my camera. We walk in tandem the rest of the way to Hot Springs. Both of us are moving at a good clip to get to town for mail drops, food, and errands—typical town stuff. We talk all the way, and the twelve miles pass quickly. Magic Rat apologizes for not having made room in the shelter. He is hiking with two guys and two girls. The girls, Nova and Bear Bait, were not feeling well, so Curtis had given them a ride from Standing Bear Hostel up to Hot Springs, where the group will get together again. Meanwhile, Steve O. has been tagging along, hinting at his need for money, and the guys don't want to be saddled with a moocher.

Within a mile of town, when rooftops are first visible through the trees, I feel the return of the ache in my knee. Also, my Achilles tendon is stiff, causing me pain when I flex my ankle. There are steep stone steps descending the last fifty yards to the street. I hobble down them. Magic Rat looks back to see why I've fallen off the pace. How suddenly and causelessly these troubles arise.

Hot Springs is a main-street town. Every restaurant, barbershop, and bar has an address on Bridge Street, the street with a bridge over the French Broad River. The street is marked with white blazes, from the south end of town where we arrived to the north end, where the trail crosses the river and dips back into the woods. Here, the choices of efficiently standardized America are not available. The most popular restaurant has honey-stung chicken on the menu instead of value meal number four.

There's a large subset of people with a connection to the trail. It is not uncommon for trail towns to have at least one former thru-hiker who has returned to take up residence. Outfitters, post office workers, and hotel and hostel owners all know and cater to backpackers. A procession of new thru-hikers maintains a transient presence. In towns as small as Hot Springs, add a few dozen hikers, and it seems like they are everywhere. Thru-hikers are easy to spot; they shop wearing rain suits while laundering their trail clothes; they wear sandals exposing feet papier-mached with moleskin and duct tape. Most men make the trip without shaving.

I'm staying at the Sunnybank Inn, otherwise known as Elmer's Hostel. The place and the person are legends on the trail. The inn is a Victorian home on the National Register of Historic Places. There are seven bedrooms, one phone, and no TV. Elmer has run this place for over twenty-five years. IIe is gruff, in his midsixties, with unkempt gray hair and an untucked Oxford shirt. He lets out a puff of air when a hiker asks if there is a computer in the inn. Elmer is proud of his anachronistic ways, yet he is no simpleton. Books are everywhere, and he is more comfortable the deeper the conversation delves.

On a scale at the outfitter's store I weigh 157. I weighed 172 when I started the trail and thought I was trim. I assumed I'd lose about ten pounds over the length of the trail, and this thing tells me I've lost fifteen pounds in less than three weeks. It is an old scale; it must be here only for show. While I'm still perusing the store, I see a nonhiker family near the scale. The father steps on the scale, so I move close enough to ask him.

"Is that right?"

"No," he says, "ain't no way I weigh that much!"

"It reads heavier than you think it should?"

"Naw, I only wish it was wrong. It's right on."

So 157 it is. That might explain the appetite.

I have a gourmet vegetarian family-style dinner with Elmer, his helpers Paul and Casey, and five other hikers. Dinner has a communal feel. Elmer explains that each night they come up with a question and circle around the table hearing everyone's answer. "If you could choose one musical group or artist to eliminate—it would be as if their music never existed—who would you choose?" Paul asks. Much conversation ensues, and we get around to the subject of trail magic.

Nova, one of the girls from Magic Rat's group, is a pretty young girl with wavy brown hair and a stellar smile. She has a flower-child demeanor and says "peace out" in place of "goodbye." "We were on Clingmans Dome," she tells us, "and kinda wanted to go into Gatlinburg, you know, so I went up to a couple next to their Suburban and asked, um…could we get a ride? They were really great. They gave us a ride into town, and then took us out for a huge steak dinner. They paid for everything. It was really great. Then, in the morning, they came to our room and gave us a ride back to the trail. Oh, they bought us breakfast, too. It was so cool."

All the while I think of my fruitless experience at Newfound Gap. I tell them I'm feeling sorry for myself for not receiving any trail magic. If only I looked like Nova.

"You go too fast," she says.

Cimarron is rooming with me. Cimarron is small, wiry, sharp, quick to smile, and eighty years old. "You know what people under seven or over seventy have in common?" He then answers himself: "The first thing they tell you is their age."

The next morning I'm with a group of hikers waiting for breakfast, and through the window we see Steve O. restocking from the hiker box. It's a peccadillo to take from a hiker box at a place where you are not staying. No one cares about this, but his presence sets off a discussion about him. Everyone has a Steve O. story. Or more accurately, everyone has an incredible story that they've heard from Steve O. He has told people that he hiked the Pacific Coast [*sic*] Trail. He had all his gear stolen in Mexico. His wife died of cancer and her dying wish was for him to hike the AT. We rationalize the hiker gossip as a safety issue. We want to know who is out in the woods with us.

Steve O. himself joins the circle of hikers inside. I had not seen him leave the hiker box. He doesn't appear to have overheard. He's wearing a green boonie hat, with the side flaps tied up. It's a flattering look for him, which converts his worn look to a look of ruggedness. He launches into a story of his son being killed in Iraq. Park rangers tracked Steve O. down on the trail to tell him, but they were not able to find him until after the funeral. "There's no sense in me getting off the trail now to go to Arlington," he says. "My son's already buried." Steve O. tells of his son's death in graphic detail with the emotional detachment of a reporter. I don't know what to make of it.

I've decided to take my first zero day here, to give my knee a rest. I ask Elmer about doing work around the inn in lieu of payment for another night. There is a trail term for this, too: "work-for-stay." Elmer is tentative. He wants to know what kind of work I can do.

Most people running hostels do it as a business. They are doing thru-hikers a favor by providing lodging cheaper than what is available to anyone else. But recipients of favors tend to develop higher expectations. In many cases, hikers look upon work-for-stay as a nominal amount of busywork for a free night's stay: another handout. Some hostel owners don't mind giving up a bed for work that they don't need done, but other owners rightfully expect the arrangement to be mutually beneficial. This is the undercurrent of my exchange with Elmer.

He lays out a plan where I will get an hourly rate that I can apply to my bill. I know he is hedging. If I'm not doing anything useful, he'll be able to say "that's enough" without committing to the full value of a night's stay. I'm a worker, and I know how to fix nearly anything in, on, or around a house. I'm glad that he expects something from me, because that means he will appreciate my work.

By noon I've replaced the screens on two doors, planed the front door so it opens more easily, and fixed some wobbly chairs. There are more things to do. Elmer and I rush down to the hardware store for fittings before it closes at noon on Wednesday, as do most other stores and the post office.

Things are going well. In the afternoon Elmer takes me, Paul, and Casey out to his organic farm, where we plant corn and butternut squash. I get a tour of the property while Paul feeds me every edible plant he can find: sourwood leaves (taste like citrus), cucumber plant (not a cucumber, but roots taste just like it), ramps (really strong onion), and chives. Elmer is building a home for himself on the farm. The walls are made from cords of wood packed in mortar.

We load a malfunctioning tractor into the bed of Elmer's small pickup, taking all the bed space where Paul and I had sat on the ride to the farm. So I end up riding back into town sitting in the seat of a tractor in the bed of a pickup, pretending to steer, feeling very much a part of this small town.

Meanwhile, more hikers have come into town. Crossroads, Snail, and Patience are here. I walk down to Paddler's Pub in the evening and hear a few calls of "Awol!" from hikers surprised to see me again. Magic Rat and his friends (Nova, Bear Bait, Moss, and Tito) are in the pub, having spent another day in town. "We have a ride to Damascus!" Moss says, in reference to Damascus, Virginia, where a weeklong hiker party called Trail Days is under way. "We can come back here in four days."

"Or not," Nova adds, implying that they could just continue north from Damascus.

This is a scenario I would see thru-hikers get themselves into, I thought unnecessarily so. It would be anticlimactic to reach Katahdin, then come back and "finish" my thru-hike by walking fifty miles in North Carolina. It would also create travel and planning logistics more difficult than hiking it while I am here. I am skeptical of hikers actually returning to do the mileage, and often the hiker making the claim seemed to be saying as much: "Yeah, I'll do it later," they'd say with a wink. Moot point. In my observation, hikers who broke the continuity of their hike were much more likely to go off the trail altogether.

I am reinforced in my belief that walking a continuous path and sticking with the white blazes is the best way for me to hike. My attitude about this is not rigidity for the sake of principle or unfeeling discipline done out of habitual compliance. More at issue is doing things in a way that enables me to sustain purpose and drive. I will do some things on this hike that will make purists cringe. But if I were to blue-blaze away a chunk of trail, or leave miles to be done "later," then it would be tempting to pare away even more of the trail, eventually concluding that there is no purpose to it.

Gumption is the most important thing for a thru-hiker to maintain. Compare rounds of golf, one played while keeping score and one in which you hit a mulligan every time you are unhappy with a shot. In the latter case, being on the golf course loses significance. Rounds that are memorable are the ones that you make count. In a broader context, all rounds of golf are of no consequence, whether score is kept or not. But you are the center of your own universe. You are free to create meaning for yourself.

When you attempt to capture the highlights without burdening yourself with the tedium, the highlights lose the foundation that elevates them to the status of "highlight." Analogies abound because a focused attitude defines the quality of all that we do. In playing a game, dieting, or hiking the AT, you benefit most when you commit yourself to it, embrace it.

❋ ❋ ❋

Stretch is the most athletic person I've met on the trail. He's two years out of college, where he played soccer. He and I seem to be the ones most concerned about stopping our weight loss, but I can't match his eating: six pancakes, two bowls of granola, cantaloupe wedges, and probably stuff he snatched from plates on either side of him.

Fourteen hikers are having breakfast at Elmer's. One of them comments that he has to stop taking these zero weeks.

Hot Springs is a hard town to leave. "Would you consider staying a while longer?" Elmer offers. "I'd like to build a bay window in that farmhouse, and I could use your help. You could stay at the inn, and your knee would get more rest."

The offer is tempting, but I'm determined to keep to my fast hiking plan. Before leaving home, I had laid out my plan on a spreadsheet. The plan had me hiking over eighteen miles a day with no zero days, and finishing in 116 days.[17] It was a crazy plan. At the time, I had never backpacked, run, or even walked unburdened on flat Florida ground eighteen miles in any single day. Remarkably, upon arriving in Hot Springs on May 13, I am still on schedule.

Leaving Hot Springs, I see Steve O. on the other side of the street, talking to another hiker. He doesn't have his pack with him. "Good," I think to myself. I plan on walking a few long days. I'll never see him again.

---

17   I would finish the trail in 146 days. I hiked on 128 days, averaging about seventeen miles per day, and took eighteen zero days.

4

Hot Springs to Damascus

From the French Broad River, I follow the trail along switch-backs up to the rocky cliffs of Lover's Leap. At the cliffs, the narrow path bends along a vertical rock wall. There is a view back to the river and the city I have left behind. In Hot Springs I had time to stand at a pay phone in the middle of town and talk with my wife and say hello to my kids. As I look back on the town, I miss this connection to home.

I take my time at a stream crossing, getting water, eating lunch, and writing a letter to Juli. A young man in sandals and day pack walks by, carrying a butterfly net. He sees that I am writing, nods, and continues on. The trail bends at the stream, so I am able to see him in profile up ahead. He slows, pauses, and slaps the net down over nothing on the side of the trail. It's best if I stall and let him move on. Now he sits and starts writing. Okay, I can get ahead of him.

Forgoing the urge to compliment him on the nice batch of dead leaves he snagged, I ask, "What are you looking for?"

"Oven birds. There is a nest right there," he says, point-ing to where his net landed.

He shows me a hole about the size that would be made by stabbing the handle of a shovel into the ground. Inside there are three eggs, but no bird. He is a naturalist gathering data on the small, ground-nesting birds. If a bird had been in its nest, it would attempt to fly out and trap itself in the net. This encounter is a tip to be more observant; surely there is much more wildlife I pass without noticing.

The AT just north of Hot Springs, North Carolina.

Tenderfoot is one of the few hikers on this section of trail today. She does not come as far as Little Laurel Shelter, so I have it to myself. It's a lonely transition from the crowd at Hot Springs. Soon after I settle in, an hour-long tempest begins. I cook on the sleeping platform of the shelter, having to back away from the open front to avoid the spray of pounding rain. Lightning shocks the sky with light. I wonder how Tenderfoot is doing out there.

I leave the shelter at 7:30 the next morning, and about a half hour later I hear an animal crashing through the woods. A small bear is running away from me. By the time I get my camera, the bear is out of sight. I chide myself over missing the photo—that may be the only bear I see. I should be more attentive. I put my camera away, and as soon as I take another step, two more bears drop from the trees and bolt in the same direction as the first.

Near the three-hundred-mile mark, there are headstones for three boys killed in the Civil War—the Shelton brothers and Millard Haire. Three bears, three hundred miles, and three weeks on the trail. Twelve miles into my day I feel drained, exhausted. I roll out my sleeping pad at Flint Mountain Shelter and take a nap. I wake an hour later, feeling fine, and hike nine miles to Hogback Ridge Shelter, arriving at dusk. This was the only time I would sleep midday during my hike. I saw no other hikers on the trail, but there is an overflow crowd at the shelter. Thru-hikers Cimarron and Wall Street are here, along with a handful of section hikers. The section hikers have a campfire going, and I take note of the fact that this is the first campfire I've seen. Cimarron has just finished his longest day, fourteen miles. He groans in his sleep: "Arrrgh…oooohh…my achin' body."[18]

On the early part of my hike out of the shelter, I feel strong and convince myself to go for Erwin, twenty-seven miles away, mostly under the influence of my stomach, which is calling for a big meal. My average hiking speed has been two miles per hour, including breaks. I should be able to get to Erwin before dark with my 7:00 a.m. start. But it

---

18   Cimarron had to leave the trail a short time later with a bad knee. This would be the last time I saw him on the trail. In 2004 he resumed his hike and sent me a postcard in September of that year: *"Well I finally finished doing the AT on Sept. 7. It was the hardest thing I have ever done. I was the oldest (82) person on the trail. It was a perfect day when I went up the Big-K. Hope it makes me a better person."*

sounds unrealistic to carry a backpack over mountains for a distance longer than a marathon.

The biggest climbs of the day are within the first ten miles. Big Bald (fifty-five hundred feet) is an expansive, double-peaked bald, totally covered in windswept fog. I struggle with these climbs. My Achilles tendon is still tight. On the same leg, I feel shooting pain in the tendon on the outside of my knee. I walk with a limp and with an aversion to bending my right knee. Distress affects more than my gimpy knee; it takes the wind out of me. It doesn't make sense that I should be out of breath because my knee hurts. I argue with my body, contending that I should be doing better aerobically because my sore knee slows my pace.

On the downside of the mountain, I duck into Big Bald Shelter and gulp down water and ibuprofen. I recover quickly and make good time. The trail stays sidehill for a pleasant stretch, maintaining roughly the same elevation as it passes through a pine forest. The trail is never straight and level for very long. When the elevation is somewhat constant, the trail is usually on the side of the hill, bending along the contours of the mountain to stay at the same height. It is common to cross streams running down the crease formed by the intersection of hills on the same ridge. Sidehill trails sag downhill where the trail is not supported by the root system of a trailside tree. The profile of the trail hangs between supporting trees like the scalloped fringe of a curtain.

Imperceptibly, the woods change from pines to hardwoods. The surface of the trail changes from needles to gravel. Switchbacks mark the beginning of the descent to Erwin. There is a break in the trees, and the lay of the town is evident. Looking down at the base of the mountain, the Nolichucky River and railroad tracks run perpendicular to the trail. Highway 23 is parallel to my path, off to the left, forming the western border of the city. Straight ahead, puffy green treetops hang over the city like clouds.

I am worn from the effort of covering sixty-seven miles in three days since leaving Hot Springs. Over these days, other than at the shelter last night, I've seen more bears than hikers. I look forward to rest and the company of people in the town below.

Near the trailhead there is a bunkhouse and a small store. The place is called Uncle Johnny's Nolichucky Hostel, run by a man of the same name. A few miles into town, Miss Janet runs a hostel. Word has spread among hikers that the competition between these hostels has gotten ugly. I had planned to stay at Miss Janet's. Her listing says to "call from the trailhead" to get a ride into town. The pay phone at the trailhead is on the porch of Uncle Johnny's.

Last year a hiker calling Miss Janet from this phone was chased away by Uncle Johnny. One guidebook removed a reference to Uncle Johnny's Hostel on account of complaints from hikers. So I sheepishly try calling Miss Janet from Uncle Johnny's phone and get an answering machine. I loiter a while and try calling again. No one is there. I start the walk into Erwin, sticking my thumb out whenever a car passes. I need to get out to the highway, walk a few miles up to the next exit, and find my way through town to Miss Janet's. I make it to the highway by the time a van stops for me. There's a sign on the side of the van: "Uncle Johnny's Hostel." The driver is Uncle Johnny himself. Before getting in I come clean: "I'm going to Miss Janet's Hostel."

"That's okay, get in. I won't take you to her doorstep, but I'll get you close." Uncle Johnny's tone is repentant. His business has been damaged by the guidebook omission and by negativity coursing through the hiker grapevine. I am the beneficiary of his contrition as he strives to get back into the collective good graces of thru-hikers. Still, he drops me off at a gas station near the highway. It's more of a walk across town than I want to make this late in the day. By now I've learned that jaunts made in cars are deceptively far on foot. Possibly drivers assume that hikers don't mind trivial walks. If you walk twenty-seven miles in a day, a few more blocks should make little difference. Not so. All off-trail mileage is anathema.

A young man in a pickup pulls up to a gas pump just before I start walking. Pickups are ideal rides since I can throw my smelly pack (and self) in the back.

"Do you know how to get to the Sonic drive-thru?" Uncle Johnny had told me directions to Miss Janet's, the last part of which was to go one block behind the Sonic. I'm asking for information that I already know, but there is a point to this.

"Go up to the light and turn right, then it's up the road, on your left."

"How far do I go after I turn right?" I choreograph this question with a move to sling my pack on my back, wilting under the weight and the prospect of a long cross-town walk.

"Do you want a ride?"

Finally he catches on.

Unlike any other hostel I would see on the trail, Miss Janet's is on a street in town among other homes. It is a framed house with wood siding, a picketed front porch, and a crawl space below. It is locked, no one is home, and a sign on the door says that they've gone to Damascus for Trail Days. My mail drop is inside.

I walk over to an eclectic Mexican restaurant, Erwin Burrito, and eat a burrito the size of a small dog while listening to a soundtrack of Johnny Cash singing covers of Depeche

Mode and Nine Inch Nails. I consider my options. It's been a long day, and it's still light outside. I'm eager to see other hikers; maybe I could take a zero tomorrow and stay with the crowd at Miss Janet's when they return tomorrow night. I could resupply and get cleaned up. But before buying anything, I want to see what's in my package.

Back at Miss Janet's, I walk around the place, looking for a way in, trying not to look like a criminal. I climb through an open window into a bedroom. The bedroom has been converted into a bunkroom, with a pair of bunk beds fashioned out of unfinished lumber. It's cramped, with gear strewn about. The carpet is matted and musty. I smell dog. I make my way to the front of the house. Where is the dog? I see two dry piles left by it and take the time to pick them up and flush them. Hostels look grubby when empty.

The foyer closet is packed with cardboard boxes, and I find mine among them. It's starting to get dark. I strap the box to the top of my pack and head back toward the highway. There's a motel out there. I'd better hurry, it's starting to sprinkle. The road crosses a railroad track, and a train is passing. Rain falls more heavily, and it's dark now. Standing roadside, waiting on the train, I am a sad sight to the people in the cars lining up beside me. I wonder if I look like I feel—run down, ticked off, and all wet.

❀   ❀   ❀

In college I owned an aging VW Beetle. Its red paint had faded to orange, and leaking battery acid ate through the floor under the back seat. The gas gauge no longer worked. Driving through a rainstorm one afternoon, the Beetle stalled in the middle of a flooded street. I stepped out into water over my ankles, assuming the water had killed the engine. It was still raining heavily as I pushed the Bug off the road to higher ground.

I had taken for granted the insulated little bubble of existence that a car provided. Life outside a car was shockingly different from life inside on a day like that. Outside I was pelted by cold rain, and I sloshed around in shoes full of water.

I tried to start the car again, only to hear the spin of the starter. Then it dawned on me what the problem was—I had run out of gas. Just coincidentally it happened at the deepest point of a flooded street, at the most inopportune moment. The gas gauge needle was always on empty, and for once it was right. I knew what I had to do: walk until I found a gas station, buy a can, buy gas, walk back, and hope I could get the Bug started. There was no gas station in sight, so it was sure to take a while.

On my walk in the rain, I came to the odd realization that I was happy. I would be okay. Being annoyed at my misfortune had been overtaken by my sense of coming alive when presented with obstacles. I was pleased with myself. I felt resilient and resourceful. Nearly every other day of my life would contain nondescript commutes, but not that day. That day was valuable, a day I'll always remember.

❁ ❁ ❁

At the motel, I look at the blister on my left heel. It is much the same as the one on my right heel that I popped when I was at Standing Bear Hostel. This blister is a little larger, and the bubble of skin is taut with pressure from the fluid inside. I sit on the lid of the toilet in the motel and poke it with a needle. A stream of clear fluid sprays the side of the tub. I take a look at my right foot, where the twin blister has peeled away and healed over with tender pink skin.

Erwin, Tennessee, has the unusual distinction of being the only town in America to have hung an elephant. That was in 1916, and the elephant had it coming. Since then there have been no more elephant incidents. It is Sunday and most stores are closed. Bad timing for my zero day. I do what I can—write, call home, and laundry. I take a walk down to the grocery store and look over its meager first-aid aisle, trying to find the ideal bandage to stifle these blisters.

Periodically, I make return visits to Miss Janet's, impatient for her return. Late in the afternoon, Muktuk, a thruhiker, lets me in. One other hiker is there, sleeping on the couch. Miss Janet pulls into the driveway, and hikers hung over from Trail Days spill out of her van. Miss Janet is a big lady with long, kinky brown hair, a tie-dyed shirt, and round glasses.

"We're all filled up," she says apologetically, "but I'm sure we can find a place for you."

"Probably on that carpet," I'm thinking. As welcoming as Miss Janet sounds, the whole scene is too Bohemian for my mood.[19] Back to the motel.

I speak with my sister on the phone. My mother recently had a blood test. She has been given these tests periodically over the course of her cancer treatment. My sister relayed that the results were not what the doctors had hoped for.[20]

Back on the trail, I am dispirited. My zero day wasn't what I wanted it to be, and I'm still nagged by assorted aches and pains. A toenail has broken loose and causes me pain whenever it gets moved (every step). I wrap a strip of duct

19   Miss Janet even wrote me after my trip to apologize for the inconvenience, exhibiting the good will that has made her extremely popular among thru-hikers.
20   The information turned out to be inaccurate. She is in remission.

tape around the toe to hold it down. After getting the tape on, it occurs to me that there will be no way of getting the duct tape off without taking the toenail with it.

I think of my mom. Snippets enter my mind, like Mom crying when I left for college. Once, at the beach, she swam out to rescue my beach ball that was pulled out by the current. I stood wailing on the sand. A toddler at the time, it seemed to me that she was out impossibly far and would never come back. I remember her helping me, my brother, and sister put tinsel on a Christmas tree while we played forty-fives. There is no continuity to these images. They come out of time sequence, and some replay many times over. I make no effort to control my thoughts or make sense of them. I'm just allowing myself a session of melancholy reminiscing. Alone, cruising serenely through the woods, is a situation that nurtures emotional liberation. In the bustle of everyday life there is no time for frivolous thoughts. If they come, they contend for attention with thoughts of what needs to be done at work, getting the car in for service, and paying the bills.

Distracted by my thoughts, the morning passes quickly. I have lunch on top of Beauty Spot, a bald mountaintop with a view back to Erwin. Mounds of boulders push up through the grass, making for ideal seating. I make peanut butter and jelly sandwiches using a bunch of single-serving jelly packets pilfered from restaurants and a loaf of bread purchased in Erwin.

More hikers are on the trail, resuming their hikes after returning from Damascus. Cherry Gap Shelter, seventeen miles from Erwin, is full when I arrive near 5:00 p.m. Crossroads is here, sitting outside looking forlornly at the full shelter.

"There will probably be six hundred more hikers coming here tonight," he hyperbolizes.

"There's a hostel a little further along," I say, implicitly asking him if he'll come with me. I haven't even paused to take off my pack.

He shows a bit of inclination to go, then says, "It's too late to go seven more miles." His boots and socks are off, and I see his blisters. Putting boots back on those feet would take more resolve than he has.

I am alone for the rest of my twilight walk. Hundreds of crickets are in patches along the trail, feeding on fallen leaves. As I pass they scatter; it's like wading through popping black corn. Beyond this, there is little sound, accentuating my aloneness. I feel uneasy, cautious. Just beyond Iron Mountain Gap, someone has spray-painted brown paint over the AT's white blazes. Seeing this heightens my wariness. I take some comfort in noticing that the vandal did not continue very far from the road and did a sloppy job of obscuring the blazes. "It must be a recreational vandal, maybe teenagers, not someone with a serious grudge against hikers," I rationalize to myself.

On the peak of Unaka Mountain, there is a grove of towering spruce trees. Like giant arrows shooting up from the ground, every one is perfectly straight. Short and bare branches are on most of the lower trunks. Near the tops are arrowheads of needles, the only green on the trees. The trees are tightly packed, choking out ground cover. Pine needles blanket the forest floor. This feels like sanctuary, and I am no longer wary. As soon as I am clear of the trees, I am treated to a field of golden wildflowers.

The guidebook directions to the Greasy Creek Friendly are: "From gap go right (downhill) on old jeep road, then take first left, and then the next right, go past old barn and around metal gate to first house on right."

There is no sign at "the gap," so from the start I am uncertain about heading down the side trail to my chosen destination. The trail is little used, overgrown with weeds, and hardly distinct from the surrounding woods. I need to push some shoulder-height branches out of the way to stay on anything resembling a path. I'm no longer taking the directions literally, I'm just picking the clearest downhill route. I nearly turn around but then see the metal gate. Beyond the gate, the jeep path is still in use, and it separates the only two houses in sight. The house on the left has a large yard enclosed by a tall chain-link fence. I'm glad it's there when two menacing, barking, mixed-breed dogs charge from the house. The house on the right stands in a sea of weeds. As I enter the yard, owners Pack-Rat and CeeCee come out to greet me.

They've named this place "Greasy Creek Friendly" as a pun on the word "hostel." "Why would you want to stay where it is hostile?" They've purchased this land as their own home, knowing its proximity to the trail, hoping that hiker business will provide Pack-Rat with full-time employment. CeeCee works as a nurse. I am the only hiker here tonight, and I'll stay in a bedroom of the main house.

CeeCee cooks nachos for me while I watch from the dining room table. "Do you want jalapeños?" she asks as she cleans the lettuce. Pack-Rat sits behind me on the couch, shiftlessly fumbling with lawn mower gears and watching news of the Martha Stewart trial. The setting makes me aware of what odd situations this trip has put me in, this time in the family room of a tiny house with a couple living in the mountains of North Carolina. CeeCee works to stay chipper, seemingly to offset Pack-Rat's depression.

They have been fighting to get permission from the local trail maintainers to post a sign on the AT to mark the side trail to their place. They aren't allowed to paint markers on the side trail, cut branches, or maintain it in any way. It has been a very slow year for them. I am the only hiker coming in tonight. Another sore spot for Pack-Rat and CeeCee is their quarrelsome neighbor, the one with the dogs.

"You hear that lawn mower running over there?" Pack Rat asks. I hadn't noticed it when I came in, but now that he asks, I can hear the drone of a mower, and I realize I've heard that noise ever since I've been inside. "Every day he parks that thing as close as he can to our place, and lets it run 'till it runs out of fuel." When I leave in the morning, I see that the neighbor had boarded over a section of his fence, on which he has spray-painted insulting graffiti.

Roan Mountain is the last mountain over six thousand feet until New Hampshire, and it is a hell of a climb. I pass Muktuk and the other hiker I saw sleeping on the couch at Miss Janet's Hostel, now struggling up the mountain. I also see three enviable thru-hikers walking downhill with barely filled daypacks. They got a ride to the top of Roan Mountain and are hiking south; tomorrow they'll get a ride back to the top and go north and avoid climbing the mountain. Some hostel owners provide this drop-off/pick-up service. They make money on the rides and by getting hikers back to their place for multinight stays.

For thru-hikers, walking weightless is a dream. Staying in town for a couple of nights isn't bad, either. Hiking without a full load is termed slack-packing. To purists, of course, slack-packers should be stripped of their "thru-hiker" title, and possibly dismembered. I have nothing against slack-packing, but I haven't arranged it yet. I have resolved to always walk on a continuous path northward.

After Roan Mountain, there is a series of grassy balds, providing views back to Roan. Here I meet two thru-hikers from England, Spoon and Martin. Both are strong hikers. Spoon is in his twenties. Martin is a character. He's in his early forties, small, wiry, intense, with knobby calf muscles and a smile like a terrier baring teeth. His reddish-blond hair matches his skin tone, giving him a monochromatically ruddy appearance. He is smoking, and surely he's a drinker, too. And yet, later, Spoon would tell me that Martin runs marathons. "Last time he finished, he ran right past the check-in and on into the first pub he could find."

At a fork in the trail, we go left along a blue-blazed trail a hundred yards to Stan Murray Shelter. A day hiker is here, planning to stay the night. I plan to go on to the next shelter. I head south back down the blue-blazed trail on which I came in. The day hiker says, "North is that way," pointing to the blue-blazed trail that continues north beyond the shelter.

"Yes, I know," I respond, but I continue to go back the way I came in.

Some shelters are situated with side trails coming in from two points on the trail, one south of the shelter, and the other north of the shelter. Martin explains to the day hiker that if I were to take the other side trail back out, I would not be walking the section of the AT between the two side trails. This is part of the purist thru-hiker code to which, thus far, I am still adhering. I get back to the AT and head north. I notice that I am walking parallel with the side trail, virtually retracing my steps. The shelter comes back into view, and I walk past it a mere ten yards away. The side trail was hardly necessary. I feel silly as I again wave "bye" to Martin, Spoon, and the day hiker after my two-hundred-yard diversion. They are still discussing the finer points of purist thru-hiking.

Overmountain Shelter is a defunct barn with room for dozens of hikers. Sixteen show up tonight. The setting is wonderful, overlooking a valley of cleared land. The side of the barn facing the valley is open, and downstairs there are plywood platforms for sleeping. Spoon and I lay out our bags here, but a wispy rain blows inside. I move to the enclosed upper deck—hayloft sans hay—where most of the other hikers are, spread out at odd angles laying claim to the most even patches of the rickety plank platform.

Overmountain Shelter.

Muktuk pauses on his way to the privy, full roll of toilet paper in hand. Most hikers unwind a fistful of toilet paper and stuff it in a plastic bag, hoping it lasts until their next resupply. "This is one thing you don't want to run out of," Muktuk says, mocking our preoccupation over pack weight. Now that he has an audience, he discourses on the pros and cons of nitpicking over a few ounces. "I met a hiker named

'Go Heavy' who carried his stuff in four suitcases. He'd carry two of them a hundred yards or so, leave them, and go back for the other two. He was intense. You know the kind; he had huge veins popping out on his neck and forearms." Muktuk's story is replete with hand gestures, waving a cigarette in one hand and toilet paper in the other.

I enjoy the crowd and the enthusiasm that we all have at this point in our hike. We've been on the trail long enough to make friends and to have experiences to talk about. We feel like we've been tested, and we all think we will finish. There is much ahead of us to be eager about.

Crossroads is here, on floor space next to me. We have our legs in our sleeping bags and are journaling and planning by headlamp. He has a map, and we talk of how the terrain is supposed to get easier now. I'm hoping to get to Damascus in three long days. My supplies are dwindling. I've just eaten two of my dinners, and I've finished the loaf of bread I bought two days ago. I can't get enough food. I'm shivering in my bag, and it's not that cold. I lack body fat to keep me warm.

There is barely a drizzle, as if the fog is too heavy to stay airborne, when I leave Overmountain Shelter. My feet are soaked less than an hour into the day. The first three miles are open and grassy with outcroppings of huge boulders. It probably would be scenic in good weather, but blanketed in fog it looks like a scene from *Macbeth*. The rain would last with varying intensity all day.

I spook four deer, a buck and three does. This makes me consider putting in a request for reincarnation as a deer. But I'd probably get shot so they could mount my antlers on a bunny skull at some steakhouse.

The next stretch of the trail in northeastern Tennessee was made possible by eminent domain land grabs that didn't sit well with the locals. Hikers tread lightly here. I pass with ears peeled for dueling banjos. The trail crosses a paved road, where there is an ominous sign warning of vandalism and advising against leaving cars parked at the trailhead. There are more road crossings, paved and unpaved. Few buildings are within sight of any of the crossings. Trash is dumped at one roadside where the trail crosses. I see a makeshift, handwritten "Shelter" sign, pointing down a side trail, and I wonder if it is an attempt to lure hikers off the trail. Barking hounds, distant gunfire, and rusty remnants of barbed wire fences add to my uneasiness, but my passage is uneventful.

❉ ❉ ❉

Before starting my hike, about half of the people I spoke with showed a great deal of concern for security on the trail, much more concern than I had myself. "Are you going alone?" "Are you taking a gun?" All questions showing disbelief that I would venture out unarmed among deranged, inbred mountain folk.

I went to a gun shop to buy some pepper spray. Better safe than sorry; something small just to give me peace of mind. The guy behind the counter was exactly what you might expect: big, gruff, bearded, tattoos, and one earring.

"Do ya want somethin' fer four-legged critters or the two-legged kind?"

"Both, I guess. What would you take?"

"I'd take me a gun. And a big knife, like that one," he answered, pointing to a Rambo model. "Ya see, if I wuz a low-life up there, I'd just hang out near that trail and get me some easy pickins."

So I got the pepper spray, but not the peace of mind.

❊ ❊ ❊

The trail parallels the Laurel Fork River for a few hundred yards. Near the bank, a hiker is standing in the rain like a sentinel, wearing a poncho. His pack is off at his feet, leaning on his legs.

"Hi."

"Just taking a break," he says. "Wish this rain would stop." Rain drips off the hood of his poncho and runs down his face. Droplets hang in his beard. Both of us are too weary for conversation.

I "hit the wall" after twenty miles and have a new assortment of blisters from walking with wet feet. The last six miles are a struggle. There are a number of stream crossings. The water is narrow enough to step over, but the banks of the stream have eroded, forming a deep "V" of land that I have to negotiate. Lunging across the gap hurts my feet. I stop and sit on a wet stump to put a bandage on the worst of the blisters. I have to stop thirty minutes later when the bandage peels off and forms a lump in my sock. Mud extends up the inside of my legs, where I nick each calf with the opposite foot. The large blister on the back of my heel, the one I popped in Erwin, is a mass of loose, soggy, white skin.

I arrive at Laurel Fork Shelter with just enough light to cook. Four other hikers are here already. Two are day hikers, and two are thru-hikers. None of the other thru-hikers from Overmountain Shelter did this wet, twenty-six-mile walk. I have a spot in the shelter next to one of the thru-hikers, an older gentleman with dense white hair and beard, with looks that place him between Santa Claus and Richard Harris, with the demeanor of the former. His trail name is Tipperary, named after the county in Ireland that is his home.

At this point on the trail, most thru-hikers have trimmed the fat from their packs and from their bodies. There is a notable absence of hikers who don't have it together. Few look like they don't belong, and Tipperary is one of the few. He's carrying a heavy sleeping bag and a seven-pound tent. Although he has already lost forty pounds, he is still over-weight, and he has his sore knee in a tight wrap. I introduce him to the wonder drug ibuprofen. In my mind, I unfairly judge that he won't be finishing the trail. Hearing of my long day, Tip treats me as if I am a trail master. We are both wrong.

Less than half the shelters so far have had a picnic bench, and this one does not. At most shelters, there is a fire pit out front. Hikers drag logs around the fire for seating. Here, I am seated on a skimpy branch only eight inches in diameter. It hardly qualifies as a log. I see pinholes in it, and the tiny red bugs that made them. It is an awkward place to make dinner. My stove burns isobutane, a gas that is compressed into a canister about the size and shape of an upside-down soup cup. The canister serves as the base for my stove. The stove itself only weighs four ounces and screws onto a threaded nipple on top of the fuel canister. It's just a burner with wings to support a small cook pot.

I have pasta for dinner. I cook pasta in one pot and de-hydrated sauce in the other, then dump the pasta into the pot with the sauce. The pasta pot is still considered clean. For breakfast, I make the meal that I have most often, two packets of instant oatmeal and hot chocolate. I don't carry a cup, so I mix hot chocolate in the smaller of the two pots. When I finish the oatmeal, I pour hot chocolate into the pot I ate from. This cleans out the oatmeal; I drink the dregs in my hot chocolate.

It is raining again today. I make a short day of it, hiking only six miles to Kincora Hostel. I wanted to stop here anyway, since it is a renowned trail stop. Owner Bob Peoples has built the hostel in a building adjacent to his own home, a few hundred yards from where the trail crosses Dennis Cove Road. Bob is retired and works as a trail maintainer. Thruhikers stop in to shower, wash clothes, and stay the night, all for the charitable price of four dollars.

Bob drives a truckload of hikers into town, and we quiz him about his work as a trail maintainer. He says the dumping of trash that we've seen near road crossings has gone on for years. He has picked through the trash, looking for anything that might identify the perpetrator, but the trash has always been scrubbed of identifying material. The animus towards hikers in this region comes in part from Irish landowners who had their land taken away to make the AT corridor more than twenty years ago. A long time to hold a grudge? Not for families who have owned the land for generations. Bob himself is Irish; Kincora is taken from the name of a castle in Ireland.

Next year, Bob will be rerouting part of the trail south of here. He assures us that the new trail will maintain a low grade and won't go over peaks unless there is a view. I'll believe it when I see it.

A group of us are early enough to make it to the lunch buffet at Chopsticks Chinese Restaurant. Later, when another wave of hikers arrives at Kincora, Tipperary and I tag along for a second trip to town. Spoon is here for this trip, and he and I split a pizza. Then he eats half a dozen doughnuts.

There is a talkative bunch at the hostel, happy to have reached the four-hundred-mile mark and eager to get to Damascus, Virginia, just fifty-one miles away. We load up the couch and every other sit-able surface for a group discussion. Tipperary wings me with his elbow whenever he is tickled by the conversation, which is often. I do surgery on my shoes. The tendon just above my left heel is raw because the padding on that part of my shoe has deteriorated. I cut a lumpy seam from the inside back of my shoe. The Dude has the same problem. His solution is to get a ride to Damascus to buy new shoes. He's a handsome young man, with utter confidence in his ability to charm his way to Damascus and back.

I am the first one up in the morning, so I can cook pancakes for the crowd. Spoon is up a little later and cooks a second breakfast of scrambled eggs and toast for everyone. Yesterday, I spoke with Juli, and she relayed a statement made by our oldest daughter, Jessie. "Mom, you know what I miss about Dad? His pancakes." The thought of my family having breakfast together at home recurs throughout the day.

North from Kincora the trail weaves through a small gorge formed by the Laurel Fork River and Waterfall. Just past the waterfall, the trail follows a ledge between the river and a rock wall. From there, the trail turns skyward for an arduous climb up to a plateau known as Pond Flats. Nine miles into the day, I reach Watauga Lake. There is a road and a picnic area.

In the vicinity of the picnic area there is a bit of litter that didn't quite make it to the trash can. It is a minimal amount of trash that I may not have taken notice of had I arrived by car. On the trail today I had seen small, square Jolly Rancher wrappers at regular intervals. I cursed the hiker who was thoughtlessly dropping them, and I put them in my pocket along with the wrapper of a candy bar that I ate while hiking. I go to the trash can to unload my pocket full of wrappers and find that my own wrapper is not there.

It must have been dislodged when I was stuffing the other trash into my pocket.

I follow the trail on an arc along the shoreline, then across Watauga Dam. The dam is more like a dike—mounded earth topped by a gravel road crenellated with boulders. On the climb up from the dam, I catch up with Tipperary. He has stopped with three hikers who were going to hike through the upcoming weekend (today is Friday). One of the weekend hikers is ill, and they plan to get off the trail as soon as they can. The two who are well have stuffed most of the sick hiker's gear into their packs.

"Awol, would you like to take some of their food?" Tipperary asks. "They are unloading whatever they can."

The food is a major score for me, but I try not to look too greedy at their misfortune. I take four breakfast bars, six bagels, a tuna packet, and a Little Debbie cake. Tipperary and I walk along with them until they reach the next road crossing. As soon as they are out of sight, I dig in. Of course the Little Debbie is first to go, then three of the breakfast bars. It is a long afternoon. By the end of the day, I have eaten five of the bagels and the tuna fish.

Vandeventer Shelter is nicely placed along a rocky ridge. Two thru-hikers are sitting on boulders behind the shelter, looking north to Virginia. They warn me that they have just seen a bear, and they believe the bear is still near the spring that is the water source for hikers using this shelter.

I am motivated to stretch the day, with hopes of getting to Damascus tomorrow. I hike seven more miles to Iron Mountain Shelter, and I am here alone. Recent entries in the shelter register tell more bear stories. A bear or bears have been lurking in the area between these two shelters, rummaging for food.

I have about twenty-five feet of string, with a carabiner tied to one end. After dinner, I toss the carabiner over a tree branch and clip on my food bag. I lift the food by pulling on the free end of the string, using the branch as a pulley. Then I tie the free end to the tree trunk, leaving the food suspended.

This technique is standard practice for thwarting bears. There are still drawbacks. Hikers lose food that has been hung too low; this was the case with Jean, who lost her food on her first night out. Bears push over trees that are too small and allegedly are smart enough to gnaw on the rope. In Georgia and a little way into North Carolina, campsites would have been adorned with hanging food bags. By now, most hikers have tired of the routine and tired of leaving their food out in the rain. Most of us just hang our food from the shelter rafters, as I have generally done from the start. But tonight is the exception, as I don't want to wake to the sight of a bear in the shelter playing piñata with my food sack.

Woods are never silent. Pine cones drop, branches rub in the wind, squirrels skitter. Any of these sounds, amplified by darkness and the absence of other hikers, could be mistaken for a foraging bear. Most of the suspect rustling comes from the unviewable back side of the shelter. To the right, there is a dense stand of rhododendron; perfect cover for a stealth attack. I lie down, uneasy, and pull one trekking pole by my side. The trekking pole is not enough. I slip out of my sleeping bag and gather up the rest of my arsenal: pocketknife, mace, and a whistle.

Morning comes without a showdown. Daylight emboldens me, and now I wish I would see more bears on this hike. A slab of fungus on the side of a tree glows bright orange as it is hit by a ray of the rising sun. Damascus, the most famous of trail towns, is my goal. All days on which there is a town stop are exciting, this day more so because I will also be crossing into Virginia, the easy state. It will all be downhill from here. I have a long day (twenty-six miles), and I want to arrive before 6:00 p.m. so I can get my mail drop from the Mount Rogers Outfitters. I'm eager for the challenge. I'll make a game of racing the clock.

The trail is conducive to a fast pace. There are only minor hills in the early part, and the last fifteen miles into Damascus is the easiest long span so far. To speed things up, I've put a protein bar and a bag of trail mix in my pockets and filled my water bottles, so I can eat and drink while walking.

I carry a two-liter water bag and a one-quart hard plastic bottle. My water bag has a tube that I thread through the top of my pack and over my shoulder. It rests in a loop on my pack's shoulder strap. At the end of the tube, there is a "bite valve," a soft plastic mouthpiece with a slit in it. When I pinch it with my teeth, I can suck out water. When I'm not drinking, it dangles at the ready without leaking. I learned of water bags with bite valves when I started gearing up for my hike, and I consider them to be the best innovation since my last extended hike ten years ago.

The one-quart hard bottle is good for mixing drinks. Infrequently, I will mix a protein powder shake or powdered Gatorade. I also use the bottle for getting water; my water filter screws onto the threaded bottle top. The filter has a pump at the top and a tube that dangles down into a water source. With this setup, I can pump a clean quart of water out of the murkiest puddle in less than thirty seconds.

My water bag has the brand name Camelbak, and my bottle is made by Nalgene. These makers are the dominant suppliers for these items. It is common for hikers to refer generically to a water bag as a Camelbak or call any bottle a Nalgene, just as we call a facial tissue a "Kleenex." I doubt that I ever heard the word "canteen" on my hike.

Typically, I start the day with my bottle empty and my bag nearly full. At around three pounds, a full water bag is the heaviest single item in my pack, so I always give some consideration to how much water I'll need. If I have less than ten miles to travel, I'll be tempted to take less than a full bag of water. Sometimes in the final hour before I expect to reach a town, I'll pinch the bite valve with my fingers and drain the unnecessary weight. Springs are abundant. Only on rare dry parts of the trail would I head out with water in my bottle as well. Those days are still far ahead of me.

Since 1987, Damascus has been home to Trail Days, an annual mobbing by thru-hikers past and present. For past thru-hikers, it is a reunion. For current thru-hikers, it is a party. There is dancing, drinking, talent shows, and of course eating. Some hikers stop for the entire week of festivities. Vendors set up booths to present new gear and capitalize on the extraordinary collection of hikers. As many as twenty thousand visitors come to town, a town that only has about one thousand full-time residents.

Trail Days ended the Sunday before I arrive, and the outfitter is low on stock. There are no trail shoes my size. I poke around the store for anything that will lessen the foot pain and blisters, or anything that will lessen my load. I buy new blister bandages, the fourth type that I will try, and new socks.

I eat at the Side Track Café, a diner with a bar and a row of computers hooked up to the Internet. Hikers sit at four of the machines, eagerly checking e-mail, typing their own journal entries, and looking up journals of other hikers they have met on the trail. Even though pay phones are available in every town, I prefer to send e-mail rather than to talk with friends on the phone. Using e-mail, I still retain a degree of separation from the "real world." With family it is different. I talk with my family on the phone at every opportunity. Tonight, I speak with Juli about plans for her and our kids to come visit me. They will fly into Richmond and drive over to wherever I am on the trail seventeen days from now.

Dave's Place, the hostel run by Mount Rogers Outfitters, is my home for the night. The small contingent of hikers lounges out front in the evening. A gregarious couple, Jason and Shelton, share their beer with the rest of us. The hostel caretaker, a hiker himself, edifies and entertains us with the techniques of shitting in the woods. He demonstrates the positions: sitting with your back leaning on a tree, squatting facing and holding onto a tree, unsupported full squat, and my personal favorite, the half squat.

The caretaker tells an anecdote about a hiker always intent on putting a good distance between himself and the trail to ensure excretory privacy. The hiker bushwhacks down, down, down from the trail until he finds his spot. He goes leisurely about his business, assured that this bit of nature is his alone. In the clean-up phase, a backpacker walks by and says hello. A switchback had brought the trail to within a few yards of where he thought he had privacy.

I look for my spot on the downhill side of the trail, preferably where I can walk down far enough to use the curvature of the land to conceal my situation. I certainly get further from the trail than is necessary. I always shed my pants without taking off my shoes, taking off one pant leg and leaving my shorts hanging on the other knee. An oft-muddy shoe will make two passes through one pant leg.

Going off the trail provides a truer feel of the wilderness. The ground is spongy with moss and duff. Branches and deadfall impede the way. I get poked by stray limbs and harvest spider webs. Undergrowth can completely fence me in. Without the trail, I quickly lose my place in the woods. I try to remain attentive to landmarks and keep my path simple. Even so, I rarely return to the same point where I left the trail. Our ribbon of beaten path—the AT itself—is a luxury afforded us in the wild.

There are more outhouses (most often called privies) along the trail than I expected. They are at most shelters and some campsites. Inevitably there are times when I have the urge soon after leaving a place with a privy or leaving a town, and I admonish my body for its poor timing.

In my pre-hike talks with acquaintances, more than a few drew the line at porcelain. Hiking they felt they could handle. Sleeping in a shelter, okay. Shitting in the woods, no way. In truth, I feel completely at home with this aspect of hiking. There are a few tracts of the trail ingrained in my memory specifically for having made a relieving trip into the bushes.

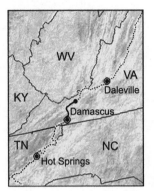

5
Damascus to Bland

The waitress is skeptical. "You sure you can eat all that?" she asks, referring to the Barn's Hiker Breakfast that includes massive blueberry pancakes, scrambled eggs, a half plate of hash browns, two slices of ham, a biscuit and jelly, a big bowl of grits, coffee, and orange juice. She should be skeptical, because I look pretty scrawny now, weighing well less than 160 pounds.

The meal is such an impressive spread I am tempted to take a picture of it, but I am too embarrassed to do so in front of the other customers. About thirty seconds later the waitress returns for the empty pancake plate. "You're doin' great; remember to chew." I polish it all off, except for a few spoonfuls of grits so I wouldn't look completely barbaric.

The AT heads north from Damascus on the Creeper Trail, an old railroad bed running parallel to a sizeable creek. The AT cuts into the woods and runs up and down the hills parallel to the Creeper Trail, staying so close that I can often catch an enticing glimpse of the wide, level path below. Twelve miles later the two paths end up at the same spot.

I walk leisurely most of the day. Over the past week, I have been constantly stretching to reach one destination or another. Today I am starting out with an unplanned foray into Virginia. I spend time chatting with a trail maintainer. He is out with a sickle, battling kudzu for ownership of the trail. It starts to rain, so I pull in to Lost Mountain Shelter. I meet two other thru-hikers who are staying here tonight. Old Bill is a fiftyish police officer from England. Crash is about half his age.

Old Bill has a compendium of motivations and goals. He decided to hike in part because of job dissatisfaction. While in North America, he'd like to see New York City and Washington, D.C., and he talks of venturing into Canada. This all cannot fit into the time he has available if he hikes the entire trail. Old Bill admires another hiker who he perceives to be having a more spiritual adventure, stopping and lounging in his hammock whenever the mood strikes him. Old Bill would like to spend more time contemplating. He is also proud to be fit and is aware of the hike as an athletic challenge. It probably worries him that meandering along the trail could have the negative connotation that he can't keep up with the young bucks.

Crash, Old Bill, and I walk much of the next day together. In the early hours, fog and sun fight for control of the skies. There is a light drizzle. By the time we enter Grayson Highlands State Park, the sun has the advantage. There is a sign marking a side trail to the summit of Mount Rogers. Crash pulls out his guidebook and reads, "Left one-half mile to summit. No views."

"I think not," Old Bill says. We get a laugh out of the invitation to walk another mile out of our way to visit yet another mountaintop covered with trees. The AT is sometimes referred to as the "green tunnel" for the endless miles of trail that are shrouded by trees. Another reason that we pass on the side trail is that the next ten miles are a highlight of the southern section of the AT.

Much of the trail through Grayson Highlands is grassy and open. For the first time I can see long stretches ahead, cutting through the grass and up conical hills. Rocky outcroppings erupt from the hilltops. Some craggy monoliths stand over twenty feet tall. The trail passes through a body-width split in a huge boulder, in a tunnel-like pass of about thirty feet. The isolated trees are shapely evergreens. Trees and scrubs in this region gather around the rocks, projecting a landscaped appearance.

Wild ponies roam the park, keeping the shrubbery in check and providing us with this welcome break from the green tunnel. We pass three herds, all with about a dozen ponies and some foals. The most daring of the ponies approach us for food; one chews on the loose end of my salty shoulder strap.

As we exit the park, we pass through herds of cattle. Late in the day, we pause at Wise Shelter, a large, comfortable shelter with a clean privy. It looks like the three of us would have the place to ourselves, but we move on to Old Orchard Shelter, which is old and full. A mile of the trail between the shelters is intertwined with a shallow, ill-defined stream, so I end up saturating my shoes in ankle-deep water. My feet feel bruised from the rocky trail.

A hiker is in the shelter, lying "rest-in-peace" style, wearing headphones. I recognize him as Russ, the hiker I last saw plotting a blue-blaze around Standing Indian Mountain. I have not seen him since and assumed he was well behind me.

"Russ! How'd you get here?" I ask.

Russ lifts an earphone and answers curtly, "I walked." He lets the earphone spring back over his ear. End of conversation.

Did I offend him? My question was really just stated as a greeting. Only after his reaction do I realize that he may have interpreted my question as an accusation or condemnation of blue-blazing. I regret that I did not phrase it more aptly, like, "How has your hike been since I saw you last?" When I spoke with him a month ago, he had been candid about his plans to take an abbreviated course along the trail, so I didn't anticipate his defensiveness. Maybe he just didn't feel like talking.

I set up my tarp in a field in front of the shelter, with eight other tents. A crowd gathers around the campfire, telling trail stories. A group of three section hikers are here, and they have pieced together more of the trail than we have traveled. I make a pan of Jiffy Pop popcorn over the fire. One of the section hikers pulls out a bag of extra Snickers bars he carries for encounters with hungry thru-hikers. Retreating to my tarp, I notice how late we've stayed up; it's 9:30 p.m.

I get off to one of my best starts yet and cover fourteen miles by lunchtime. Crash and Old Bill catch up to me at Partnership Shelter, where we all stop for the night. This shelter is one of the more elaborate shelters on the trail. It is a two-story structure with a steeply pitched wood shake roof and a solar-heated shower. By the time I take a shower, it is a torturous, cold, icy spray, and I dance around trying to wash myself with minimal water exposure. The shelter is adjacent to a ranger station that has a pay phone and vending machines outside. The phone number for a pizza delivery service is posted by the phone. Hungry Hiker, yet another hiker from Israel, already has his pizza. This is our first meeting, but I had been taking notice of his elaborate drawings in shelter registers. He carries his own pen for his artwork. He's young and not yet filled out, except for a big toothy grin, which has grown ahead of the rest of his body. He is thin with a pale complexion and red hair cut to stubble.

I don't feel too worn after covering forty-eight miles in the last two days. An assortment of foot pains nag at me, but otherwise I feel as though I am hitting my stride. I get up early and drag my unpacked gear up to the visitor center so I can cook my breakfast without waking anyone. I buy two sodas from the vending machine to carry on the trail with me.

When I hit the trail, I see Crash starting his walk, too. I have enjoyed his company. He also left an engineering job to hike, so we relate on the tedium of cubicle confinement. He is tall and lanky, and his pace is compatible with my own. He perplexes me when he tells me that the two days we just walked have been his longest, and that he started the trail much earlier than I did. He must be wise to walk well within his capabilities, or he has become more capable as his hike progressed. The name "Crash" is from the Kevin Costner role in *Bull Durham*, though he actually bears a stronger resemblance to the character played by Tim Robbins. Halfway through our day, I surprise him with the smuggled soda.

We stop again to look at Settlers Museum. There is an open but unmanned schoolhouse exhibit. There are even undisturbed textbooks on the desks. Hot Dawg is taking a break at the schoolhouse. He carries his pet, "Stubby Cat," atop his pack, and he poses while we take pictures of them.

Hot Dawg and Stubby Cat.

The cat is a star at shelters, where he has caught sixteen mice. Hot Dawg grins widely and speaks just a little slowly, like he is feeling no pain. Literally. "I took eight Advil this morning," he tells us. The rest of the walk into Atkins is mostly through waist-high fields of grain. There is just enough of a downhill slope that my steps land heel first. Pain builds in my left heel. What first feels like the prick of a splinter grows to the feeling of a bamboo shoot thrusting into my heel on every landing. With town in sight, I shake it off and press on.

All that we see of the town are a few businesses near an off-ramp of Interstate 81. It is the typical cluster of businesses that serve passing traffic: a gas station, a restaurant, a Dairy Queen, and a motel. We would visit them all, starting with the motel. As Crash checks in ahead of me, he shuffles

Awol south of Atkins, Virginia.

through a small stack of bills and cards kept in a Ziploc bag, the hiker version of a wallet. Wordlessly, he extends one of the cards to me. The card has a picture of a clean-shaven young man, heavy, with a round face. I don't know why he is showing me this person. Finally it dawns on me that it is a picture of *him* on his driver's license. That's how he looked before the hike.

Crash started out with a good bit of weight to lose. He struggled early on. People from home doubted his ability to thru-hike, and before getting through Georgia, he started to agree with them. It was tough, he was lonely, and he started to wonder why he was doing it. He hitched to Blairsville, and from there he arranged a bus ride back to Atlanta. As it happened, he had to wait a day for the bus's departure. In that day, he had time to reflect on his situation. He didn't want people to be right about him. He didn't want to go back feeling like a failure. He put his pack back on and returned to the trail.

Our motel is a simple one-story motel with a single row of rooms. More rooms have backpacks, boots, and hiking poles parked out front than cars. I get clean and take a look at my troublesome left heel. The bamboo shoot pain I had was in the same location of the blister I had in Erwin. Dead skin from that blister has peeled, leaving a circle of ragged skin around an inflamed red area. In the center of the whole mess is a new blisterlike abscess. All my other blisters I have treated with apathy, but I put effort into this unhealthy-looking wound. I clean it, coat it with antibiotic ointment, and paste a bandage over the top.

Crash and I have dinner at the restaurant and dessert at Dairy Queen with two other thru-hikers, Jeff and "Double A" (written as "AA" in shelter registers). I tell AA that she should have the trail name "Snow White" instead. She has jet black hair, a pale complexion, and looks that are too clean and soft for a thru-hiker. She has heard this suggestion enough times for it to raise her dander. AA is simply the initials of her name, Allison Allen. I comment on the coincidence that my next door neighbor has the reverse name: Allen Allison. I go on to explain that I always had difficulty with the neighbor's name because the previous neighbor in the same house had the last name "Allen," like AA. To further compound the coincidence, we learn through our conversation that AA went to a small college in Georgia (Toccoa Falls) with Lisa Allen, the daughter of my previous neighbor.

We talk of motivations for thru-hiking. "I've always wanted to thru-hike," AA says. "My dad and I hiked some when I was little." Answering that you want to do a thing because you have always wanted to do it seems somewhat circular, but it is as common as any other explanation.

Writing daily journal entries is a welcome part of my routine. I also write a newspaper article every two weeks for the *Florida Today* newspaper. Writing for the newspaper does not come easily. I must submit an article before leaving Atkins, so I spend the morning collecting my thoughts and getting them composed into e-mail. At the moment, I regret having committed to writing the articles, and I am dismayed that the act of recording is interfering with the trip that I have proposed to record, but these thoughts are temporal. I am glad that I write. Experience is enriched by reliving it, contemplating it, and trying to describe it to another person.

This is the first time on my hike that I feel burdened by tasks I put on myself. Back in the real world, I routinely enlisted myself in an excessive array of activities. I recall a formative decision I made soon after starting my first job out of college. An acquaintance had asked if I would reroof his mother's home. I spent two days pondering the decision. I had a job programming. I didn't need to labor on roofs anymore. When the decision finally came, it was an epiphany. No way was I going to allow myself to settle into an ordinary life because it was the easy thing to do. I didn't want to be pigeonholed, defined by my career, growing soft and specialized behind a desk. I would continue to resist specialization and stretch myself by undertaking new endeavors.

If not for that attitude, I wouldn't be here. But because of that attitude, I can be too demanding of myself. Now I see an unexpected benefit of thru-hiking. It is an escape from me. It is a forced simplification of my life; being on the trail limits the opportunities for me to pull myself in multiple directions.

By the time I leave Atkins, all the other thru-hikers who were here last night have left, and a few new ones have trickled in. After I check out, I pass the open door of a room full of hikers, catching a glimpse of one with a green hat. I don't pause to do a double-take, because unmistakably it is Steve O., the hiker I believed—hoped—I had seen for the last time in Hot Springs.

It is raining when I head out, and it rains on and off all muddy day. The first two miles are through waist-high grain, and it is like walking through a car wash. The trail goes through a number of cow pastures, each time entering and exiting the barbwire-bound fields over stiles: wide, stubby, wood ladders with three or four steps. The path in the pasture is rutted, about the size of a bowling lane gutter, with red clay showing where the grass has been pounded away. The bottom of the gutter is muddy at best, or flowing with a stream of orange water. I try walking on the shoulder of the gutter, but a misstep catches the rain-slicked clay and I slide, toppling over on my side. Venturing off the trail, I get thrashed by tall grass, splatter through a few piles of manure, and find that the ground below the grass is also uneven.

I reach Knot Maul Branch Shelter at 4:30 p.m. It is a full house, and the water source is far from the shelter. Crash is laying out his sleeping pad. I tell him of my plan to head for Chestnut Knob Shelter, another nine miles north. I will be in for a twenty-three-mile day, long under any circumstances, but particularly so since I wasn't on the trail until noon today. Late in the afternoon, I reach an extensive, somewhat open ridge, feeling as though I should be near the shelter but never getting there. Heel pain is excruciating now, even on uphill steps. It was a poor decision for me to push on. Wind-blown clouds limit visibility and dump a steady rain on me. The grassy top of the ridge has just enough trees to avoid being called a bald. Ghostly looking trees stand back from the trail, obscured by the foggy mist. Wet, windy, high, and exposed is a good recipe for hypothermia, and I feel increasingly chilled, despite the sweaty effort of walking.

A spring-fed puddle is off to the left. I recall from the guidebook that this must be the water source for my still-unseen shelter. As much as I desire to reach cover, I know I need water to cook, and I won't want to come back later. I take off my pack and balance it in an upright position on the long, wet grass since there are no trees in the vicinity. In the brief moment of pulling back my pack cover to get out a water bottle and filter, rain dampens the upper contents of my pack. I pump a bottle of water with numb hands and a shivering body. When done, I turn to see that my pack has toppled, spilling more gear onto the wet ground. Frustrated, I stuff it all in the pack, losing all pretense of keeping anything dry.

I am lucky that there is room in the shelter, more so since it is a rare, fully enclosed, concrete shelter. A half hour later, Crash arrives. I am flattered that he was inspired by me to extend his day. His entrance makes me think of this shelter as an Arctic outpost, where the weary, bundled traveler opens the door and enters with a burst of howling cold wind. Then the wind slams the door behind him and there is silence and safety.

The pain in my heel is agonizing when I walk out to pee in the morning. For the past few days, my heel pain has intensified as the day wore on, so I don't like the way this day has begun.

After spending considerable time cleaning and rebandaging my heel, I decide I need to get off the trail and see a doctor about this problem. All but one of the other hikers head out while I'm looking over the guidebooks for the next easy access to town. The last remaining hiker is a young man who was asleep in the bunk above mine when I arrived last night. To my knowledge, he had not stirred in the twelve hours since that time. Now he has retrieved a cigarette and lit up without leaving his bag. The smoke pervades this small enclosed building, but I say nothing.

The best choice for getting off the trail is at road U.S. 52, which leads into the town of Bland, Virginia. This road crossing is twenty-two miles away, a daunting prospect considering how I feel at the moment. At first, there is a rocky but manageable descent from the shelter, then a climb back up Garden Mountain. On the climb, the smoker-hiker passes me. I step aside and finally say hello. He flies by without a word. On the downside of the mountain, I come upon him and another thru-hiker. His friend had camped by the road last night. The two of them look over a map, scheming to hitch out on this little-traveled road. Smoker-hiker remains reticent, but his gregarious friend explains the plan. "If we can just figure out which way to walk, [right or left on the road], someone will eventually come along and give us a ride."

"How will you get back here?" I ask, only getting laughter for a response. Of course they don't intend to hitch back out on a dirt road. There are plenty of well-traveled access points further up the trail.

In the middle part of my day, the trail is an obstacle course of mud, blow-downs, and a bunch of stream crossings. Actually, I believe it is only one stream that the trail planners crossed back and forth a dozen times. On the home stretch to civilization, the AT follows a gravel road, where I pass hiker "Dirt Nap" playing his guitar. He indeed looks like a man woken from a nap on the ground. Gear jangles from his pack as he strolls along. Given the width of the road, I'm free to walk alongside, pass, or walk backwards diagonally in front of him, as a dog might explore perspectives of a walking companion. His words have the wispy, deliberate tone you would use to induce hypnosis. We speak about his guitar, music. On other topics he is vague.

"When did you start the trail?" I ask.

Dirt Nap responds, "I don't know."

Surely he knows when he started hiking, but giving a concrete answer would undermine his enigmatic persona. The appropriate response here would be, "Awesome." "Awesome" is a sweeping adjective used by the younger generation. In this context, "awesome" is equivalent to the "far out" of the older generation. If I say "awesome," it would mean, "It's cool that you are so much at one with nature that you have lost your sense of time and self. Far out." Semantics aside, I'm in a bit of a snippy mood, and I don't want to let Dirt Nap off easy.

I test his ability to be creatively evasive with, "Where did you stay last night?"

He's taken aback, stumbling over my breach of protocol. "I...I don't remember."

When I get to U.S. 52, the first car I see pulls over and the driver gives me a ride to the Big Walker Motel in Bland, Virginia. Smoker-hiker and his friend are here, telling me of their success in hitching out from the dirt road, even though they had chosen the wrong direction to walk. Steve O. is here, too.

"Hi, Steve," I say.

"Awol—I thought that was you I saw in Atkins," he responds.

In the midst of our greetings, it dawns on me that he shouldn't be here yet. It was only yesterday that I left Atkins, and Steve O. was just settling in. How is it that he is here one day later? Actually, it is almost as improbable for me to be here. He saw me at noon yesterday, and here I am forty-four miles further north the next evening. For all he knows, I am a kindred spirit in taking a less literal approach to thru-hiking.

The incongruity has dawned on him as well, and he explains, "These guys I'm with, they've hiked that part already. Those miles are trash. I'm not gonna let it bother me. Hell, I'll be walking two thousand miles—nobody cares about a few miles."

The name Bland is apropos for this town. Scanning the phone book, I see few businesses. My choices for medical care are just a couple of private practices, and it is now Saturday morning. I have poked into the bulging infection on my left heel, as I did in Erwin, but now instead of clear fluid, a sickly yellow puss seeps out. Indecisive about what to do next, I talk on the phone with Juli and then with my parents. They encourage me to walk into an emergency room for medical care, a thought that never dawned on me. I think of hospitals as places for people who are seriously ill. The nearby town of Wytheville has a hospital. There is also a rental car agency that will shuttle me to Wytheville if I rent a car.

❄ ❄ ❄

I lie on my stomach while the doctor and his assistant have a go at my heel. They cut and squeeze with much success. They whisper to themselves, not to keep me from hearing, but because they are concentrating.

"Look at all that," he says, referring to the puss they've extracted. He makes another cut.

"There is another pocket over here." He squeezes to the extent of his strength, then regrips and squeezes again. I know just how he feels, on the cusp of accomplishing a total purge. In spite of the pain, I want him to do this. I want the infection gone. I am silent, but my leg tension breaks the doctor's focus.

"Oh, sorry," he says, as if suddenly aware that the heel in his grip is attached to a person.

The doctor sends me away with antibiotics, bandaging tape, and gauze, and he reprimands me for continuing to walk with my foot in this condition.

"You should not hike until you've finished the antibiotics. The real problem for you will be the wound. Even if it has started to heal when you hike again, it will be very easy to reopen the injury."

The antibiotics will last a week. I can't take a week off. In my mind, I've already cut the doctor's suggestion back to four days, maybe even three. His other, more worrisome sentences ring true. This infection stemmed from a blister that I popped twelve days ago in Erwin. I thought it was on track to heal, and then the infection appeared. How can I prevent this weakened area from becoming a perennial problem?

From being on the trail, and from my prior reading about thru-hiking, I know that this is how a hike ends. It only takes one injury that won't go away, and I've already dodged a handful of injuries that had hike-ending potential. Also, taking multiple days off will break the momentum that I had. I will have the distraction of nursing a sore foot. Will I maintain the motivation to continue? Even if my heel ceases to be a problem, I've come to expect that there will be another injury or pain to take its place. I feel like my chances of finishing the hike are fifty-fifty. My assessment of the situation is objective. I'm not unmotivated at the moment. I won't really know how my head or my heel will react until I hit the trail again.

Assumption, even about your own state of mind, without immediacy of action is guesswork. During the yearlong planning of my hike, I mostly felt positive anticipation about the things I would be doing and places I'd be seeing, just like anyone does looking over vacation brochures. As my departure date grew near, worries about leaving work mounted. For at least four months I would be a spender with no earnings. Then came the day I actually walked away from my desk and turned in my badge. It was really happening. I felt like a truant, having broken free in midday, midweek. Instead of looking forward to 5:00 p.m., I was looking forward to adventure. The doubts I had about voluntary unemployment were washed away by the tide of excitement. It wasn't until then that unadulterated emotion escaped and I was certain of my decision.

I'm determined to do all that I can to get myself back on the trail with the best chance of staying the course. I find a motel in Wytheville willing to put me up for half price for taking a room with poor TV reception and agreeing to stay at least three nights. I buy Epsom salts and soak my foot for fifteen minutes three times a day. I wear camp clogs all the while, keeping the area free from friction or confinement.

I drive a car for the first time in over a month, taking my rental car north to an outfitter in Blacksburg, Virginia, to buy boots. Heel blistering occurs on my trailing foot during the walking motion, when my heel lifts off the ground but my shoe resists bending like my foot does. I reason that boots can be attached snugly at the ankle, alleviating some of the heel friction.

I purchase molefoam, a thicker version of the popular blister-protecting material called moleskin. Molefoam comes in patches about the size of an index card, about one-eighth of an inch thick, and has one adhesive side. It is applied by custom cutting a donut shaped piece and pasting it to your foot with the hole over the blister. The molefoam around the blister absorbs impact and friction that would otherwise befall the blister.

During my stay in town, I never tire of eating large meals at restaurants. Four days of bingeing hardly adds back any of the weight I had lost. I watch the movie *Finding Nemo* at the Millwald Theater, the oldest continuously operating movie house in Virginia, open since 1928.

I try my hand at trail magic and anonymously leave a cooler where I got off the trail near Bland. I want to see hikers, but no one passes in the half hour that I wait. When I retrieve the empty cooler later in the day, I see that Tipperary left a note of thanks.

The next day I head for a trail crossing further south, on a road I remember crossing before reaching Atkins. I navigate the back roads, pairing a road map that doesn't show the trail with a trail map that doesn't show the roads. I gain a better understanding of the effort others go through to meet hikers at trailheads. From the city of Marion, Virginia, I head up a tiny road that is supposed to cross the trail.

A short way out of town, two hikers are walking the road, still far from the trail. I'm not expecting them, and they are just as surprised to see a car. Not many hikers go into Marion because the trail leads directly into Atkins less than twenty miles away. The hikers are a couple in their midfifties. They are dressed alike in blue shorts, white shirts, and white Gilligan hats. The woman turns and backpedals, waving superfluously to get my attention. Her feet slide down a grassy shoulder of the road, and she falls forward onto her hands. Both have short black hair peppered with gray. I can't help my impressions. They look too clean, too civil, and they've come off the trail at an inconvenient road to go into a town no hiker visits. They must not know what they are doing. On the remainder of my hike, I would see much more of them and learn how wrong my impressions were. For now, they introduce themselves as Ken and Marcia.

6
Bland to
Daleville

The break did not make me feel like quitting. If anything, having the injury and time off added to my motivation. I had my hard times and expect balance to be restored. I now know that I have the drive to finish the hike and realize that I must take better care of myself to make it happen. I averaged twenty miles per day in the twelve days of hiking from Erwin to Bland. I no longer want to push to make miles. My self-imposed four-month schedule is sure to be extended.

It's raining. Not too bad really, and it clears up by noon. The trail feels different, more organic than the trail I left four days ago. The ground has rich, dark, wormy soil. Kudzu and its kin are covering the floor of the forest with green runners. I see three sizable black snakes at separate locations.

The cuts made by the doctor have not closed completely, but they are not bleeding. My heel does not hurt when I walk. I'm not used to hiking with shoes that come over the ankles, so I feel constrained by my new boots. Even though they are no higher than the average hiking boot, it feels like I am walking in ski boots. After a couple of miles, I start experiencing discomfort, especially when going downhill. On the downslope, the top of my boots put painful pressure on my Achilles tendons. Unfortunately, there is no way of knowing how shoes or boots will work until you try them out. After using them, they are difficult or impossible to return, and usually you are a day or more away from being able to swap them out. If I stick with my current plan, I would reach Daleville in a little more than a week, where I could visit another outfitter. After about eight miles the pressure on my Achilles tendon is unbearable. I cut a line an inch and a half vertically down the back of each boot to loosen the "collar" around my leg.

At 3:00 p.m. I arrive at Jenny Knob Shelter. Boot alterations alleviated the stress on the back of my leg, and I never felt any irritation on my heel. At the shelter, I take off the bandage and see that there is no bleeding or undue redness. The day thus far was a success.

Two section hikers are in the shelter, and more thruhikers come in after me. Andy is a thru-hiker I'm seeing for the first time. His clothes and gear give the impression he is traveling on a limited budget. He is young and from California. My short twelve-mile walk is exactly what I need to be doing while I'm nursing my heel and coming back up to speed on the trail. Andy packs up and continues down the trail. Rain clouds have dissipated, and I can see blue sky through the treetops. I get restless. The weather is perfect and I feel fine. Indecision paralyzes me until 5:00 p.m., then I get up and go. Six miles from Jenny Knob Shelter I'm ready to stop, but now I'm too close to a road. Head-high brush near Kimberling Creek laps across the trail. When I push them aside, thorns snag my shirt and cut thin red lines into my arms and shoulders. I'm wearing down and wish I had not left the shelter. My first day back and I've already made a bad decision and walked another twenty-mile day.

Darkness is falling, and I finally find a clearing in which to camp. It's on the side trail leading to Dismal Falls. Andy comes back from the falls and sets up his tent in the same clearing. Andy is good company; he is talkative, gregarious, and agreeable. He had met some locals having a party on the other side of the falls, and he had rock-hopped across to join them.

Dismal Falls is a short, wide cascade. Water drops only ten feet over a concave arc of rock. The creek is running low, exposing broad slabs of rock on the unused portion of the streambed. Our little clearing among saplings, with the din of the falls, is calm and comforting.

I return to the falls in the morning to get water and see a few of the locals asleep on the slabs of rock, one of them less than an arm's length from the falls. Andy is still in his tent when I leave. Before lunchtime I reach Wapiti Shelter, the location where two hikers were murdered in 1981.[21] The shelter faces away from the trail, as if embarrassed by its past. It is a worn, old-looking shelter. Inscriptions are on the walls and in the shelter register, some mourning the victims, some expressing outrage that the murderer was set free in 1996. It is a sad place to be, and I don't stay long. Sad, but not spooky; visiting this site does not change my visceral feeling that the trail is safe.

The trail passes through a zone in which all the trees are saplings, no taller than a dozen feet high. Their young leaves are a luminous light green. Undergrowth is dense here, still getting a share of sunlight that they will be deprived of when the trees mature. The effect is that of having

---

21   Jess Carr, *Murder on the Appalachian Trail* (Radford, VA: Commonwealth Press, 1984).

a wall of green on either side of the trail, like a corridor through an oversized cornfield. A deer is in the corridor, less than twenty yards ahead of me, also walking north. He looks over his shoulder at me and then lazily jogs ahead on the trail until he is out of sight. I catch up and see him grazing on trailside shrubbery. Again, he only goes far enough to lose sight of me. On my third sighting, he grows impatient and leaves the trail for cover of the saplings. An hour later, the trees are taller and sparser, so I have clear vision of three deer galloping on a path that will bring them closer to me as they cut across the trail. They don't alter course even though they must be aware of my presence. I have a fleeting feeling of being disrespected since they show no fear of me—then I think better of it, content to believe that I am somehow passing through their woods with a nonthreatening demeanor.

The trail, now on a ridge, has changed direction from earlier in the day. Looking at the map, I see that the change is much more severe than I perceived while walking. A ten-mile section of trail is in the shape of a wide, flattened S curve. When the trail finally resumes its northeasterly bearing, I stop for a break at Doc's Knob Shelter, where I am perplexed to see Andy. He sheepishly admits that he took a blue-blaze trail that lops off one loop of the S, shortening the walk by about five miles. I do my best to help him understand that I don't condemn blue-blazing. Andy is a great guy to have on the trail, an asset to the trail community. In many ways, he is more wholly taking in the experience than I am as a white-blazer.

The trail leading away from the shelter is a wide straightaway, mildly downhill, lined with rhododendrons. The rhododendrons are blooming pink, like giant bouquets overstuffed with flowers. The path is carpeted with pink petals. Nine beautiful, dreamlike miles pass. From the ridge, a patchwork of fields is visible in the valley below. Then there is the two-mile-long, foot-jamming descent into Pearisburg.

On the downhill, my toes cram forward into the unforgiving toe box of my new boots. I stop, take the boots off, and let my feet breathe. After the break, I walk only a hundred yards before the pain resumes. I try walking backwards, to make my feet slide toward the heel of the boot. I try loosening the bootlaces at the eyelets nearest my toes, hoping that my forefoot would feel less constricted. Tightening the boot laces near the ankle to hold my toes back from the front of the boot doesn't help. Nothing works; the descent is torture on my feet. The failure to solve my foot problems with $140 boots is a huge disappointment.

The trail enters Pearisburg near the Rendezvous Hotel on Highway 100. I hustle over and get a room, eager to forget my difficulties. I walk down the street to a bar and am thrilled to see other thru-hikers. I see Stretch for the first time since Hot Springs. Jason and Shelton, a couple I met in Damascus, are here. No Pepsi and others come and go as the night wears on.

I wake early, feeling no ill effects from the drinking. I have a plan to get out of these boots. Although there is no outfitter in Pearisburg, there is a car dealer across the street from my motel. Correctly assuming that they rent cars, I get a rental and once again head for Blacksburg. Getting the car was time consuming, and I'm starving. Before leaving town, I pull into a little diner to get breakfast.

Steve O. is sitting at a cleared table with his pack, either not eating or having finished breakfast. Ladies from an adjacent table hand him a few dollars. I had missed out on whatever story earned him the money. A waitress eyes him, probably for the dual transgressions of occupying a table and soliciting customers.

"Awol!" he says, as surprised as I am to meet again.

"Hi, Steve O."

"Just my luck," sarcastically runs through my thoughts. I imagine he thinks the same thing without the sarcasm. I wonder if he might ask me to buy him breakfast.

"They're calling me Elwood now," he says, as if the choice for changing his trail name was not his. Changing names is not always dubious, but in his case I suspect him of sweeping over his tracks.

"Where are you going?"

"I rented a car, and I'm going to Blacksburg. These boots aren't working out for me, so I'm looking for new ones." Normally, I would be more guarded about my plans, but I assume he's headed back out to the trail. We will be parting ways, and I don't feel as though I need to concoct a story.

"Great!" he replies. "That's where I wanted to go." I've shown my hand, and now I'm stuck with him.

Elwood has a different backpack from the one I last saw him using. His clothes are new, too. He tells me of all the things he has been given along the trail. "And when I told her about my son, killed in Iraq, she said 'Elwood, I want you to have this backpack.'" He continues to the next story, but his words fade from my attention. His reason for going to Blacksburg must have been one of the things I missed. I deduce that he is getting away from a person or situation in Pearisburg. "Where will you go from here?" I ask.

"I can get back on the trail up by Four Pines [a well-known hostel near Catawba, Virginia]. I'll come back later and do this section."

In Blacksburg, I pick out lightweight trail shoes, similar to the pair with which I started. Even though it is 5:00 p.m.

when I return to Pearisburg, I head back out on the trail. It was only three days ago that I was laid up in Wytheville. The AT parallels Highway 100 for a weed-ridden half mile before returning to the road to cross a river on the auto bridge. Here, I meet thru-hiker Bigfoot, who is coming out of a grocery store at the north end of town. Together we head uphill, back into the woods.

Bigfoot is tall and lanky, just out of college, where he ran cross-country all four years, perfect preparation for the AT. He started May 5 and is the first hiker I've met who is this far along having started later than I did. We walk seven miles nonstop while climbing seventeen hundred feet, talking the whole way. My new shoes are definitely an improvement over the boots. I am content to follow him up the trail since I want to reach a shelter before dark. I try not to let on that I am winded keeping up with his pace.

Our ascent levels off, and we enter a cow pasture. Off to the right, just outside of the barbwire, is my destination, Rice Field Shelter. Bigfoot continues to hike, planning to tent a little further along. Hungry Hiker is at the bench in front of the shelter, creating an elaborate sketch in the register. Indiana Slim is asleep and would still be sleeping when I leave the next morning. Andy, Dude, and Gray Matter come in just about dark. They spent the day lounging around town. Andy and Dude brought along thirty-two-ounce White Russians mixed in their water bottles.

Andy scurries into the shelter, convinced one of the cows is chasing him. "Awol, you want a drink?" he offers.

After pouring about eight ounces into my bottle, Dude stops him. "What are you doing?"

"I'm giving Awol a drink," Andy answers defensively.

"Yeah, but that's my bottle," Dude chastises him. "Now give him some of yours."

This shelter register has a theme; hikers are encouraged to submit jokes. Andy, Dude, and Gray Matter take turns reading the jokes aloud until rain drives everyone to bed. Dude stays awake, sitting at the foot of the shelter reading the register jokes with his headlamp and alcohol, giggling into the night.

It is still raining lightly in the morning. There are no views, and I trudge along dodging mud puddles and watching water gush out of my shoes. By lunchtime, it is a constant, drenching rain. I take a long lunch break at the aptly named Pine Swamp Shelter. While I eat, I am joined by Jason, Shelton, their dog, Mission, and Gray Matter. All of us thirst for a bit of dry time.

This shelter, like many others so far, has the message "SMOKE WEED" scratched on the ceiling in big, bold, charcoal letters. I can't imagine that nonsmokers are converted by this commandment, or that those who do bring pot are waiting to be told. On cue, another hiker enters the shelter and lights up, offering to all present. I've been on the trail less than two months, and already I've been asked more than a handful of times if I'd like to share a joint.

We all move ahead four miles to Bailey Gap Shelter to stay for the night. I give some attention to my soggy, prune-wrinkled feet. One broken toenail has come off with my sock. Another toenail is broken at the base of the nail, and I'm trying to dislodge it by flapping it side to side.

"If you get that off," Jason says, "I'll take it for my collection." Soon enough it does come loose, and I hand it over. "The skin still hanging from it is a nice touch."

We litter the shelter with wet clothes and gear. All shelters have an assortment of pegs and nails, and often there is a web of strings forming makeshift clotheslines. On wet days, there are never enough nails or lines. I drape wet socks over my muddy shoes and stuff them under the shelter floor.

Another hiker, Vic, arrives, and five of us are cramped in the small and damp shelter.

My shoes and socks aren't a bit drier in the morning, nor is the sky. Gray Matter is the first one to head out into the drizzle. The rainfall increases. Vic leaves minutes later, and again the rain intensifies. "Rain on the Appalachian Trail is proportional to the number of hikers on the trail," Jason submits.

I am in a positive mood in spite of the dreary weather. I put on wet footwear and head upstream. I am as strong as I've been since leaving Damascus, and I have minimal pain. Dead skin falls off of my once-infected heel in soggy chunks, but the redness is gone. Juli and the girls will be here in three days.

I sit on the platform of War Spur Shelter for a lunch break, with my food bag just inches from me. A huge black snake emerges from inside the shelter, brushing my leg as he slithers between me and my food. I'm too stunned to react. He drops to the ground and proceeds into the woods at an unhurried pace, as if I were inanimate.

A few miles beyond the shelter, near an intersection with a dirt road, the trail passes over a stream on a foot-bridge. Someone has left cans of beer in the stream. The first thought that pops into my head is "calories," indicative of how my thoughts on food and drink have changed since starting the hike. After gulping down two cans of calories, I begin a long uphill segment of trail. Mountain laurel crowds the trail with dense green leaves and abundant white blooms.

Gray Matter marches uphill ahead of me, legs like pistons, arms pumping in synch with trekking poles. I envy his youth. For a while I keep up, using his pace, as I did with Bigfoot, to pass difficult miles quickly. But I fall behind. Looking up at him making the climb accentuates the steepness of the trail. In that moment I make the mistake of despairing over the difficulty of the task at hand, rather than just doing it. I opened the check-valve on my gumption and feel my energy drain away. Thoughts are the most effective weapon in the human arsenal. On the upside, it is powerful to realize that goals are reached primarily by establishing the proper state of mind. But if allowed the perspective that our endeavors are propped upon nothing but a notion, we falter.

For most of the day, the trail bounces up and down between twenty-four hundred and thirty-six hundred feet. The fantasy of easy walking in Virginia has not materialized. The rain has subsided, though, and my clothes, even my shoes, have started to dry.

I descend into a grassy pastureland, bisected by a road. Looking ahead to the road, still a mile away, I see a car stop to pick up two hitching hikers. The last fifty yards of pastureland are submerged ankle-deep in water, and my shoes get soaked once again.

A lone cherry tree has more low-hanging fruit than I can eat. Time in the pastureland is all too brief before another long uphill segment. I stop twice to snack, trying to power my way up with a sugar boost. Atop the ridge there are a number of stone piles, mounded up to five feet high. In the late afternoon, the mounds have the eerie appearance of funeral cairns. Sarver Hollow Shelter is off the ridge, reached by a precipitous downhill side trail. The shelter is new and sizeable, with a roof large enough to cover a picnic bench in front.

Soon after I reach the shelter, a thunderstorm erupts. Lightning drops like bombs. Bigfoot arrives in the midst of the storm, barely able to see through his wet and foggy glasses. He is covered in mud. "On this shelter trail my shoe strap broke, and I slid down," he explains, followed by curses about the steepness of the side trail. His running shoes are secured by Velcro straps instead of laces, and I look down to see the offending strap flopped to the side of his shoe.

Well after dark, we awake to the sounds of two hikers singing in the rain as they approach the shelter. The hikers call themselves Riff and Raff. They are the same two hikers I saw earlier, getting a ride at the road through the pasture.

Early into my morning walk, I nearly jump out of my shoes when I am startled by a sound like a baby's cry amplified through a foghorn, coming from ten feet away. Lucky for me I used the privy before leaving the shelter. The sound is so unnaturally loud I first suspect a hiker is hiding up a tree to play a joke on me. It is a fawn about two feet tall, waking up scared and bleating for its mother.

A fawn bleating after I startle it.

Near the top of the ridge, the trail passes over large slabs of stone. The trail is slightly off the peak, making the walk precarious on about a forty-degree side-hill slope. I look for cracks in the stone for good footholds. Only small, sparse trees gain purchase in the limited soil, so I have open views to the east. The sky is clear. Another ridge, parallel to the one that I am on, is a few miles away, rising about three thousand feet from the plateau that separates the ridges. The side of the ridge facing me is rippled with valleys, sharply contrasted by the stark midmorning sun, but the top of the ridge is surprisingly level. A trail running along its peak could go on for miles with little elevation change. I hope my ridge is like the one I see in the distance.

Fire pink, a delicate red wildflower, adorns tufts of grass along the sides of the trail. A rusty metal wheelbarrow sits abandoned in the middle of the trail, suggesting backpack replacement. The air is filled with a droning hum, similar to the sound of power lines, of the seventeen-year cicadas. The insects are about two inches long, with transparent wings, a thick black body, and beady red eyes.

Ahead, the trail leads directly into a pond. In the middle of the pond, there is a tree whose trunk is deep in water. Higher on the trunk there is a white blaze. I explore to my right and to my left, looking for any signs of how hikers ahead of me have navigated this mess. Often when there is an obstacle such as this, the best path around it is indicated by the trampled ground on the detour most often used by previous hikers. Here, there is no uniform detour; this flooding must be fairly recent. Current is discernible toward each end of the "pond." There is a stream under all that water, vastly overflowing its banks because of the daily rainstorms. I take some deadfall and try to drop it across the water, but it floats away with the current. After wasting fifteen minutes searching for dry footing, I've already soaked my feet with missteps. I do what I should have done to begin with: march straight ahead through the knee-deep water.

I catch up to Gray Squirrel, another thru-hiker that I have seen almost daily over the past week. Gray Squirrel has the look of an old-timer, lean and leathery with bright white hair and beard. I pass him in a zone of blooming white mountain laurel, where he blends perfectly. Gray Squirrel walks at a slow and steady pace, so all of our meetings on the trail have been like this, me passing him as if he is standing still. The first time I met him, I was sure he'd never catch up. But the next day, I found him ahead of me again. He starts early and walks late into the day. He sleeps in a hammock, so almost anywhere on the trail is an acceptable campsite. I'm more inclined to end my day when I come to a shelter or a town, not necessarily at nightfall. We will continue our tortoise and hare routine until Daleville, when I take a few days off. I will not see the tortoise again after that because I will never catch up to him.

Over the past week I've also crossed paths with a young woman hiking southbound as I continue north. Incongruously, we crossed paths going in opposite directions three times. I had the same experience with a young man twice in the same week.

On passing the woman for the third time, I stop to ask how it was that we continued to meet like that. She and her husband are thru-hiking the trail together, and they have their car with them. On most days, one will drop the other off at the south end of the trail to hike north. The driver then drives to a point where a road crosses at the north end of the trail, parks the car, and hikes south. They meet at midday on the trail. The northbound hiker will reach the car at the end of the day, and drive back to the south end

Gray Squirrel on the trail through a thicket of mountain laurel.

of the section to retrieve the partner. Having the car offers them many options; they can camp, sleep in the car, or drive to a nearby town. They carry little more than a water bottle and lunch.

My favorite cartoon of those that Hungry Hiker has drawn in shelter registers is the one he titled "Evolution of a Hiker." The first frame shows a hiker after two miles, taking long strides and saying, "I can do twenty miles today." The next frame has the hiker settled into a walk after eight miles, saying, "This is nice." After twelve miles, the hiker is stooped over, saying, "I'm hungry." Finally after sixteen miles, the hiker is in a sprawling crawl with the caption, "Shelter... where's the shelter?"

That's how I pass many a day, including this one. The last major obstacle of the day is the climb up to Dragons Tooth, which begins after I've already hiked eighteen miles. I crawl ahead and rest frequently, not caring how late I'm on the trail today. I take my pack off and sprawl out on a boulder, waiting for energy to return to my body. I see Bigfoot hiking by, so I put my pack on and follow him to the top. We both take a short side trail to Dragons Tooth, a spectacular pointed monolith jutting more than thirty feet high. He climbs the rock, but I'm too tired for the diversion. I want to move on, and I meander back toward the trail. From above, Bigfoot tells me about the views, and how the last bit of climbing was tricky. I can sense a little fear in his voice, so I wait for him.

Bigfoot climbs down without incident, and we walk the rocky trail together. The descent from Dragons Tooth is steep, often made by sliding down rocks on hands and butt. This descent is steeper and longer than the climb up Albert Mountain. From the rocky ridge, we see where we are headed: it is a house in the valley with four tall pine trees out front. Moving specks of people are visible and, unbelievably, we can hear some of the hootin' and hollerin' going on below. This registers slight concern with me, curious about what kind of a crowd we are about to join.

Four Pines Hostel is set up in a three-car garage behind a ranch house. At least twenty-five hikers are here for the night. Half the floor is covered with cots and cot-sized mattresses where hikers laid claim to floor space. Some are sorting through their gear, and there is a line waiting for the single makeshift shower in the corner of the garage. Other than the ratty attire, the scene is similar to any other house party; small groups mingling, drinking beer, nibbling on food. A few bottles of harder stuff are circulating.

Indiana Slim is on a lawn chair just outside one of the overhead doors, offering up a bottle of whiskey. He looks a little impaired, so I ask if he remembers meeting me.

"Oh, sure...Awol...I've got you here in my list." He fumbles through a tiny pad on which he has recorded the name of every hiker he has met. Good idea, I think of his list. He really is slim, no facial hair, so boyish-looking he could be sixteen. He insists on having me drink from his whiskey bottle. His smoking and drinking play like an attempt to harden his soft shell.

Another hiker approaches and blurts out, "Slim! How'd you get here?"

"Well, I hitched a ride, of course," Slim answers jocularly.

I'm happy to be back with some of the familiar crowd. AA wants to know how I got behind. Stretch and No-Hear-Um are here. I meet Popsicle and Moose once again. They are keeping to themselves at a bench outside, and set up their tents on the lawn away from the garage. Tipperary is here. Tipperary always makes me feel as if there is no person he's happier to see. I am greeted with a hearty "Awol!" and an engulfing hug. His unshakable good nature makes him popular among thru-hikers and certainly improves his chances of staying on the trail. On this trek, his temperament is more of an asset than conditioning or know-how.

One large group of hikers that I have been hearing about is here. The group is centered about the repeat thru-hiker Green Man. This bunch is all about having fun. They spent two weeks at Trail Days. There is beer wherever they go, noisy hotel stays, making a bit of a wake as they plow through the trail. It is a boisterous crowd, and FUBAR is the most outlandish of them, with his bare-chested exhibit of tattoos, hair cut in a Mohawk, and the demeanor of a wild man. His voice bellows without constraint. Clearly it is him we heard up on the ridge. His young wife is here, too. They were married at Trail Days in Damascus.

It is 11:00 p.m.—way past hiker bedtime—and only blissfully deaf No-Hear-Um is asleep. A circle of people just outside are passing around a guitar and doing an acoustic set. Two of them are excellent singers. Tipperary, who is not, sings anyway. Roman Around is incoherent, curled up in a chair with a near-empty bottle of vodka. The sprinkle of curse words in conversation has turned into a downpour. The circle is uproarious when Tipperary the priest joins in with an F-word of his own.

Suddenly, everyone is out of their seats, grouping over to one side of the circle of chairs. With little warning or apparent provocation, FUBAR has come behind the still-seated Indiana Slim and put him in a choke hold, and others in the crowd are trying to tug him loose. The party mood is broken, and most people head for bed. FUBAR and Slim stay just outside, now playing the roles of drinking buddies slurring out a disjointed conversation.

Slim's topic alternates between "I love you, man" and "Why you wanna' choke me?" FUBAR's words are impossible to categorize. In a final act of reconciliation, FUBAR holds Slim's head in his hands, forehead to forehead, making a final vow of friendship. Then they are bumping heads firmer and firmer, until they have a full-fledged head butt. Indiana, initially tickled over the bonding, is upset again when he finds that his head is bleeding.

The episode drags on nearly an hour, with hikers shouting at the two of them to go to sleep. The lights go on and off a number of times. More angry words, then FUBAR badgers Slim to "come take a walk" and heads out into the dark without waiting for a reply. Slim sits confused, pondering aloud what FUBAR wants from him. We all know FUBAR wants to administer a beating unimpeded by the rest of us, so we coax Slim back into the garage.

FUBAR wanders the grounds making noises, doing God knows what. Slim refuses to sleep. FUBAR's wife goes out to rein him in, while hikers inside take turns trying to console Slim and guide him into his bed. One female hiker attempts to talk Slim through his troubles over a cigarette, adding smoke to the suffering of the rest of us. Outside, FUBAR's screams and curses rise to a new level. We hear another voice, I assume Mrs. FUBAR, screaming for someone to call the police. A few of FUBAR's handlers head out and round him up. Shortly, they are back inside, telling us the police are on the way to get FUBAR.

Few hikers are able to sleep. Stretch and I sit up and talk about what to do. Roman Around comes out of his slumber and decides that he and Slim need to have a drink. Stretch packs up and hikes out into the night. It is well past 3:00 a.m. when I finally get to sleep.

I am one of the first hikers awake on a dewy, quiet morning. I take a bike lying in the yard and pedal down empty streets to a convenience store to get a breakfast of donuts, chocolate milk, and coffee. Back at the hostel, I see Popsicle and Moose fixing breakfast at the picnic table. "You two were lucky. You missed out on all that craziness last night... did you hear it?"

"We weren't so lucky," Moose replies.

The woman's voice calling for the police last night was Popsicle. She was kept awake by the ruckus and left her tent for a bathroom break at the same time FUBAR was in the yard upchucking his whiskey. He wasn't happy with the encounter, so he tried out his choke hold on Popsicle. FUBAR chose the wrong person to pick on this time. Not only did Popsicle get the better of the scuffle, she was intent on pressing charges. But the ordeal would be the end of her thru-hike.[22]

McAfee Knob is one of the most photographed locations on the Appalachian Trail. Near the peak of the mountain, there is a shelf of rock cantilevered above an unbounded, view of the mountains and valley below. Stretch and No-Hear-Um arrive shortly after I do, and we help each other to get photos of ourselves in this wonderful setting. The walk up to the knob was not demanding. There were even smooth pine-needle-covered pieces of trail that were delicious to walk on. The trail to Tinker Cliffs is also benign, yet rewarded with additional excellent views and interesting cliff-top hiking. I am fortunate to have good weather. On the whole, this day provided the greatest visual payoff (for the effort) of any day I would spend on the trail.

McAfee Knob.

Between the two highlights, I meet with a group of hikers celebrating on an inconspicuous piece of trail. "Congratula-

---

22   Or so I thought at the time. Popsicle actually did continue, and she completed her thru-hike. She concocted the story about getting off the trail in case there was any attempt at retribution. The story worked; I did not learn about Popsicle's ruse until the final draft of this writing.

tions!" they say in greeting. "You are at the seven-hundred-mile mark, about one-third of the way to Katahdin."

I hike along with one thru-hiker from the group, Footslogger, until he turns off to stay at Lamberts Meadow Shelter. Near the shelter, Elwood (aka Steve O.) is fetching water. I say hello, content to have a cordial relationship with Elwood, but happy to be moving on. Footslogger knows Elwood as well, and they begin a typical hiker exchange, each asking how the other's hike has been since they last met. Elwood gives sparse detail, obviously not intending to say anything of the ride I gave him four days ago. I move along, allowing Elwood to dissemble in private.

The day ends with an unexpectedly challenging rocky ridge walk down to Daleville. My long day (twenty-five miles) and paltry sleep probably contribute to my perception of the difficultly. Hikers have to manage their expectations during walks into town because it always takes longer than you want it to, and many times you can see, hear, smell, and taste the town long before you get there. In this respect, Daleville has been the worst, since the town can be seen six miles before arriving. The last few miles of the descent are in a corridor of land parallel with power lines. Vandals have painted graffiti on boulders, making the land feel more like an unwanted extension of the city than part of the forest.

As much as I'd like to sprint down the trail and be done with my day, my feet will not cooperate. Again my feet hurt on the descent. Although these shoes are lightweight, there is rigid plastic around the toe box, so I feel the same clamplike pain on the front row of toe knuckles as I felt wearing boots. The pain is similar to the hand pain caused by shaking hands with a prankster who squeezes as tightly as he can. I lie on a graffiti-blemished boulder and wallow in my discomfort, picking up shards of broken beer bottles and flinging them into the woods.

The trailhead hits town on a main road just a few hundred yards from a hotel. I am exhausted but still have much work to do. I shower, eat, do laundry, make phone calls, and don't get to sleep until 2:00 a.m. I wake during the night with leg cramps and foot pain, and I decide I will be taking a zero day here in town.

In preparation for hiking the AT, I purchased the full set of guidebooks and maps from an advertisement in *Appalachian Trailway News*. I decided against carrying the maps before getting out of Georgia, so the maps themselves gave little return for the money. However, I gained more than my money's worth by meeting the seller of the maps, 2002 thru-hiker Arrow. Arrow kept in touch throughout my planning process, during my hike, and beyond. He had encouraged me to call him when I reached Daleville so he could put me in touch with the Witcher family, friends from his 2002 hike.

Homer Witcher maintains a section of the trail for the Roanoke Appalachian Trail Club. He put me up at his home and let me use his car to run errands. Homer, his wife Teresa, and their two children thru-hiked the AT last year. The kids, whose trail names are Cascade and Rockslide, were eleven and eight years old during the hike. At dinner they tell of the challenges of keeping the kids motivated. Cascade and Rockslide are filling out questionnaires about their thru-hike for yet another magazine article. Both kids are sincerely happy to have completed the AT.

I speak with Juli on the phone about our plans for tomorrow. I will hike nineteen miles from Daleville to Mills Gap Overlook, one of the places where the AT crosses the Blue Ridge Parkway. During roughly the same time frame, Juli and the girls will drive thirty miles from our home in

Titusville to the airport in Orlando, fly 667 miles to Richmond, rent a car, and drive 175 miles to our meeting place.

In the morning, Homer drops me off at the trailhead. I hike with my pack but take only what I need for the day, leaving my tent, sleeping gear, and stove with the Witchers. With a light pack and much anticipation, I fly down the trail. Near lunchtime I pass Elwood, who has paused for a break, leaning heavily on his hiking pole. Elwood has a new set of clothes since the last time I saw him and has added gaiters to his ensemble.

As I cross a streambed, I scan the smooth pebbles along the bank. All along the trail, I have been picking up rocks as souvenirs. I select rocks that have an interesting shape or color and are near the size of a quarter. I collect only a couple each week, and when I reach a post office, I mail them home. I'm not sure if my actions are environmentally sound. I've asked other hikers what they think of me taking the rocks, and they wish I'd ship home some of the larger ones. Luckily, I spot a near-perfect heart-shaped rock in this pile of pebbles. It is the fourth heart rock I've found so far, one for every girl I will be reunited with this afternoon.

Toward the end of my hiking day, the AT crosses the Blue Ridge Parkway a half dozen times. The trail and the road run parallel for the next two hundred miles until reaching the north end of Shenandoah National Park. The road is known as the Skyline Drive in the Shenandoahs. My expectation had been to see a convoy of vehicles carrying binocular and camera-wielding tourists. But this is not the case. All of my trail crossings on the Blue Ridge Parkway are at lonely overlooks and vacant parking areas. The parking area at Mills Gap Overlook is empty when I arrive, so I lie down for a rest, using my pack as a pillow. Within minutes, Juli pulls up in a rental van, and Jessie, Rene, and Lynn pile out for a joyful reunion. "You smell," Rene says, soon followed by the observation that I look old.

Even though I have washed my pack a couple of times, foul odor is hopelessly trapped within and released by the heat of my body when I walk. The same is true of my clothes. Going unshaven has aged my appearance, but I will keep the beard to Katahdin (and beyond). The brown hair on my head still holds firm, but gray hair has made significant inroads in my beard.

We drive back to the Homeplace Restaurant in Catawba, a family-style restaurant serving country food of great renown among thru-hikers. I dazzle Juli with my newfound eating prowess. We have three and a half more days to spend together.

Jessie, Rene, and Lynn walk with me for 1.8 miles from Mills Gap to Bearwallow Gap, in a token bit of adventure sharing. The trail is misted over by fog, but the girls are giddy, skipping along, singing their impromptu song which consists of the five-word lyric, "We're hiking the Appalachian Trail," repeated until their dad asks them to stop.

Even though our walk will take less than an hour, I bring food and my water filter so we can stop at a stream and take a break, just like I would do on my own. During the seven weeks I have been hiking, my daughters have seemed to be doing fine. That is what they say when I talk to them on the phone, and that is what Juli tells me. To dig deeper into their thoughts, I pose a question to them: "Would you like for me to come back home, or would you like me to continue hiking?" I don't really know what answer to expect. It would hurt me to know if they felt strongly about me coming home.

Lynn is reticent, but Jessie and Rene answer resoundingly, "We want you to finish the trail!" Having braced myself to hear of how they have missed me, I am surprised by the "you better not be thinking of quitting" tone of their answer. They have seen newspaper articles about my hike, and they talk about it at school. They have taken ownership of the endeavor, and it is fortifying to know that they are proud of what I am doing.

Juli meets us with the van at Bearwallow Gap. She brings many varieties of Little Debbie snack cakes, a cooler full of sodas, and some fruit, so we are able to do trail magic for a group of hikers: Bad Ass Turtle and Footslogger, Ballou, Rumbler, Skidmark, Beth, and Jersey. Many other thru-hikers pass through town during our stay. I see Old Bill for the first time since Grayson Highlands. The Dude, No Pepsi, and No-Hear-Um are here. We are all doing the same errands—going to the outfitter to mull over equipment changes, picking up mail drops, resupplying our trail food, cleaning up, rejuvenating for the next leg of the AT.

I buy yet another pair of trail-runner type shoes, recalling my painful descent into town. Thus far, I have alternated between using a Mountainsmith Auspex and Kelty Satori backpacks. Both are lightweight internal frame backpacks. Both are serviceable, and both have their shortcomings. The Mountainsmith pack, which I have been using most recently, has a less padded hip belt and has bruised my hips. I will use the Kelty pack for the remainder of my hike. It has detachable side compartments and a removable mesh pouch on the back of the pack. I remove one of the side compartments and hang my water bag to the side of the pack with carabiners. Another addition I make now is to buy two pouches the size of a paperback book that attach to the front of my waist belt on either side of my camera case. The getup has an ammo belt appearance, but is very functional. I have no hesitancy to take pictures since my camera is readily available. I will keep snacks in one pouch, so I can snack on the move. In the other pouch I carry my knife, spoon, toothbrush, and toothpaste. I brush my teeth while walking.

I do not have a strict "finish what you start" attitude about completing the trail. Nor would I end my hike after having a bad day or even a bad week. I know that there is a large component of delayed gratification in hiking. I am likely to appreciate it as much or more after I am here, so it is unwise to quit on a whim. Before starting my hike, I read to Juli a passage from a thru-hiker journal about a hiker who wearily called home and told of how he was having a difficult time of it. His spouse told him he had done enough and he should come home. That was the end of his hike. I wanted Juli to be prepared for times when I might sound ready to give up. Staying motivated could be dicey, so she should not encourage or endorse any thoughts I might have about quitting the trail.

The closest Juli ever came to breaking this rule is in Daleville. The morning before returning to the trail, Juli is in the shower at the hotel, and I am talking to her through the curtain. "When I woke up, my legs were still sore. I'm surprised that I feel this way after taking off three of the last four days."

"David, we'll be proud of you whatever you decide to do," Juli answers, thinking that I am considering getting off the trail.

I don't feel like quitting. Sometimes I want to be done faster; always I want it to hurt less. I haven't had any day that has been entirely bad, and I've yet to have a day when I wished I was back at my job.

7
Daleville to
Front Royal

The Appalachian Trail in Virginia is 535 miles long, roughly
one quarter of the overall trail length, and longer than the
trail through any other state. It is said that the trail in the
state is easy, but that has not been my experience. I reached
Damascus in less than a month, but my progress has sput-
tered since then. It is June 15, I've been in Virginia for twenty-two days, and I still have 156 miles to hike before leaving
the state. Thru-hikers are so often worn down by this stage
of the hike that there is a name for it: the "Virginia blues."

On the morning that Juli, Jessie, Rene, and Lynn are
to fly home, we dawdle, using all the time they can spare
before returning to the airport. I had been looking forward
to their visit and had not contemplated the fact that I was
setting myself up for another painful parting. They drop me
off at featureless Bearwallow Gap, fittingly, in the rain. Before being engulfed by the woods, I look back to get a last
look at my daughters. The view of them waving through de-
parting car windows is reminiscent of them back in Georgia,
but my attitude is entirely different. In Georgia, all was new

and exciting and imprinted itself in my memory. Here, I am resuming the long walk through Virginia, and no detail of the trail, other than rain, makes an impression on me. On my first break of the day, I discover Juli and the girls have slipped drawings and notes of encouragement into my pack.

The water source for Cornelius Creek Shelter is a wide, shallow stream on the path leading to the shelter. While I pump-filter water, I take in the view. Sparkling water glosses over a bed of softball-sized rocks. The stream meanders among rhododendrons, and the pink flowers reflect off the water. Andy, Meredith, and Roman Around are at the shelter. I comment on the beautiful stream, and Andy tells me he sat by the stream for three hours before settling in to the shelter. Friends think I am free-spirited to have gone on this hike, but in that regard I don't compare with Andy and others, whom I observe to have much greater skill at the art of smelling the roses.

When I wake, I don't need to look at my watch to know it is 6:30 a.m., my habitual wake-up time on the trail. Rain is pinging the shelter roof—a sound known, but not loved, by hikers. All of us lie in our bags hoping for a break in the weather. A couple of hours later I grow impatient and hike out into incessant drenching rain and lingering fog. My camera stays tucked away, dead weight in my pack. There are few overlooks, anyway. The trail is never clear of trees, and there is heavy undergrowth. I resign myself to simply covering miles.

The miles don't come easily, with the trail climbing a number of peaks near or above four thousand feet, and descending all the way down to seven hundred feet at the James River, the lowest point on the trail so far. Before reaching the river, I stop to rest at Matts Creek Shelter. A hiker is in the shelter, asleep in his bag set on top of a two-inch-thick

Therm-a-Rest. I've yet to see another thru-hiker with a sleep pad this luxurious.

The last entry in the register confirms what I suspect, that this is the thru-hiker who has been venting his unhappy experience in lengthy entries. I had yet to meet him, but I've heard other hikers comment on the melodrama of his hike, and I've read some of his writing. Here, he's taken the better part of two pages to record his misery and depression, clearly suffering the Virginia blues as much or more than the rest of us. He had come to this shelter last night in the rain. The shelter was full, so he spent a restless night trying to stay dry in the muddy crawl space below the shelter. He had decided to thruhike after his last failed relationship. No longer a young man, he feels he has accomplished nothing of which to be proud. He had come to the trail to make something of himself. An AT thru-hike would give him "something to hang his hat on." Early on his hike, he met a young woman with whom he hoped to build a lasting relationship. Things aren't working out. The young woman is off hiking with someone else. His pack is too heavy, his feet aren't holding up, and every step is agony. Downtime has separated him from all other thru-hikers that he knows. He has nothing to look forward to on the trail, and has no life at home.

I imagine how I will recall these words a week from now, if he was to take a leap into the James River. I write a register entry of my own, sharing thoughts I've had about a thru-hike:

Anything that we consider to be an accomplishment takes effort to achieve. If it were easy, it would not be nearly as gratifying. What is hardship at the moment will add to our sense of achievement in the end.

By the time I'm done, unhappy hiker sticks his ruffled head out of his bag. After introductions, he asks if I've seen other thru-hikers recently, asking specifically about the hikers associated with the female hiker he has yet to give up on. In Daleville I had been told that the woman had jumped ahead on the trail to discourage his advances, so I avoid talking about her.

"I read about your foot pain. My feet are killing me, too," I say, addressing a problem to which I truly can relate. "This is the fourth pair of shoes that I tried."

"My boots are great. I've had them from the start. They're not the problem."

I take it that he's already been encouraged to try new shoes and he's having none of it. We talk a little about pack weight, and he only wants to tell me how much he likes and needs all the heavy stuff. He couldn't live without the mattress he's carrying. He moves on to other problems, equally insoluble.

"I just wish I could catch up to the guys I've been hiking with. I took days off trying to get better, and they are probably way ahead. It sucks being alone."

"Why don't you skip ahead and hike with them?" This really isn't a question. He's ready to ditch his thru-hike, so I'm trying to convey that it is okay to stay on the trail without walking every mile. Doing sections is a softer landing than just heading home.

"I don't want to skip. I want to thru-hike. I probably couldn't keep up with them anyway."

My most recent days have been a challenge. The positive attitude I project in my attempt to rouse him was only an act. I may have been of no help to him, but role-playing a better mood actually made *me* feel more upbeat. Also, the rain has stopped. I pack up and move ahead another four miles to Johns Hollow Shelter. The remainder of the walk is mild, traveling along the shoreline of the James River and crossing the river on a fantastic, long, and sturdy footbridge.

AA and Strider are at the shelter. The shelter is set in a flat-bottomed bowl of land at the foot of the mountains, a setting that helps me to understand the use of the word "hollow." Strider has a campfire going and uses it to cook his dinner. We all sit around the fire and talk of our experiences and plans, partaking in the simple pleasures of camping.

Strider started the trail with a purist mind-set, but soon joined with a group of hikers who are having a more social experience of the trail. He spent two weeks partying with them in Damascus. The group is ahead at Rockfish Gap, preparing to travel by canoe to Harpers Ferry, bypassing the trail through Shenandoah National Park. Strider is torn between going with them and hiking the entire trail. "I can still come back and hike the Shenandoahs later," he says, echoing a common refrain.

My morning begins with a two-thousand-foot climb in the rain. Same as yesterday, I am soaked before even walking a mile. Cold raindrops peck at my hands. I hunger for a protein bar, but my fingers are too numb to unzip my belt pouch. Everything is wet; I don't want to sit down. That would make me colder anyway. I am complacent about the struggles of the day. I am just making miles through the long, wet green tunnel. I knew there would be monotonous stretches. Hike on—that's the "solution" to which I keep coming back.

I was apathetic about planning when I left Daleville two days ago. Consequently, I am nearly out of food. Father-and-son section hikers are waiting for a ride where the trail crosses the Blue Ridge Parkway, making the sensible decision to cut their hike two days short to get out of the rain. I linger at the parking area where they are waiting, unloading trash from my pack and dropping hints about how I have used up all my food. They must have leftovers. Or maybe they'll give me a ride. They offer neither.

The trail runs along and over a number of large, scenic creeks leading down to the Lynchburg Reservoir, where there is a lake formed by Pedlar Dam. The trail crosses the lake on the dam, then inclines steadily up an unnamed peak on freshly cut trail with nice switchbacks. However, the ground here is smooth red clay, made slick by rain. Clay has embedded itself in the tread of my shoes, transforming them into muddy foot-long skis. On every upward step, I lose some of the ground I have gained to slippage. I walk duck-footed for better traction. I imagine I am entertainment for the trail gods, who have a boundless variety of obstacles to place before me.

Out of energy by the time the mudslide ends, I drift through the valley of Brown Mountain Creek, where there was once a settlement of freed slaves. All that remains is the detritus of a rock wall. I lie on the floor of the shelter by the creek, pondering my muddy legs, immobilized by indecision. Should I stay here tonight, or get into town and resupply? I am alone in the shelter, as I was on the trail today. Sluggishly, I drag myself on to the next road crossing.

A Boy Scout troop is at the roadside rest area when I reach U.S. 60. They look tired and restless waiting in the rain for their ride home. I move up the road far enough to dissociate myself from the group—lone hitchhikers fare better—and stick out my thumb. My destination, the town of Buena Vista, is nine miles away and is not a popular stop for hikers. And there is the drizzle of rain. Who wants a wet, smelly hiker in their car? Despite these factors, only a couple of cars pass before one stops to give me a ride. "Hey, look at that!" one of the Boy Scouts shouts, envious of my quick departure, as astonished as I am at my hitching good fortune.

In town, the motel clerk allows me to check out the "only" room they have available, a smoking room. A chubby white youth is strolling through the parking lot, wearing an oversized baby blue University of North Carolina basketball jersey and midshin-length shorts, the brim of his baseball cap turned sideways. I search for his parents, but there are no people or cars in the lot. "Want some weed?" he asks, using his best Eminem accent. I return to the office after surveying the room to say I can't handle the overwhelming smell of smoke. The clerk does a cursory shuffle of her reservations and says, "I can give you this room."

In the morning, the parking lot is still empty and there is a new clerk. "The lady who checked me in last night said all the nonsmoking rooms where booked, but it looks like there are a bunch of empty rooms. Are most of the rooms smoking rooms?"

"No. She saw that you were a hiker, and most hikers smell worse than the smoke. We don't want them [hikers] to mess up our good rooms."

Trail angel William, a retired gentleman who has lived in Buena Vista all his life, gives me a ride back to the trail. The birds are chirping, the sun pokes through the clouds, my foot pain is short of agonizing, and I have a belly and pack full of food. This is a good day. There is a long climb, gaining two thousand feet in less than three miles up from the road, and I handle it easily. Jason, Shelton, and their dog, Mission, are atop Bald Knob. Clear skies on the open summit provide the first views I've had in days.

It starts raining when I am fifteen minutes from the shelter, and I make a dash for it rather than stop to put on my pack cover. No-Hear-Um and Leaf are at the shelter.

No-Hear-Um is retired, but he is fit and I consider him to be a strong hiker. I've seen him sporadically since Kincora Hostel. He has decided to do a "flip-flop" hike. In Harpers Ferry, he will meet his wife and travel to the north end of the trail. From Katahdin, he will hike south, planning to finish his thru-hike at Harpers Ferry.

The AT progresses through Virginia with still more challenges. I hike up Priest Mountain, down to the Tye River (below one thousand feet), and back up peaks higher than four thousand feet. The terrain is rocky and, again, it rains. I don't leave the shelter until 9:00 a.m. to avoid a heavy morning rain.

Tye River Footbridge.

Gnats, flics, and black flics swarm mc at cvcry brcak on my walk over Three Ridges. Gnats fly into my eyes, nose, and mouth. Sunglasses fail to deter them. I eat three gnats; with effort, I could probably suck in a couple dozen. If all hikers consumed a few dozen gnats a day, would we put a dent in their numbers? Would they leave us alone if they feared us as predators?

It is getting dark because it is late and because another surge of rain is imminent. My guidebook tells me about landmarks I should pass every mile or so, and I'm not seeing them as soon as I think I should. I curse the landmarks for not being there and berate the guidebook for giving me erroneous information, but I know the fault is mine. I'm trudging along much slower than usual. I've walked over twenty miles. I am in the middle of a sixteen-mile stretch between shelters. My feet hurt and my legs are spent, and I need to find a place to camp. The trail is a narrow ribbon through waist-high undergrowth studded with rocks and tree roots. Even if the ground was clear, it would be too sloped to camp.

Finally I reach the top of Humpback Mountain, capped off by a monolith of stone thirty yards wide and twenty feet high. At the base of the rock wall is a flat spot the size of my tarp and a ring of stones for a campfire, typical of commonly used tent sites. I set up my tarp in the fading light, lucky that this is nearly the longest day of the year. Minutes after crawling in to sleep, the tarp is pelted by rain. Comfortable in my bag, my mood shifts from harassed and bedraggled to feeling lucky for having found this priceless speck of flat ground.

Having a rough time on the trail is not the same as the irredeemable frustrations of urban life, such as being stuck in traffic or wading through a crowded store. Difficulty on the trail, like this long and rainy day, is usually reflected upon fondly. There is the soothing, rhythmic beat of rainfall, the feeling that the woods are being washed and rejuvenated, the odors of the woods awakened by moisture. There is appreciation for the most simple of things, such as a flat and dry piece of ground and something warm to eat. There is satisfaction in having endured hardship, pride in being able to do for myself in the outdoors. There is strength in knowing I can do it again tomorrow.

Thirty minutes into my morning hike, I am caught in a downpour. I am immediately drenched and cold. My destination is Rockfish Gap and the town of Waynesboro, thirteen miles away. I walk faster to stay warm. On the way down Humpback Mountain, I have to pick my way through wet rocks, like walking down a streambed. As soon as I clear the rocks, I am off to the races, literally jogging on the most level tracts of the trail. I reach the gap in less than five hours, and then I gimp around on sore feet. No one would guess I just backpacked thirteen miles before lunch.

The Rockfish Gap Information Center has a visitor package for hikers, complete with a list of restaurants, places to stay, and a map of Waynesboro, which is four miles from the trailhead. I choose to treat myself with a stay at the Tree Streets Inn Bed and Breakfast. At sixty dollars it is expensive by hiker standards, but owners Bill and Nickie pick me up from the trail, let me use a bike to get around town, set out free snacks (butterscotch brownies) and sodas, and the room has the most comfortable down bed I've ever slept on.

After a fantastic breakfast, Bill from the Tree Streets Inn returns me to Rockfish Gap. At the gap, the Blue Ridge Parkway transitions to the Skyline Drive. A four-by-four-inch concrete milepost etched with a zero marks the start of the Skyline Drive. I pause to take a photo of myself next to the post, feeling that it is also a fresh start for me. The trail stays atop the ridge of mountains through the Shenandoah National Park (SNP) without too much elevation gain or loss. The Skyline Drive parallels the trail, and waysides on the road sell meals and dry food, so I can travel light. I look forward to visiting friends when I am halfway through the park and when I reach Harpers Ferry days after leaving the park. The forecast I saw before leaving Waynesboro predicted days of clear weather.

Progress in the 387 miles since leaving Damascus has been hard to quantify, devoid of milestones. Now I feel the motivational benefit of having intermediate goals. There is a discrete chunk of miles through the Shenandoahs. Soon after, the trail in Virginia will be behind me. Also within reach is Harpers Ferry, and the halfway point of my journey.

It rains, but not enough to soak through my shoes. When I stop to refill water bottles in a spring, I lie back and look up through the poplar trees. I see only slivers of blue sky through the canopy of leaves. The leaves are illuminated by the sun and cast down filtered lime-green light. I linger on a grassy hillock, where someone has planted steel tractor seats in a semicircle. Thru-hiker "Bearable" charges past, headphone music loud enough to be audible ten yards away.

After a smooth twenty-mile day, I reach Blacktop Hut. Shelters in the Shenandoahs are called huts, although they are still simply three walls and a roof. The huts are larger than most shelters. Every one that I will stay in has two levels of sleeping platforms. Tonight the space is needed because other thru-hikers Bigfoot, Ken and Marcia, Bearable, Steppenwolf, and Lumberjack are here, along with three section hikers. I set my pack down and try to decide where to claim space. A rat scurries under the shelter from a bush out front, so I take a spot at the other end.

This is the first I've seen of Ken and Marcia since giving them a ride when I was laid up in Bland. Bearable, Steppenwolf, and Lumberjack are all new to me. Lumberjack stands out as looking more urbane than the typical thru-hiker. The name doesn't fit. Even after two months on the trail, he looks as if he's been just a few days away from the office. The other hikers shuffle their sleeping spaces to be further away from him in the shelter, teasing him about his snoring. Lumberjack is so named for his nightly routine of "sawing logs."

Marcia mentions a bear paw print she saw embedded in the trail. I saw it too. It was as large as my hand with outstretched fingers. The size and perfection of the imprint made me suspect that it was a hoax, but we have heard that bears are plentiful in the park. This hut, like the others in the park, has a steel flagpole-looking device near the shelter for placing food beyond the reach of bears. Bars are welded to the top of the pole, extending like tree branches, with hooks for hanging food bags.

Eagerly, I am on the trail in the morning, hoping for a late breakfast at Loft Mountain Campground. A concrete post, similar to the mileposts on the Skyline Drive, marks a side trail to the campground. The side trail ends on a road through the camping area, with no store in sight and no directions to it. I take a roundabout detour through the campsites before making my way down to the store. The grill is yet another mile away. I leave my pack outside the store and grudgingly make the hot asphalt walk downhill to satisfy my hunger for blueberry pancakes. "Is it worth it?" I ask myself, thinking of the return walk and my hot feet. The pancakes are disappointing, carelessly and cheaply made, but not cheap. They are filling, though, and I luck into a hitch back to the store. Bearable, Lumberjack, and Steppenwolf are sitting outside gorging on store-bought junk food, their simple plan for a second breakfast much more efficient than my own.

The AT passes within sight of the camp store. If I had ignored the posted side trail and stayed on the AT, I would have come within thirty yards of the store. Rather than meandering back through the campsites, I take a side trail out from the camp store, causing me to miss about a half mile of the AT. It's the first time I've wavered from purist white-blazing, and I feel no guilt about it.

"You can't throw a rock without hitting a deer," Bearable comments. Deer are noticeably more plentiful and less readily spooked since we have entered the Shenandoahs. A deer with a fawn stands only fifteen yards from the trail, frozen as I pass. The fawn stands under the safety of its mother, their bodies perpendicular.

A bear, startling, shiny black, steps out onto the trail ahead of me from the right. I freeze, and the bear bolts across the trail. A cub follows and dawdles long enough for me to get a picture. Then a second cub comes out and the two take curious steps towards me. I hear mama bear rustling in the woods to the left, probably trying to figure out what to do. I try "shoo" hand gestures on the cubs, imagining that mama bear would not want them too close to me. The sound is now running; mama bear is rushing back. She gets on the trail fifteen yards beyond the cubs, running towards them and me. I take a few steps back, feeling in my belt pouch for the pathetic lipstick cylinder of mace. I will not be able to get it out in time anyway, so I lift my trekking poles into a defensive position. When mama bear reaches the cubs, she cuts back into the woods and the cubs follow her.

Most of the crowd from last night are together again at Hightop Hut. Bearable arrives early in the morning while the rest of us are fixing breakfast. He had chosen to walk through the night to mix things up, and to walk in cooler weather.

Cubs in Shenandoah National Park. Mother bear is unseen in the woods to the left. She would soon return.

I make great time in the morning, covering twelve miles before arriving at Lewis Mountain Campground for lunch. I spend two hours at the camp store, making phone calls and plans. For lunch, I buy a prepackaged sandwich, chips, packaged snack cakes, two sodas, and ice cream. Carrying so little food and eating like this is bliss.

Many thru-hikers who are hiking with another person will walk separately so that they can walk at their own paces. They will wait for one another at designated points along the trail. Married couples sometimes hike in this fashion as well, but more commonly, they will walk in tandem, staying within earshot of each other the entire day. This is the style of Ken and Marcia. I catch up to them late in the afternoon, and I walk with them for the final six miles into Big Meadows Campground. I've been looking forward to getting to know them better, and we engage in conversation that lasts the rest of the day.

Ken and Marcia Powers are from California. Ken was able to retire from his job as a database administrator in his early fifties, and since that time they have backpacked an impressive number of miles. When they complete the AT, they will have accomplished the "triple crown" of backpacking, which also includes the Pacific Crest Trail (PCT: 2,658 miles) and the Continental Divide Trail (CDT: 2,764 miles). Both trails are less traveled than the Appalachian Trail.

With all their experience, they are in great hiking shape and are very efficient hikers. They plan well and stick to their plan. They don't carry any more than is necessary. On one break, I observe them counting out their ration of cookies. Hiking as a couple also helps to keep their pack weight down since they share a tent, stove, and food. Most of the time, they both have backpacks weighing twenty-five pounds or less. They do not walk fast. Marcia confides that "everyone passes us." But they are regimented and are further along the trail than most thru-hikers who started earlier. They pack quickly in the morning, and they walk late into the day. They walk few short days and rarely take days off.

Big Meadows Campground is set upon a plateau skirted by rocky cliffs. The trail passes over the cliffs as it heads into the campground. The hard surface, the heat, and the long day are wearing on my feet. We've been walking nonstop since I joined Ken and Marcia. They seem unaffected, but I am eager to get this pack off my back and to get my hot feet out of these shoes. We share a campsite and walk over to the lodge for a meal at the restaurant—the same restaurant that we will return to for breakfast.

The next morning, I don't make it far from Big Meadows before my feet are aching again. My feet are sending me messages, all of them bad: they are hot, sore from bruising, itchy from blisters, and squeezed as if cramped into shoes that are too tight. I stop on a rock outcropping, take my shoes off, and ponder my future. It concerns me that the pain is starting so early in the day. Taking a larger view only makes my outlook bleaker. Even if I tough it out today, I still have many more days ahead. I'm not even halfway to Katahdin. From this precipice where I have stopped, I have a view over green hills extending to the horizon. The setting, like so many others, is beautiful and serene. It is unfortunate that the pleasure is inseparable from the pain.

My feet are ugly. Even my wife and mother think so. Not because they've been ravaged by the hike; they've always been this way. They don't have enough meat on them. When I walk barefooted on smooth ground, my feet hurt for lack of adequate padding. I have a thick callus on the middle of my foot pad from a history of blistering there. My left bunion juts out, and blisters form where the bunion pushes on the shoe. My right foot bears a scar from bunion surgery. The skin on my feet is pale and thin, so a network of veins shows through. A friend once said, "If you drop anything sharp on your foot, you'll bleed to death." My feet are too long for my size. A few years ago, I wore size 10½. After bunion surgery, I'd occasionally buy size 11. Now, swollen by walking, anything less than 11½ is unthinkable.

Only my pinky toe is fleshy. It gets crowded where shoes taper in at the toe, and this toe was the first to blister on the hike. The next smallest toe is hammer-toed, curving in toward, and a bit under, my middle toe. Both toes blister as a result. My middle toe blisters on the underside, between the padded tip of the toe and the pad of my foot. This blister is most painful since it is on the sensitive area of the toe. The toe next to my big toe is longest and bears the brunt of impact with the front of my shoe, especially when I stub into rocks and roots. The toenail turned blue and fell off within the first weeks of my hike. My big toe is raw from contact with the adjacent toe. The toenail of my right big toe is cracked but holding firm. The left big toenail is one of only two that are still intact.

I tire of hiking in pain. Over the course of my hike, I've dealt with knee pain, a strained Achilles tendon, shoulder and hip bruises from pack straps, and an infected blister on my heel. But my feet are far and away my greatest physical liability. Foot pain is constant and exasperating. I expected to endure aches and pains during the first few weeks, but then toughen up and hike with relative ease. It hasn't happened. I am getting more worn down by the miles.

As kids we dared each other to jump off the roof of our house, antics I escaped without injury, but I remember the pain. On landing, I felt the impact on the soles of my feet, as if I had stomped them on a concrete surface. My knees folded up into my chest faster than anticipated, and my ankles were sore from the jolt. Jumping off a roof is what comes to mind as a comparison to the wear I feel from backpacking this far.

After resting, my foot pain is more tolerable. The trail moves onto softer, more shaded ground. The pattern is familiar. My aches approach the limit of what I am willing to bear. I rest, take ibuprofen, and, fortunately thus far, the pain subsides. It doesn't take a debilitating injury to end a thru-hike. At the moment, it is easy to see why hikers choose not to continue walking when it causes such discomfort. It is a tough decision to make. Wisdom is knowing when perseverance will be rewarded.

By noon I have reached Skyland Lodge and Restaurant and continue the wonderful string of store-bought and restaurant-prepared meals. I get a seat in the large, air-conditioned restaurant by a window overlooking a creek. Indiana Slim and a thru-hiker friend are at the restaurant, too. I use a pay phone downstairs to call my friend Scott Strand, who will meet me later at Thorton Gap. Indiana Slim's friend is on the pay phone next to me, and Indiana stands nearby waiting.

"What's up, Indiana?"

"We're making plans to get a ride out to Luray. From there we'll aqua-blaze [take a canoe] up to Harpers Ferry. I'm ready to get out of the Shenandoahs."

I have heard more disparaging remarks from thru-hikers about the trail through the Shenandoahs than about any other section. "I hate it," one of them went so far as to say. The Skyline Drive, and the traffic that it brings, is one point of contention. Thru-hikers act at times as though they should have exclusive or preferential access to the AT. The attitude of thru-hikers can be downright uppity when confronted with a significant tourist presence, such as it is here, in the Smokies, and concentrated around the huts of the White Mountains.

I have no complaints about my time in the park. The treadway is smoother and less eroded than in most places on the AT. I've enjoyed hot meals and carried less food. Wildlife is abundant.

I see two more bears during the remainder of my day, about an hour apart. The first is very close when we notice each other's presence. He lopes away about twenty yards and glares at me indignantly from behind the bushes, making me uneasy. He is rotund with a dusty coat. His disheveled look and carelessness in letting me get so close spur me to personify him as a couch potato of the animal world—a bear with a loose grip on his vices. The next bear I spot walking along on a jumble of rocks about one hundred feet downhill from the trail. He is refreshingly clean-coated and has simian agility on the uneven terrain.

Two day hikers are headed in the opposite direction of me, and I tell them of my bear sightings. They proceed, thwacking the brush with their hiking poles. I wish I hadn't told them.

Scott picks me up at Thorton Gap and takes me to his home in Culpeper, Virginia, about an hour away. Scott has been my friend for over twenty years, dating back to when he taught me how to juggle in high school chemistry class. He is following the journal entries I make on the Internet, so he's well aware of what I need most: food, a shower, and laundered clothes. I have a restful evening relaxing with Scott, his wife Carolyn, and their three kids. In the morning, Scott is awake to cook me a big breakfast and gives me even more food to pack for the trail.

Summer has begun, and we are all feeling the heat. Other than the warmer days, weather in the park is ideal. I'll gladly trade a little more sweat in exchange for rainless days.

I arrive at Elkwallow Wayside at midday, feeling lethargic from the heat. I eat lunch, write, and mingle with other hikers who trickle in and congregate around the camp store, all conceding the middle part of their hiking day. Some of us stay long enough to down multiple milkshakes. Many of us depart near the same time, making for an unusual late-day group hike into Gravel Springs Hut.

I have just met the couple Superman and Torch, and I walk nearest to Superman in the chain of thru-hikers headed to the hut. Time passes as I have an interesting, wide-ranging conversation with him. He is a well-versed, budding minister, and I am intrigued by his unorthodox views on religion. When hikers meet it's not unusual to quickly delve into each other's background. Where are you from? What sort of work do you do? What brings you to the trail? We digress into discussions about layoffs, broken marriages, religion…all within an hour of meeting. In the real world, we don't open conversations with, "Where are you from? What brings you to Walmart?"

Stretch and Tipperary are here. Crossroads arrives when we are all set up at the shelter, drop-jawed at seeing me again for the first time since Tennessee.

I am a rotisserie sleeper, periodically turning so all body parts share time being compacted on the hard sleeping surface. Tipperary is next to me in the crowded shelter. I worry that the noisy rustling of my bag is keeping him awake; I hear him stir every time I turn. I apologize for it in the morning. "No, not to worry," he replies. "I turned when you did so you wouldn't have to listen to me turn."

All seven other people in the shelter clear out before me. Usually, I am one of the first on the trail around 7:30 a.m. It is getting hotter during the day, so hikers are motivated to do their walking early and late. Ten miles north, at Tom

Floyd Shelter, there is a tent set up inside the shelter. Three hikers who stayed here last night still haven't left and don't look as if they will be leaving anytime soon. Elwood is one of them; the other two are a couple out for a few days. Both the man and woman are pale-skinned, riddled with tattoos, and have dyed hair. "Hello, Awol," Elwood says in his raspy voice, smiling because of the odd coincidence of us meeting so often, and giddy with the company he has found. The three of them are ribbing each other about hanging out here all day. I make a trip to the privy and to get water while Elwood and his bawdy buddies cackle about "getting back into the tent."

The trail is all downhill from the shelter. Below, I see a young bear in the woods, unaware of my presence. I lose sight of him in the trees, but I suspect he is on a course that will intersect with the trail below. I get my camera out and continue stalking downhill as quietly as I can. I see the bear emerging from the trees out onto the trail a short way ahead. He turns his head to look uphill and freezes momentarily when he sees me, giving me a perfect opportunity to snap his picture before he runs away. Sadly, this picture, and all other pictures that I took in the latter part of the SNP, were lost in my attempt to mail home a digital camera card from Front Royal.

I hitch into Front Royal from U.S. 522 after leaving Shenandoah National Park. Again, I have a ride within minutes. My driver is a young man in an eighties-era muscle car. He spends his spare time and money getting his car into racing form and gives me a sample of its acceleration on the short ride to town.

I get a shower and set out to explore the town. The chamber of commerce has free goody bags for hikers, similar to what was given out at Waynesboro, but also including granola bars and single-serving cereal boxes. I head out to a restaurant at the west end of town, walking nearly a mile on the hot pavement. Along the way, I stray off to visit with other thru-hikers. By some coincidence, they are all couples. Superman and Torch are lying under the shade of a tree in a park; Ken and Marcia are at the library updating their journal; Doc and Llama and their dog, Coy, are at a café.

I circle back by the hotel and then head for an outfitter on the east end of town. Again, my walk is nearly a mile, this time on streets without sidewalks. I try hitching, half-heartedly because it is such a short distance. No one stops, anyway. It is much more difficult to hitch within town than it is to hitch from a remote trailhead. My backpack, which I don't carry around town with me, is my ticket to hitch.

I look over trail shoes, insoles, and socks at the outfitter, but I see nothing that looks promising. I don't know what I was expecting to find. I've already worn four different pairs of shoes. I've tried many different types of socks, wearing two pairs of socks, and different types of inserts. There is no magic insole, no wonder shoe in which I will be able to backpack twenty miles a day and feel as if I hadn't.

8
Front Royal to Pen-Mar Park

Doc and Llama are on their second thru-hike of the AT. They did the PCT the same year as Ken and Marcia. They are in the small sect of thru-hikers that could be dubbed "career hikers." During the off-season, Doc does landscape work and Llama waits tables. These aren't jobs with "a future"; they're jobs that will fund their next adventure.

People living normal lives are ruffled by folks like Doc and Llama. Nonconformity is an affront to those in the mainstream. Our impulse is to dismiss this lifestyle, create reasons why it can't work, why it doesn't even warrant consideration. Why not? Living outdoors is cheap and can be afforded by a half year of marginal employment. They can't buy things that most of us have, but what they lose in possessions, they gain in freedom.

In Somerset Maugham's *The Razor's Edge*, lead character Larry returns from the First World War and declares that he would like to "loaf."[23] The term "loafing" inadequately

---

23   W. Somerset Maugham, *The Razor's Edge* (New York: Penguin Books, 1984).

describes the life he would spend traveling, studying, searching for meaning, and even laboring. Larry meets with the disapproval of peers and would-be mentors: "Common sense assured...that if you wanted to get on in this world, you must accept its conventions, and not to do what everybody else did clearly pointed to instability."

Larry had an inheritance that enabled him to live modestly and pursue his dreams. Larry's acquaintances didn't fear the consequences of his failure; they feared his failure to conform.

I'm no maverick. Upon leaving college I dove into the workforce, eager to have my own stuff and a job to pay for it. Parents approved, bosses gave raises, and my friends could relate. The approval, the comforts, the commitments wound themselves around me like invisible threads. When my life stayed the course, I wouldn't even feel them binding. Then I would waiver enough to sense the growing entrapment, the taming of my life in which I had been complicit.

Working a nine-to-five job took more energy than I had expected, leaving less time to pursue diverse interests. I grew to detest the statement "I am a..." with the sentence completed by an occupational title. Self-help books emphasize "defining priorities" and "staying focused," euphemisms for specialization and stifling spontaneity. Our vision becomes so narrow that risk is trying a new brand of cereal, and adventure is watching a new sitcom. Over time I have elevated my opinion of nonconformity nearly to the level of an obligation. We should have a bias toward doing activities that we don't normally do to keep loose the moorings of society.

Hiking the AT is "pointless." What life is not "pointless"? Is it not pointless to work paycheck to paycheck just to conform? Hiking the AT before joining the workforce was an opportunity not taken. Doing it in retirement would be sensible; doing it at this time in my life is abnormal, and therein lay the appeal. I want to make my life less ordinary.

❀ ❀ ❀

From the start of the day, I am sluggish, and I struggle even on undemanding climbs. The drenching rains don't help. At Manassas Gap I stop to adjust socks on my hurting feet, and it starts sprinkling. I have to unload most of my gear to get my pack cover and rain jacket from the bottom of my pack. This day I'm peeved by these simple inconveniences. Why did I leave town? I could still be sleeping in a comfortable motel bed in Front Royal. The feeling is comparable to wanting to turn your car around midway into the morning commute.

This day would turn out fine, even though I wouldn't regain any spunk. The terrain isn't too tough, and I enjoy the company. I cross paths with Ken and Marcia a few times. No-Hear-Um is taking his lunch break, and he shares carrots he brought from town. This is the last I would see of him on the trail. I meet section hiker Molly, and she tries to help me out with powdered Vitamin C.

I flop down in Dicks Dome Shelter, a small dome-shaped experiment of a shelter. The arching roof provides less headroom than a typical shelter; it is low enough for me to extend my legs and rest my feet on the trusses. The leaky roof has left water stains on the ceiling and floor, so already I know I don't intend to stay here. Molly enters and starts setting up her sleeping bag awkwardly, perpendicular to my position. The oddly-shaped floor space does not lend itself to a uniform sleeping arrangement. Elwood is here, too.

I head on into the late afternoon. There is dense undergrowth and no room for a tent. I don't mind, since I am covering miles in cool weather and putting distance between myself and Elwood. A side trail to Sky Meadows State Park branches off to the right. At the intersection of the AT and the side trail, there is an open piece of flat ground and a park bench. The little bench is a convenient place to cook and eat. The ground here is dark, packed dirt studded with pebbles and hard to penetrate with a tent stake. But as expected, I don't feel the pebbles through my air pad. I settle in for a memorably comfortable night of solitude.

Harpers Ferry is thirty-six miles away, and I intend to get there by noon tomorrow. I've arranged to meet my friend Tim Kesecker, who is visiting his parents in West Virginia. Tim is on vacation from the same workplace that I quit at the start of my hike. In the early going, my desire for rapid progress is waylaid, first by muddy trail, then by the Roller Coaster.

The Roller Coaster is a nine-mile-long series of hills in northern Virginia over which the trail ascends and descends, as the name implies, straight up to the peaks and straight down to the valleys. Although no peak is higher than fourteen hundred feet, there is five thousand feet of elevation gain and loss. The first part of any uphill climb is the most difficult. It takes time for me to establish a pace that I can sustain. Especially hard is the transition from walking downhill to walking uphill. On the downhill my pace accelerates, momentum carries me into the uphill, and then I make the panting realization that I'm headed uphill at a near-jogging pace.

The last ascent of the Roller Coaster ends on a rocky plateau called Bears Den Rocks. I take a short side trail to Bears Den Hostel. The hostel is in a beautifully rustic stone building that houses the hostel caretaker and a small supply store. Stretch is at a park bench out front eating a pint of Ben & Jerry's ice cream. Stretch has a friend, Justin, out to hike with him this week. Elwood is also sitting at the table.

"Elwood, you beat me here!" I exclaim.

"Hey, you know it, man. I got up early and hauled ass," he says.

I camped ahead of him and never saw him pass me, so I know there is some other explanation. Stretch and Justin head back out to the trail, and I leave soon after. "Until next time," Elwood says, alluding to our continuing encounters on the trail. This time, there would be no next time.

The trail stays atop Bears Den Rocks for the next half mile. On this stony ridge, there is a steep drop-off on the western edge with many overlooks. At one of these overlooks, Stretch and Justin are taking in the view. I pause to take a picture for them.

"Back there when Elwood told you that he 'hauled ass'..." Stretch says, not bothering to finish the sentence. "We were sitting right there when a jeep pulled up and dropped him off." I suspected that Elwood was again having a Rosie Ruiz day, but his brashness in telling the lie in front of people who knew better renews my wariness of him.[24]

The trail dips down to Snickers Gap and then ascends steadily. Near the peak, I say hello to a couple of teenagers wearing daypacks walking in the opposite direction. Soon after, there are more small groups of teens and parents, obviously all part of one troop. A man and woman shepherding a distressed youth are straggling behind the rest. The adults are more likely counselors, judging by the patience with which they are handling the young man. The boy is

---

24   In 1980 Rosie Ruiz "won" the Boston Marathon by jumping out from among the spectators near the end of the race. She finished the New York Marathon by taking the subway.

overweight, red-faced, and listless. In an obvious attempt to engage me in their efforts to motivate him, the adults stop me with questions.

"How close are we to the top?"

"You're almost there. Another hundred yards, then it's mostly downhill."

The woman turns to the boy. "See, honey, we're nearly there. It'll be okay." And then she says to me, "How far to the road?"

"Oh, I passed the road about thirty-five minutes ago."

"Are you a thru-hiker?"

"Yes."

They continue with questions about when I started, how much weight is in my pack, how many miles I walk per day, and so forth pursuing this conversation to show the young man by inference, "See how long he's been hiking? It's not so hard." But I don't think the strategy is helpful, so I don't cooperate. The young man is deflated; I don't know how anyone could inspire him at this point. Anything said will cause him to search for the counterpoint, to rationalize why he's miserable, entrench himself in his position. If help is coming, it will be from within.

I've encountered many large groups, and within each there are always one or more kids not happy to be there. Do I see this because kids have less patience for hiking, or because they are more likely to be here against their will? Adults with the same aversion to the outdoors—if they came at all—would get fifty yards down the trail, decide it is "not their thing," and go home.

Not everyone needs to be a hiker, but using "not my thing" is too convenient. Activities that even momentarily cause discomfort, that don't provide immediate positive feedback, are subtracted from the realm of experience. We are outraged when we are constrained by others, but willfully, unwittingly put limits on ourselves. There are better solutions. The boy I saw struggling that day could conclude that he will get in shape so that he won't need to avoid physical activity. Or he may realize that the outing was not as bleak as he imagined and resolve to keep a better attitude. These are solutions that build confidence and put no bounds on future opportunities.

There are many thru-hikers on the trail late in the day. This is unusual. Ken and Marcia, Bearable, Torch, Superman, Doc, Llama, and Tipperary are still hiking past 7:30 p.m. All but Ken and Marcia take the side trail down to the Blackburn PATC (Potomac AT Club) Center. The Blackburn Center is located steeply downhill, about one-third of a mile from the AT. As we descend on switchbacks, music floats up to meet us.

A wedding has just taken place on the lawn of the Blackburn Center. A sign posted on the side trail told us so and informed us that hikers were welcome to come anyway. A modular dance floor is assembled on the grass and covered by a white canopy. Next to the canopy a band is playing to a crowd of about fifty people outfitted in suits and dresses. A few diehards still dance, but most have moved on to eating and drinking, scattering among a dozen linen-covered tables. The transition from the trail to this celebration is striking and exhilarating. What good fortune.

Crossroads and two other thru-hikers have already checked into the hostel and have been delegated the job of greeting hikers and showing them to the bunkrooms and tent sites. They say the time is near for us to dig into the reception leftovers. Many nights on my hike I would spend alone, or with few other hikers. By wonderful coincidence, most of the hikers that I've enjoyed spending time with through the Shenandoahs arrive here on the same night, camaraderie culminating at the moment we stumble into a beckoning party.

The bunkroom is one of the outlying structures of the Blackburn complex. There are other buildings for storage and equipment. The main building, a large, square building with a wraparound patio, is the caretaker's residence. Bill, a former thru-hiker, is the caretaker.

Bill tells us we are welcome to drink from the keg. We set up at picnic tables on the perimeter of the reception area, eyeing the buffet like vultures. Before long we are brought a tray of leftover meat and rolls. When guests take notice of us, they trickle out to mingle. The wedding photographer takes pictures of this anomalous intersection of people. Upon seeing how quickly the food dissolves, the guests take it upon themselves to bring more. We are treated to a re- markable feast of smoked pork, turkey, salads, deviled eggs, wedding cake, brownies, cookies, and champagne.

After the wedding party leaves, we move to a linen- covered table and continue to work the keg and talk with Bill and a couple of lingering guests. One of the guests brings out a bottle of his favorite whiskey, and we pass it around until it is empty. The same fate meets a second bot- tle. We discuss hiking, blue-blazing, politics, and the war in Iraq with logic and earnestness peculiar to those who have drunk alcohol in quantity. Bill has a proposition that we all accept: stick around in the morning to clean up after the wedding, and he'll drive our packs to Harpers Ferry.

I wake, confused, to the sound of running water. There's no stream outside and no water inside this bunkroom. May- be the sound is from a dream. There are only two sets of bunk-bed platforms with floor space in between. I am in one of the upper bunks. The hiker in the upper bunk on the other side of the room asks, "Is someone urinating in here?" I hear that clearly. I'm not dreaming. The sound is someone urinating. A drunken hiker sleeping on the floor had made it to his knees, but couldn't struggle free from his sleeping bag before the urge to pee overtook him. He passed out, clunked to the floor, and started to drag the sodden sleeping bag back onto himself. I struggle too, between overwhelming grogginess and the desire to get up and help. I retrieve my watch and push the "illuminate" button. It is 1:30. Thankfully, another hiker gets up and takes the bag outside.

At seven in the morning, a bunch of hung-over hikers are out of bed cleaning up after yesterday's wedding and reception. We spend about an hour picking up trash and packing folding chairs and tables. Even the hiker whose sleeping bag is out to dry is working. Bill heats up leftover potatoes, peppers, and bread for breakfast, along with much coffee. By nine o'clock most of us, sans packs, are headed for Harpers Ferry, twelve miles north.

I am so tired I sleepwalk through the miles. The grade is fairly level, rocky in places. Someone has assembled twigs to form a square frame on the trail. Inside the frame, pebbles are arranged to spell out the number "1,000." I've been hiking for one thousand miles.

On the final stretch into town, I cross the Shenandoah River on the long, bending bridge of Highway 340. I am isolated from the cars by a concrete barrier, but I feel propelled by their breeze as they whip past, like I am on a victory lap. After crossing the bridge, the trail enters woods on the outskirts of town. I take a side trail that leaves the woods, crosses the grounds of Storer College, and leads to the headquarters of the Appalachian Trail Conference (ATC), a nonprofit organization that builds, protects, and manages the trail. A staff member is out front taking pictures of thru-hikers, using the building's facade as the backdrop. The ATC keeps a photo album for each year, with a photo and a blurb of information on every thru-hiker passing this point. I am the 528th thru-hiker this year.

Laurie Potteiger takes a picture of Awol in front of
ATC headquarters in Harpers Ferry, West Virginia.

I hear "Awol!" yelled from down the street. Tim, my friend from Florida, is doing as the Romans do by using my trail name, yet it is odd to hear it from him. He is here with his parents, Dan and Wilma Kesecker. They take me back to their home in Martinsburg, West Virginia, twenty miles to the west.

I have only met Tim's parents on two occasions before this. They are exceedingly friendly and caring, the type of couple who seem like parents to us all. I am treated to a shower, a home-cooked dinner, and a comfortable bed. Tim talks about how projects have progressed since I left the workplace. There is much work to be done, and they are likely to be hiring in the fall, when I will be finished with my hike. He believes that the company will be willing to rehire me. I am content knowing that decision is still months away.

The day starts out great with Wilma Kesecker making me the best pancakes I've ever had. The Keseckers return me to the ATC Headquarters building, and I take the blue-blazed trail out of town and back to the AT. The AT wiggles briefly through the woods overlooking the Shenandoah River, and then reenters Harpers Ferry on the north end of town. I cross the Potomac River on a wire-fence-enclosed footbridge. From the bridge, there is a view down to the convergence of the Potomac and Shenandoah Rivers. The merged river keeps the name Potomac and flows east through Washington, D.C., about fifty miles away.

The Potomac River is the northern border of West Virginia, so upon stepping off the footbridge, I start my sixth state on the trail, Maryland. The state begins with the easiest two and a half miles on the AT. This bit of trail is on the Chesapeake and Ohio (C&O) Towpath. The towpath is a wide pathway of packed dirt, similar to a dirt road, but thankfully without tire ruts. The towpath and the shallow canal parallel to it were constructed as a trade route between Washington and towns in the Potomac Valley as far west as Cumberland, Maryland. A team of mules driven along the towpath pulled barges loaded with cargo. The towpath was last used commercially in 1924. Now, it is a 184-mile-long national park.[25]

A hundred yards down the towpath, I turn to look back at the footbridge. There the Keseckers stand, waving goodbye. All the towns through which the trail passes are distinctive and inviting. When I hike in one day and out the next, as I have done here, it feels rushed. I would return

---

25   Towpath details from the Chesapeake and Ohio Canal National Historic Park Web site: http://www.nps.gov/choh/.

to spend more time in Harpers Ferry—sooner than I could have imagined.

Thru-hiker Kodiak passes me on the climb up Weaverton Cliffs; we both stop a short distance later at the Ed Garvey Shelter, a fine new bi-level shelter. Kodiak started a thru-hike in 1999 but quit halfway through for lack of funds. He regrets not finishing the hike on his previous attempt and is determined to finish this time. This year he started the thru-hike with his wife, who decided to get off the trail at Harpers Ferry. This is his first day hiking without her, and he seems caught up in his thoughts.

The first half of the trail through Maryland is a nice stroll in the woods. The terrain is fairly smooth, and the grade is mild. Trees and undergrowth are pleasantly green, but not suffocating. When I arrive at Gathland State Park, a small, grassy park, I see enough sky to determine that rain is coming. There are soda machines at the park under a small overhang on the porch of the bathroom building. I huddle under the overhang with four other thru-hikers, getting our feet wet by the slanting rain. I buy a soda and, with it, eat all of the treats Wilma packed for me.

Dahlgren backpacker's campground is my stop for the night. There are restrooms with showers, picnic tables, and a tenting area large enough for at least a dozen tents. Kodiak, Ken and Marcia, and more than a handful of other thru-hikers are here. I fix and eat my meal at a table with Orbit, whose situation is similar to Kodiak's. Orbit was hiking with his girlfriend, who got off the trail yesterday.

Harpers Ferry is a major milestone. Thru-hikers consider it the halfway point, even though it is eighty miles short of the trail's midpoint. A number of hikers have chosen the Harpers Ferry milestone as a drop-out point. Ken tells me, much to my surprise, that Bigfoot is off the trail. Some hikers have taken time off to visit Washington, D.C., and still others, like No-Hear-Um, head up to Katahdin to walk the second half of the trail north to south. The rest of us continue north with our mood receding from the elation of making it this far. We are a bit more serious, down to the business of focusing on the next goal. I always feel apprehensive when thru-hikers decide not to continue, particularly at this time of mass defections.

I am up and away early, opting to walk an hour to Washington Monument State Park before making breakfast. I cross over two walls made of stacked stone. This part of the country is rich with history, detailed by frequent plaques and monuments. Seeing these stone walls in the dewy, peaceful morning woods gives me a more visceral feel for history than any of the plaques. Civil War soldiers hunkered behind these walls as the opposing side approached. The harsh percussion of bullets on rock would be a devastating departure from the stillness of the woods. How could a man function from behind this explosion of splintering rock and smoky lead?

The original Washington Monument, built in 1827, is a sturdy stone building thirty feet tall, shaped like an upside-down drinking glass. I walk a staircase that spirals upward along the inside wall of the cylinder, exiting on the flat roof to see a grand view of the valley below. I descend from the park, back to the present, and cross Interstate 70 on a concrete pedestrian overpass. From the woods, north of the interstate, I look back to see Orbit crossing as a pair of eighteen-wheelers rumble underneath.

The rockiness of the trail increases as I progress, as if I am heading toward a great mound of rock from which these scatterings have been dispersed. Eventually, my feet no longer touch dirt, and I am stepping from rock to rock and weaving around boulders. I reach Ensign Cowell Shelter after fourteen miles that have seemed much longer. A small group is at the shelter, and Kodiak and Orbit arrive while I am snacking. Even though the rocks have worn us down, it is still early, and the three of us will likely move on.

"Do you think you will go all the way to Pen-Mar?" I ask Kodiak. Pen-Mar is a park on the border of Maryland and Pennsylvania.

"I might. Twenty-three miles…that would be a long day." Although Kodiak is a stronger hiker than I am, he hasn't been hiking days this long. He was hiking with his wife, and couples generally end their day when either person is ready to stop, resulting in shorter days.

"There's pizza," I add.

We know from the guidebook that there is a phone at the park and a pizza place close enough to deliver. Food is always a primary motivator. On the downside, there is no camping at or near the park. I continue on, with uncertain plans. Kodiak and Orbit will probably do the same. There are always miles to be walked.

The rocks abate for a few miles. A fifty-yard-wide swath is cut through the trees to make way for power lines that drape over the hills and extend out of sight. Huge four-legged metal giants stand in file, holding up the wires. The trail follows the clearing downhill, exposed to harsh sunlight and encroaching weeds.

The trail reenters the woods, and again rocks dominate the landscape. Earlier in the day, rock hopping was an interesting diversion. Now, having already hiked twenty miles, the rocks are an unwelcome challenge. The terrain is more difficult, with greater slope and rocks jutting up irregularly. This boulder field is significant enough to have a name: the Devil's Racecourse.

I am tired and distracted, plodding through the boulders. I recollect events of the day, as I am prone to do, when it occurs to me that I am in the midst of a protracted day. Visiting Washington Monument seems longer ago than this morning.

The trail is going steadily downhill now, so I know I am nearing the end of the racecourse. Pen-Mar Park is only a couple of miles further. I take a lunging step down from a boulder about three feet high and land unevenly. All my weight, and the weight of my backpack, comes down on the outside of my right foot. I have rolled onto the outside of each foot a handful of times up to this point on my hike, but this time it turns a little further.

I fall and roll into a sitting position, my injured leg quivering. I know immediately that I have sprained my ankle. The feeling is not so much painful as it is numb, out of whack. I look around to see what went wrong. There is no outstanding irregularity on the ground that should have caused me to misstep. Maybe there was a rock that I landed on that kicked away after I stepped on it…no, my right foot must have nicked the boulder's surface on the way down, so that my shoe turned inward before landing. My hiking poles are lying free on the ground, but I can't even recall letting them loose.

I don't even want to look at my ankle. If I take my shoe off, I probably won't be able to get it back on. I take three Advil, stretch for my poles, and get to my feet. My best chance of walking is now—waiting will only make it harder.

I can put weight on my right foot, but I have to be careful about lifting and placing it. If the ground where I place my foot is uneven, I feel a tinge of pain. It is more painful to make the slightest bit of contact with a rock while lifting and moving my injured leg. This simple sequence of lifting my foot cleanly and finding a smooth place for it to land is a challenge among the jumble of rock.

Thoughts swirl though my head as I limp down the trail. I have some anger toward the trail for taking me through the minefield of rocks, and I'm disappointed in myself for getting tired and careless. Why couldn't I stay focused? Why did I have to push myself through another long day? Then I play through all the scenarios of what I might do next. I'm not eager for another extended motel stay like my recuperation in Wytheville. It would be wasteful to spend more time away from home, especially being less sure that I'll be able to continue hiking. Am I making it worse by walking on it? I need to get down to the park and take a look at my ankle before I can figure out what to do. Maybe it's not as bad as I think; I could camp tonight and hope it's better in the morning.

I hear Kodiak steaming down the trail behind me, so I pause to let him pass. As he approaches, he comments, "These rocks are a nightmare. Someone could really get hurt on this stuff."

"Yeah, I just sprained my ankle."

He continues on without pause or reply. What I just said didn't register, maybe because I stated it so simply and he had his headphones on. This is fine, since I prefer not to be escorted down the trail. There is nothing he could do to help.

At Pen-Mar Park, I get my shoe off and have a look. Disturbing, unnatural swelling has overtaken the outer knob of my ankle joint. Kodiak, still lingering at the park, offers his assessment of my ankle: "Oh, shit!" The look of my ankle eliminates any thought I may have harbored about walking through the injury, and increases my doubts about continuing at all. Perhaps I should be thinking of ways to get back home. I call Juli from a pay phone at the park. From home, she looks up where I am and tells me of the nearest hospital in Waynesboro, Pennsylvania.

I also call Tim, who has already flown back to Florida. I wonder about returning to the Keseckers' home, but I'm too tentative about inviting myself to call them directly. Tim is encouraging, telling me that they would be thrilled to have company.

"The man at that house over there," a park ranger says, pointing to a home across the street from the park, "will give you a ride. He's taken hikers to town before."

The Waynesboro Hospital is bright and empty in the evening. I have X-rays and speak with a doctor.

"Nothing is broken," he explains. "I'd say you have a severely sprained ankle."

"That's what I thought."

"Normally, I would recommend doing nothing strenuous for a month," the doctor says as he wraps my ankle. "But I've had hikers in here before. I know you won't. Just give it at least a week."

He gives me other advice on wrapping and icing down my ankle and suggests an anti-inflammatory and a pain reliever. I am also given an Aircast. The Aircast consists of two contoured plastic splints for the inside and outside of my ankle, connected by a strap that loops under my foot, and by Velcro straps that wrap around my shin. There is a plastic air-filled pad on the inner surface of each splint. The cast not only stabilizes the injured ankle, it reduces swelling by compression. Two underworked paramedics give me an ambulance ride to a nearby hotel. The doctor's prognosis was better than I expected. I believe I can recover and resume my hike of the AT.

By morning, Juli has spoken with Dan and Wilma, and they are eager to have me back. They drive to Waynesboro to pick me up. They are gracious, welcoming, and do all they can to make me feel as though I am no imposition.

The Aircast came with the videotape, "Caring for Your Sprained Ankle." With little interest I begin the video, prepared to hear what the doctor already told me: to rest, put ice on it, blah, blah, blah. Instead, the Aircast video promotes exercising a sprained ankle right away and demonstrates exercises that speed recovery: "Even though your ankle may hurt, it's best to move it as soon as possible to help it heal." This is more good news. Hearing this spawns within me the notion that I may accelerate my return to the trail. I launch into the exercises. Also, I reason that walking is a form of rehab, which the video just encouraged me to do as soon as possible. I feel like I have more invested in the hike, as I felt when I took time off with a foot infection. Damned if I'll quit my job, suffer through knee pain, a foot infection, and now a sprained ankle, just to go home saying I did half the AT.

Dan Kesecker drives with me back to Harpers Ferry, where we spend time seeing the town. We watch a presentation about the town's history, how it thrived by the trade along the Shenandoah and Potomac Rivers, but also suffered floods because of them. Back at ATC Headquarters, thru-hiker Leaf is checking in. I look over the photo album to find out who else I might see when I get back to the trail. I feel fine limping along on smooth walkways without the weight of a pack, but my ankle is sore by the time we leave.

Wilma takes me to a sporting goods store on my quest for more comfortable shoes. The shoes must also accommodate the additional bulk of the Aircast. I settle on a lightweight running shoe, size 12 in width 4E.

The Keseckers are wonderful hosts, considerate to make sure I have everything I need. During my four-day stay, Wilma cooks delicious meals morning and night. Dan grills hamburgers on Independence Day. Despite all my indulgent eating, I hardly regain weight, and my appetite shows no signs of weakening.

Blackish-blue blood from the injury works its way down the outside of my foot and then dissipates into a jaundice yellow. The swelling, pushed around by the Aircast, manifests itself in different parts of my ankle and foot. Mainly, I am just biding time while I heal. I eat, watch TV, and surf the Internet. I have nothing to do, so I stay up late doing it.

I intercept Dan on his way out to mow the lawn. I must make myself useful. He gives me instruction on his riding mower. I've never used one, so I whip around the yard silly over how cool it is to drive a lawn mower. On the second pass, I have trouble finding a swath to follow, since I had neglected to lower the cutting blades.

I make some use of the idle time to clean my gear. I run my water bottle and pot through the dishwasher, and I wash out my backpack, emptying every nook and cranny. When I load everything back into my pack, I no longer have the stone I had been carrying with me since Springer Mountain, the one I had planned to leave on Katahdin. I don't think I lost it here and can't think of anywhere else it could be. I'm perturbed by the mysterious loss and have a superstitious uneasiness about proceeding without it. I decide to nullify the bad omen by not speaking of the lost stone to anyone, not even Juli, until the end of my hike.

9
Pennsylvania

Pen-Mar Park is bustling on Sunday morning. Families are starting their picnics early on this final day of the long Independence Day weekend. Five days ago when I left with a sprained ankle there were three other people at the park; now there are over a hundred. Dan and Wilma escort me through the crowds. I have new shoes, clean clothes, and a freshly scrubbed pack. I've lost the disheveled look that distinguishes long-distance hikers. With all the kids looking on, I feel unproven, awkwardly clean, like a kid reporting to his first day of football practice in shiny new cleats. I am ready to be moving north once again. If my ankle starts to hurt I will stop, satisfied with any amount of progress.

I start out slowly, carefully picking my steps. It is distracting to be mindful of my ankle, whose normal functioning I've always taken for granted. All of my senses are muted except for those coming from the nerves of my ankle. Walking with the added weight of my pack isn't a problem. My first uphill is not painful, and neither is the downhill. The terrain is mild with few rocks. There is nothing to make me feel as though walking on my recovering ankle is risky.

I reach a pair of shelters five miles from Pen-Mar Park in less than three hours. Both my comfort level and the speed at which I have covered this distance exceed my expectations. Continuing after a rest at the shelters, I make my first misstep, which sends a spike of pain up my right leg and reminds me that I cannot get careless. I go on to have a handful of painful steps during the day.

An excessive number of shelters are on the stretch between Pen-Mar Park and Caledonia State Park. In addition to the Deer Lick Shelters, I pass Antietam Shelter, Tumbling Run Shelters, and Rocky Mountain Shelters. In passing the last of these shelters, I feel strong and have committed to making it to Caledonia State Park. Beyond the final shelter, the trail is level, uneventful. But then it makes a sharp turn to the right, leading me into a field of rocks the size of footballs. I am unnerved encountering this obstacle late in the day, recalling that my ankle injury occurred late in the day when I was tired and careless. But after only one-half mile, the trail turns back to the left and resumes a path along the line that I was previously walking. Seemingly, the diversion was contrived to lead hikers through the rocky obstacle. My first day back concludes after 18.5 miles with no ill effects.

The trail around Caledonia State Park is parallel to a wide, slow-moving creek. I make the walk in the quiet morning on the second day of my return, passing campground tent sites and skirting the central clearing of the park, where there is a swimming pool and picnic area. I'm at Quarry Gap Shelter after a quick two-mile climb from the park.

My first day back after spraining my ankle.
I would wear the Aircast for the remainder of my hike.

Innkeeper Jim Stauch is cleaning up. He is proud of the place: "It's as good as any shelter on the AT." The shelter has two separate sleeping platforms with a table in between, all covered by one roof. Solar-powered landscape lights line the path to the spring and to the privy. The AT is what it is because of a collection of independent efforts by dedicated people like Jim.

My break has placed me in a hiker void. I saw no other thru-hikers yesterday, and would only see one today. I am content to be alone with my thoughts, hearing my own breath, shallow or deep, fast or slow, in unison with the difficulty of the terrain. My fuel canister makes muffled dings against my cookpot, so I stop to rearrange my gear. Normally, my pack is stuffed tightly and is firm to my back, making little noise. My trekking poles have rubber tips that keep them silent, unless I carelessly clang them on a rock.

I chose not to bring a radio or MP3 player, preferring to give all my attention to the woods around me. As many as half of the solo hikers wear headphones, and I'm sure I would find them addictive. However, I never feel bored on my long days of travel, as one might feel traveling by car. From a passing vehicle, miles of woods seem uniform and bland. On foot inside the woods, I am much more attuned to the sights, smells, and changes in terrain. I pass trees, rocks, underbrush, streams—same as everywhere on the trail, but always different. I see blueberries for the first time, but they aren't ripe. The trees, plants, and rocks on different sections of the trail have variations too subtle for words. Added together, the differences give each segment of the trail, each day, each hour, a substantially unique feel.

In suburbia I didn't feel harassed by noise. The din of traffic, machines, and the voices of other people were the norm. In the forest I appreciate the quiet and the clarity of thought that it induces. It is a welcome, unanticipated benefit. I feel unstressed, fit, alert, and invigorated by the blood pumping through my body.

There is plenty to occupy my mind. Nearly at a subconscious level, I am charting my footsteps, looking ahead for places to land my feet. I prefer the softness of landing on soil instead of rock. I always avoid stepping on roots, especially when they are wet. Which way will I take around obstacles like boulders and fallen trees? Even over distances as short as ten yards, I look for the path that might eliminate an unnecessary step up or down. I try to break a steep climb into more gradual steps. One lunging step will take more out of me than a hundred yards of gradual climbing. Passing a stream, I give my water bag an udder squeeze to determine if there is enough water for me to continue, and I consult Wingfoot about upcoming water sources.

I check the time frequently—at least every quarter hour—and I also take peeks at my guidebook for landmarks passed. I'll do a rough calculation in my head of how far I have walked and how long it has taken, and I'll estimate how much farther I will walk and when I will get there. Most of the time I'm fairly certain of where I will stop for the night. At any given moment I'm aware of my location, usually within a mile. I'm not proud of this. I'd like to shake the habit of obsessing over where I am on the trail.

The trail is pleasant, ranging in elevation from eight hundred to two thousand feet with steady inclines. Like yesterday, the trail makes diversions to pass briefly through rock fields. The stability of my ankle in the Aircast induces confidence. I still have intermittent pain and my right ankle is a little weaker, but it is clear that the injury will not stop me from completing my hike. Also, like yesterday, I pass three shelters and end my day when I reach a park. Today I've set my sights on Pine Grove Furnace State Park.

The last couple miles of the trail follow a disused roadbed, making for an easy walk for the rest of the day. Along this path, at an unmarked point just two-tenths of a mile before the park, I complete exactly one-half of the AT with no fanfare. At the park, I will celebrate by participating in the infamous half-gallon challenge. Tradition demands that thru-hikers celebrate their half-trail experience by consuming half a gallon of ice cream.

Before hiking, I was a modest, healthy eater. I had eliminated sodas and french fries from my diet. The only candy bars I ever ate were those I would pilfer from my kids' Halloween spoils. I'd read about the superhuman appetite of thru-hikers and their eating feats: ten candy bars a day, a dozen doughnuts in one sitting, meals on top of meals. I was going to be different. Sure, I'd need to eat more, but I'd try to eat good stuff: protein bars instead of candy bars, fruit and vegetables whenever I could get them. Healthy eating quickly fell by the wayside. A cold soda is my favorite treat. I prefer the quick energy of candy bars to protein bars. Now I sit with half a gallon of cookie dough ice cream before me, fairly certain that it won't be much of a challenge.

A small camp store at the park sells the ice cream. They have limited flavors, so wimping out with reduced-calorie vanilla is not an option. Cookie dough is the most palatable and has 2,880 calories per box. I spend fifty-two minutes eating, my progress slowed by chipping away at the frozen block. Hikers who have participated in the half-gallon challenge comment on their experiences in a spiral notebook similar to shelter registers. I bring it to my picnic table and read from it as I eat:

"That was the most disgusting thing I've done, except for the pancake challenge."   —Gazelle

"1/2 gallon peanut butter ice cream: 48 minutes. Chicken nuggets & fries: 24 minutes. Biggest bellyache of my life: priceless. Some things money can't buy."   —Mothman

"21 1/2 minutes of ecstasy in the form of cookie dough ice cream. I'm going to chuck now."   —Stretch

"16 min 21 sec. No problem. I think I'm gonna get more ice cream."   —Hungry Hiker

"I wish I could do this in every town...wait a minute... I can!"   —Trip

"29 minutes, chocolate. Washed it down with a delicious cheeseburger."   —Moo

"I don't know why I did it but I did. Heed the warning; don't go for peanut butter twist."   —Brew

I am not indisposed by the ice cream, and I eat a small dinner afterward. Ironmasters Hostel is in a huge two-story brick mansion next to the camp store and is my home for the night. It is an old building with layers of peeling paint on the window frames, a moldy basement, obsolete furnaces, and no air conditioning, mixed with vestiges of elegance like hardwood floors and a piano. Single men, single women, and families are segregated into separate spaces filled with low-budget bunk beds.

The park is named after a Civil War–era iron furnace, a trapezoidal stone structure still standing on the park grounds. I pass by it on the way out and pick up some glassy blue pebbles that are mixed in with the rock of the trail. It is slag, a byproduct of the furnace. The first eight miles out of Pine Grove Furnace are ideal, flat, tourist trail, leading me to a deli at Tagg Run Campground and an early lunch. I sit at a park bench out front to eat subs with thru-hiker Dharma Bum.[26] The next ten miles are harder. The trail goes up and down small hills and weaves through boulder fields at the summits. In addition to the white blazes, arrows are painted on some of the boulders directing me through the proper crevices. The hills are thinly wooded, so I am often in the sun on this day with little breeze. The trail exits the woods and cuts through fields of corn and soybeans for the final mile into Boiling Springs. Now in scorching full sun, I can feel the heat radiating up from the earth into my feet.

Amid this farmland, Boiling Springs, a swank little town, is built around bubbling springs that feed into a lake at the center of town. The trail passes through town, sharing the park path around the perimeter of the lake. Ducks paddle in the serene water. A few homes and businesses are nicely

---

26 Dharma Bum is an often-used trail name taken from the title of Jack Kerouac's 1958 novel.

Cornfield on the approach to Boiling Springs, Pennsylvania.

situated on the far shore. Beyond the town is a thirteen-mile stretch of the AT across the Cumberland Valley. The valley is checkered with farms and pastureland and sliced by roads. There is no camping in this section.

I go to the regional ATC office to ask about options for a place to stay. A woman at the desk is surfing the Internet and talking on the phone. She has a sign on her desk which reads, "I can only help one person a day, and today is not your day." I mill about the office for about fifteen minutes, making it obvious that I am waiting to speak with her, while she makes it obvious that she is in no hurry to speak with me.

I move on for a walk about town, exploring the places listed in Wingfoot. There are two bed and breakfasts in town. One is full, and the owner at the other suggestively tells me, "You probably don't want to stay here."

I go down the street to a convenience store, where I get hot dogs for dinner, and then to Leo's Ice Cream for dessert. Cooling down with ice cream and the dropping sun, I look over my guidebook to see what is ahead. In eight miles, the trail will cross the Harrisburg Pike, and there is an inexpensive hotel nearby. It is 6:30 p.m., but I am inspired by my impromptu plan. I can cover eight miles of farmland at sunset and avoid the heat. Full speed ahead. The trail skirts the perimeter of fields of corn, runs alongside fences, behind homes, and down a few streets. Occasionally, the trail tunnels though a narrow corridor of woods in the valley.

It is a welcome change of scenery. In the distance, over acres of broad green corn leaves, there is a farmhouse flanked by huge silver silos. In the fading light, hundreds of fireflies hover over a meadow. It is completely dark when I reach the strip of woods flanking the highway, and I don my headlamp. The AT passes over Harrisburg Pike on a footbridge. Lighted signs of motels are visible down the road to my left. I bushwhack down the embankment on which the footbridge rests. The asphalt on the shoulder is coated with loose gravel, dirt, and debris blown aside by the traffic. I hurry down to the hotel, eager to be done with my day and anxious about the proximity of speeding traffic, not knowing if the drivers can see me in the dark.

This has been one of my longest days on the trail, and I reflect on all the variety I have encountered on this day that started back at Pine Grove Furnace, passed through Boiling Springs, and ends here at a roadside motel. Inside, the lobby is brightly lit and busy. A perky couple is checking in, and they ask the clerk about places to eat. Anytime after dark on the trail is very late, but in the world of artificial light, 9:00 p.m. is still early.

In the morning, I walk over to the diner next door for breakfast. The waitress calls me "honey." Thankfully, diners are ubiquitous at the trail towns. There aren't many chain restaurants, but there are traditional diners with vinyl booths, metal-trimmed Formica tables, fluted glass sugar dispensers, and breakfasts offering bacon, eggs, pancakes, hash browns, toast, and coffee.

A shuttle bus pulls up to the hotel just as I am leaving, and I hop on to save myself the half-mile walk back to the trail. The bus is nearly full with passengers heading out to start their business day. Some have work-issue uniforms, others are in dress attire carrying purses and briefcases; I have my backpack.

For the first six miles, the trail continues as it ended last night, passing farmland, pastureland, houses, and roads. The sky is gray, and light rains add humidity to the hot and buggy day. Workers rest on the back of a flatbed truck only partially loaded with rolls of hay. The rolls are taller than I am and are dispersed across the rolling hills like hairy brown sleeping bags. They are countless, and I wonder if the farmers are disheartened or content to have seemingly endless work laid out before them. The trail reenters the woods, passing along rolling hills, with a scattering of rocks. None of the hills exceed fifteen hundred feet. The trees, taking their cue from the hills, are also of modest height. There is a clearing near the bank of a stream. A slab of rock sits in the clearing, like a centerpiece, and on the rock a hiker has used pebbles to spell the words "I miss Mom."

Rain stiffens as I near Duncannon. Streams of water run off my pack cover, uncomfortably cold as it drips down the back of my neck. I am too close to town to stop for a jacket, so I reach back and pull the pack cover up over my head like a skullcap. The trail enters Duncannon on streets on the outskirts of town, and it follows streets through the center of town. Duncannon has an aged, industrial feel. It is as if there is a layer of steel dust settled upon everything, and there has been a boycott on paint. All of the stores are packed tighter than necessary on Main Street, with restaurants, laundromats, and banks having adjacent store-fronts and shared walls. The shops are elevated two steps above the sidewalk.

The gathering place for hikers is the Doyle Hotel, known for its cheap beer and cheap rooms. Inside the Doyle, I squeeze between occupied barstools to order a beer.

The patron to my right, glancing sideways at me, asks, "You a hiker?"

"Yes," I answer simply, since he knows the answer and is asking to start a conversation in which I'm hesitant to engage. He's short but burly, near drunk, with a reddish face. Leaning with both elbows on the bar, the back of his T-shirt doesn't quite reach his jeans.

"Seen any bears?"

"I've seen a few."

"The bears up here ain't like the bears you seen already. These bears are mean. They'll get you. Snakes, too!" He looks past me to his friend, passing him an impish grin. The two of them must make a game of putting fear into the hearts of hikers.

I'm sorry I can't feign more distress, but their effort is just too feeble. "I'll keep an eye out," I promise, and depart with my beer.

Some of the same crowd of thru-hikers who were part of the rowdy night at the Four Pines Hostel are in the bar at the Doyle, so it is an easy decision to move on. Wingfoot lists another motel two miles down the highway. The owner drives over to the Doyle and picks me up, promising to return me to town in the morning. Before leaving, I retrieve a mail drop that Juli had sent to the Doyle. Now that I am in a more populated zone of the trail, there are more food/shower/laundry opportunities than I can use. I have a few days of trail food in my pack and a new supply in the mail drop, so I opt to forgo the temptation of eating at a restaurant. I set up my tiny stove on the curb in front of my motel room and cook a meal for dinner. I repeat the process for breakfast.

From downtown Duncannon, there is still a bit of a road walk before getting back to the woods, ending with a walk over the expansive Susquehanna River Bridge. From the bridge, the trail ramps uphill into the woods for the most exerting climb I have had in days. Eleven miles from town I take a break at Peter's Mountain Shelter. Rain threatens, but I still decide it is too early to stop. At the crossing of PA 325 there is a handwritten note from a person in a nearby town, saying that he will pick up any hikers who call from this trailhead for a stay at his home. There is no phone or store in sight. A misty rain has begun.

I trudge uphill on a gravel-strewn trail that keeps an unnaturally straight line for more than a mile. Just before the rain comes down in earnest, I find a flat spot and set up my tarp. My tarp is supported by trekking poles, and the poles divide the interior space. There is room enough for me to lay out my sleeping pad and bag on one side. On the other side of the poles I have room for my backpack, my shoes, and anything I wish to unload from my pack. On this night, I unload most of the pack and set up my stove to cook inside, out of the rain.

The shoes I bought in West Virginia were my fifth pair for the hike, and I am now confident that they have been the best choice yet. I've worn them for about a hundred miles with a noticeable decline in foot pain. The shoes are the largest shoes I've ever bought and are made of lightweight material that is less constricting. I've taken the insoles out to dry. I lie on my back, extend a bent leg into the air, and look over my toes, which still suffer from blisters. I hold the insert of my shoe against the bottom of my foot. My foot is wider than the insole, even though the width of the running shoe is 4E. And the insole is pointed, tapering off much more rapidly than do my toes. I've seen no one with feet so pointed. There seems to be a fundamental mismatch between the design of shoes and the feet that go into them.

I wake in the middle of the night. Rain is still falling steadily, and water has started to flow under my tarp from the uphill side, the side where my gear is piled. I move all my gear away from the rivulets of water on my ground cloth. A thin layer of water is pooling under my legs. My sleeping pad is thick enough to keep me afloat, but parts of my sleeping bag that have flopped over the pad are wet. I can feel the wetness seeping up around my legs. A couple of hours of sleep are lost trying to scrunch away from the deepest part of the pool while keeping centered on the pad to stay dry.

Every year some part of the trail is rerouted, and guidebooks cannot always keep up. There will be changes in terrain and elevation, landmarks, and mileage. Wingfoot said the trail would dip to five hundred feet to a road at Swatara Gap. The dip doesn't happen, and I never pass a road. As well as I know my walking speed in different conditions, I have no doubt that the trail must have been rerouted in this section. I become wary about getting lost and pay more attention to the white blazes. The trail is wearing me down with some short climbs and rocky terrain. In the midst of the day's most rocky section, I see a hiker note on a sheet of paper weighted down by a stone.

"Rattlers, 50 yards ahead."

There is a sketch of two fat snakes with exaggerated fangs. Though it is little more than a stick figure drawing, it effectively abstracts the danger. There is no date or time on the note, but it looks recent, neither bleached by sun nor blotched by water. I've walked seventeen miles already—or so I think—and I'm tired, drained by watching my step on the rocks and worried about following the white blazes. Added to that, rattlers are now lurking among the rocks. I drop my pack and find a boulder large enough to lie upon, take my shirt and shoes off, and try to make myself new again.

Just before arriving at the 501 shelter, I pass a dozen or so hikers at an overlook. They've come back from the shelter to enjoy the late-afternoon view. Among them I recognize only Leaf and Bearable.

The 501 shelter, just off of State Road 501, is a large enclosed building with bi-level plywood sleeping platforms along the interior perimeter. Many hikers are here tonight. Tipperary is at the picnic table out front. He had heard about my sprained ankle, but is surprised at how quickly I have caught up. A caretaker lives in a home fifty yards away, but I do not see him this evening. I eat dinner and play cards with Bearable, Blaze, and Erica. Card playing is clumsy with the weight-saving half-sized cards Bearable carries. Erica is hiking with her identical twin, Erin, and Erin's boyfriend, Ryan, who have hitched a ride down 501 to a nearby store.

Leaf is at the table, having Treet for dinner. Treet is a canned meat product that manages to slip below the bar set by Spam. For entertainment, he reads the label. "Mechanically separated chicken and pork, sodium nitrate, hydrolyzed corn…" is as much as he reads before the heckling begins:

"If you don't separate chickens and pigs, you don't know what you'll end up with."

"Where can I buy hydrolyzed corn so I can use it in my recipes?"

This doesn't curb Leaf's appetite. He downs a can of the stuff. The card game is broken up when Erin and Ryan return from their hitch to the store. They have food and a case of beer. I climb up on my bunk and fall asleep easily, despite the noise made by the group drinking outside. When I wake, the caretaker is noisily crushing and disdaining spent beer cans, sorting them from the trash for recycling. Ryan, Blaze, and the twins are unperturbed, sleeping it off on the ground outside the shelter.

Near lunchtime, I catch up with Tipperary and Sheepstaff, who are picking blueberries near an unnamed stream. Tipperary is often the first one out of the shelter in the morning. Although he still is not a fast hiker, he gets an early start and makes good mileage by walking long and steady days.

We pass Shartlesville road, rumored to have a restaurant. Not knowing any more than that, I head left down the winding paved road, hoping to find hot food for lunch. Past the first bend in the road, there is no restaurant, no building of any kind. Maybe one more bend. I press on, less certain I've chosen the right path. Around the second bend are more bends in the road. I've invested nearly half a mile of walking, and my search is fruitless. I walk back up the road to the trail intersection and decide halfheartedly to continue on the road to the other side of the trail. For a few hundred yards in this direction, there is no evidence of development. The road heads downhill, so the further I wander, the more work I will have to return to the trail. Frustrated and hungry, I turn around.

Shortly after returning to the trail, I rejoin Tip and Sheepstaff eating lunch. I stop and eat with them, each of us exchanging some item from our food bags. Upon leaving Tip, I wonder if this is the last I will see of him on the trail. I plan to walk twenty-four miles to reach the town of Port Clinton today, and I doubt he will go that far. Signs have been posted at the last few shelters, spreading the word that a group calling itself Red Blaze will be hosting a "hiker feed"—a cookout at the town pavilion.

I spend the afternoon walking along a single long ridge, more like walking on an oversized levee than on a mountain range. The top of the ridge is sprinkled with broken slabs of stone. The rock impedes the growth of trees or vegetation, so there are often views to mostly flat land below the ridge. I see roads in the distance and wonder if they lead to Port Clinton, or if I can see Port Clinton, which now must be less than three miles away. Blaze and Erica come by as I am taking in the view. They don't have their packs.

"Ryan and my sister got a ride to Port Clinton and took our packs with them. Do you know about the hiker feed?"

"Did you see the rattler?" Blaze questions me simultaneously.

"Yes." I know about the food. "No. What rattler?"

"Right back there, less than a mile back. You walked right past it." I see snakes every day, but I've yet to see a rattler. I'd like to see one, but now I'm worried I'll step on it. I can imagine stepping over these rocks to find one curled up, hidden on the far side of the rock, striking out to get me in the back of my calf.

"We're going so fast today," Blaze says, obviously happy about traveling unencumbered by a backpack.

"I don't know," Erica says, "I kinda miss my pack."

"You can take mine."

The last hundred yards down to town are precarious, steep steps the trail builders have fashioned from stone. Steps like this are common near trailheads, and always unwelcome. The town of Port Clinton, or more fairly, the part of town within easy walking distance of the trail, is very small. By car, I could imagine this place being a one-intersection town I'd pass on a trip to somewhere else, hardly noticing that it was a named location. There are a few residential streets, a bar, and a candy store. There is an outfitter, but it is closed for the day.

The Red Blaze group has pulled picnic tables together to make a long serving table in a field near the pavilion. There are coolers of beer and soda, chips, beans, potato salad, fruit salad, cookies—a first-class picnic. A crowd of at least thirty thru-hikers is here. Shelton, Jason, and Mission are here, along with a few others I haven't seen since spraining my ankle. At least half of the hikers are new to me. Baltimore Jack, repeat thru-hiker and all-around trail bum, is at the grill, churning out hot dogs and hamburgers. A piece of red tape, roughly the same size as a white blaze, is plastered to the back of his T-shirt.

I am intrigued when I overhear a small group of hikers talking about Elwood. I move closer with my plate of food and ask if they will start the story over, from the beginning. Elwood had stayed at Bears Den Hostel (on the day that I last saw him) and left without paying for the stay and food. The people who ran the hostel called ahead to the Blackburn Center to alert them that Elwood might be on the way. Elwood must have been wary when he checked into the Blackburn Center because he checked in using the new trail name "Peg Leg." Also, he said he was thru-hiking southbound. But there were other thru-hikers who knew who he was and reported him to Bill, the caretaker. The police were called, and when they pulled up, Elwood donned his pack and made a break for the woods, only to be run down by Bill and a couple of hikers and held for the police. In addition to nonpayment at Bears Den, he had been pilfering gear from other hikers, and he was rumored to have an outstanding warrant. The police had Elwood empty his pack. His stash included a handful of pocket knives and oddball pieces, like a cookpot lid without the matching pot. Some of the stolen items belonged to hikers present at the Blackburn Center when Elwood was caught.

Everyone clusters together for a group photo, using the seats and tops of picnic benches to stand at different levels in order to get everyone's face in the picture. The photographer, a Red Blazer, leans on the open tailgate of a pickup truck. Everyone has given her cameras, so nearly thirty cameras are lined up on the tailgate. Hikers get impatient and goofy while posing for so many shots and start making different faces and gestures for each shot. They razz the photo taker when she has difficulty working one of the cameras. Many shouts of "Tipperary!" ring out, and I see him traipsing down the road, the last to arrive.

The morning is dewy and quiet; the town is asleep. There is little noise coming from the field of tents near the pavilion, just a couple of hikers trying to collapse their tents without waking anyone. I sneak down the road, under a bridge, and back up into the woods.

If the town was bigger, I would've considered a zero day. I feel somewhat ragged from walking fairly long days since leaving Pen-Mar Park. My mail drop is at the Port Clinton Post Office, which is closed for the weekend. I will call and have it forwarded when I have the opportunity, but that doesn't help my current shortage. There is nowhere to resupply. I dismiss my concerns about supplies; it feels good to be winging it, leaving my plans to fate.

I see few of the hikers who were at Port Clinton during my day. Some of the nicest views anywhere on the Pennsylvania leg of the AT are from areas called the Cliffs and the Pinnacle. The Pinnacle is an elevated shelf of rock overlooking a patchwork of farmland. The squares below stand out crisply under clear skies, all in different shades of green. There are nearly a dozen people out on the rocks, all of them just out for the day.

Coming down from the Pinnacle, the trail descends steadily for miles along the gravel road that has delivered the tourists. Near Eckville Shelter, about fifteen miles from Port Clinton, I cross Hawk Mountain Road, where a car is parked. A canopy has been erected, and there sits thru-hiker Scubaman with his parents. His parents have come to visit him and are set up to do trail magic. They've brought a handful of folding chairs, a cooler, and they are grilling hamburgers. This is the most opportune bit of trail magic I would receive on the trail: late in the day, when least expected. Before the trip I guessed my food cravings would be for pizza, ice cream, and Mexican food. All of these I have wanted at some point, but my most persistent craving is for hamburgers and cold drinks. This is surprising, since these were things I infrequently consumed in my "real" life.

The food helps power me up the last climb, through the rocks, to the peak of Dan's Pulpit. For the second time today, I stop to write. Also, I scribble down some of the items I'll need when I get to a store. Most pressingly, I need another fuel canister. For all the towns I've passed in Pennsylvania, I've not been to an outfitter. I'm lucky to have stumbled into a free dinner tonight because I only have enough fuel to cook one more meal. There is a mailbox with "register" written on the side, oddly placed on this inconsequential peak. Registers away from shelters are rare. I open the box to sign the register and find that someone has left behind more trail magic—a full fuel canister!

There were over thirty hikers in Port Clinton yesterday, and I am the only one to pick the Allentown Hiking Club Shelter as a stopping place tonight. It is odd how hikers get distributed along the trail. The last time I had a shelter to myself was back in Tennessee. It is already dusk when I lay my pack down. Fireflies play in the trees, and mosquitoes visit the shelter.

North from Allentown Shelter the going is easy, at some places following dirt roads and at other places following a path so wide and gentle that it could be used by a car. I am bothered by piercing pain under the middle toe of my right foot. I have only a small blister, but it causes insidious, torturous pain, like it has burrowed into a nerve. Twice I stop to tape and pad around the blister to little avail. I am worried about reaching an impasse so early and on such easy terrain. How will I handle the rest of the day, and all the days beyond? I pause for a rest, take painkillers, and filter water from a deep, fast-moving stream that is tea-colored from tannin. When I get going again, I am successful at getting focused on other things. But the trail gets very rocky.

I stand knee deep in boulders on Bake Oven Knob, looking back on the rubble I just ascended. Rambler is churning his way uphill, so I wait and let him pass. The boulders are large enough for me to make multiple steps on top of each boulder, gradually increasing in size until I am walking on bedrock, the source of all boulders. The surge of bedrock narrows, like the underside of a ship's hull protruding up through the surface of the hill trailed by a wake of rocks. The trail is right along the keel, elevated fifteen feet above ground. Coming to a stop at the stern, I see no blazes and wonder how I'm supposed to get down. Did I get off the trail? I can reach out and touch the upper limbs of trees rooted in the ground below, but there are no limbs firm enough to climb down upon. I notice a bulge, just large enough to get a toe-hold, and back off the rock. Near the spot where I descended, there is a white blaze, indicating that the rock scramble is the intended path of the AT.

The trail only momentarily reenters the woods before once more leading up a similar rock pile. The ridge of the second rock pile is much less uniform and more elevated, leaving a jagged cliff edge on both sides of the narrow path. The path is riddled with fissures and scree. What's more, these rocks are sloped and have a dusty layer of dried mold on them, so that footing is uncertain.

Skittles and Trace are at Bake Oven Knob Shelter.[27] I met Skittles at Port Clinton, but this is my first opportunity to speak with Trace. Skittles sits on the shelter platform with a family-sized bag of Skittles; Trace and I sit on logs outside. Trace is a young, big guy, not too many years past his days of playing college football. He has his jersey number team-mate-tattooed into his shoulder.

Rambler returns from a side trail with his water bottle, shaking his head in frustration. "That's a long way to get water…I had to go all the way to the third sign to get it."

"I should have told you," Skittles says, "that I found water off the trail between the first and second springs."

I had taken the blue-blaze trail to get water. The first spring I came to was dry, and a note had been left which read: "If spring is dry, the next spring is 0.4 mi. downhill. If

---

27   I mulled over trail names during the year I was preparing to start my hike. "Awol" was always my frontrunner, so I was devastated when I saw someone else start a 2003 journal on www.TrailJournals.com using the trail name "AWOL." I kicked myself for procrastinating on the start of my own journal. A few weeks later, the hiker decided to abandon the name. This seemed to confirm that "Awol" was meant to be my trail name. Skittles is the hiker who had changed his mind about using "AWOL."

the second spring is dry, continue approx. 0.1 mi. to next spring." I did not pursue it, inadvisably gambling that I would save myself a mile-long round trip and find a more convenient water source later. I also have a policy of keeping small the number of different locations from which I take water, believing that it will lessen my chances of drinking contaminated water. For the remainder of the day the trail never crosses a stream, and I end up having to make a long trek down a side trail anyway.

"How 'bout those boulders back there," Trace comments to the three of us. We all know what boulders he is talking about, the second stack that I had encountered.

Rambler replies, "That really looked dangerous."

"I was wondering if I was the only one that felt that way [scared]," Skittles says, sounding relieved that he wasn't the only one who was timid on the cliffs.

"I wouldn't want to do it in the rain. You fall off that, and you're going to have a lot worse than a broken leg," Rambler notes. "Don't screw around there. You could get killed."

"I thought the same thing. Slip here and you die," Trace reiterates. We laugh at the bluntness of his statement.

My three companions are fit young men, and they are challenged, at times intimidated, by the obstacles. I think how impressive it is that so many retirees, grandparents, and kids take on the AT. They have stiffer joints, shorter strides, and less strength, but still find a way to negotiate dangerous terrain like the boulders of Bake Oven Knob. There are no handicap ramps or guardrails. We are all walking the same trail.

A few miles beyond the shelter, I run out of water. The trail runs along the top of a low ridge, in places open to the hot sun. Fortunately, the sunlight is also conducive to blueberry growth. I stop frequently to harvest clumps of plump berries. Somewhere below, the Pennsylvania Turnpike tunnels under the mountains. I hear a faint rumble from the highway, but I cannot see the road. I am parched and tired and lament my decision to forgo water. The intense sun tires my eyes, and I stagger on in a dreamlike state. The sound of traffic plays on, stuck in my mind like a song, long past the point where it was last audible. Lehigh Gap is nearby, and the remainder of the trail is mild and smoothly downhill. I don't suffer much for the mistake of running out of water, but it was a mistake I should not have made. I had eliminated any margin of error. If I had gotten lost or injured, my situation could've quickly become desperate.

In Pennsylvania, the trail towns are conveniently spaced about every twenty miles, more suited to my pace than the shelters. My plan for the next three nights is to stay in Slatington, Wind Gap, and Delaware Water Gap.

In Slatington, I stay at a hotel called Fine Lodging, where the adjective "Fine" must refer to what is paid to the housing department. The hotel is not at all a hotel in the Holiday Inn sense of the word. The building is a three-story wood-frame structure with about a dozen rooms. There are narrow submarinelike hallways with matted carpet. A few additions have been made to the original structure, and where they meet the floors don't match up. Little ramps in the hallways make up the difference. The walls seem to lean, making me feel unsteady. I walk with one hand brushing along the wall for balance. I wonder if I can wobble the building if I shake hard enough. Only a few rooms are available for nightly rental.

The owner has stored excess furniture in the room where I will stay. There are three dressers, and an extra bed is propped on edge. There is no air conditioning and no room phone. There is a pay phone in a niche off the hallway, and all rooms on this floor share a common restroom and shower. I lock the door when I leave to take a shower, but I notice that slight pressure on the door will push it open anyway. My room looks down over Main Street, where boisterous youth who are loitering at the street corner yell out at boisterous youth in cars with bass-pounding radios. All buildings on the street look the same—silty, old, and forgotten. It is too hot to close the windows. I pull closed the threadbare, yellowed curtains and go to sleep to the din of slow-moving traffic.

The trail grows steeper and rockier as it ascends from Lehigh Gap. I have to pick my way around and climb over boulders, using my hands nearly as much as my feet. It is a beautiful morning, and I stop often to take in the steep view back down to the Lehigh River. On one of my stops I notice hikers coming up the trail behind me. Our slow progress up the mountain compresses the space between us, so we end up climbing together in a chain. Eight thru-hikers packed together on the trail is a rare occurrence. We stay together for the last three hundred yards to the summit of Blue Mountain, giving each other a hand up the more difficult sections, all of us appreciating the adventure, challenge, and camaraderie instead of being flustered by the obstacle.

After the climb, the trail continues for a couple of miles over rocky, deforested hills. Skeletons of trees killed by zinc smelting protrude from the rocks.

Stretch, Skittles, Trace, One-Third, and Odwalla are among the hikers on the climb. I meet thru-hiker One-Third for the first time. She is a recent college graduate who started the hike with her parents, but she is the last of the three who is still thru-hiking. Her parents had to quit due to illness, but they still hike when they can and visit One-Third periodically. Odwalla is roughly the same age as myself and is recently divorced. His trail name came from Odwalla food bars, which are a staple of his trail diet.

Odwalla and One-Third on the rocky ascent from the Lehigh River.
The AT crosses the bridge in the background.

Stretch and I break from the pack to take a side trail one hundred yards to an overlook, where we pause for lunch. I eat half a column of Fig Newtons and then offer the rest to Stretch. "Are you sure?" he responds, as if I've offered him irreplaceable riches. We walk and talk on a nearly level ridge all the way to Wind Gap. Stretch takes a short break approximately on the hour. He crosses his legs and bends to touch his toes; he lifts one foot behind himself, using his hand to pull his foot to his buttock. The habit is the source of his trail name. I do a stretching exercise designed to limber up my iliotibial band, a stretch I have been diligent about doing since having knee trouble in the early part of my hike. I believe stretching is what has kept the problem at bay.

North from Wind Gap I have the morning to myself. For miles the trail is a jumble of softball- to suitcase-sized rocks. I pick my way through the rocks. It is tedious to watch every step to avoid turned ankles and stubbed toes. It is like walking through the room of a child who has left all his toys out, but it goes on for ten miles. The trees here are modest, mostly six to twelve inches in diameter. Significant sky can be seen through the ceiling of the trees, only about thirty-five feet high. There are few views and no streams. The only wildlife I see are chipmunks.

I take a break at a clearing where boulders jut out from the trees. Another hiker comes along, surprising me by arriving so soon after I had stopped. He must have been hiking close behind me and moving at a good pace. He is a big man with a shaved head and a thick black beard. He has a scar on his face running from his brow down the outer rim of his eye socket. I would've been more concerned had I not seen him at the hiker feed in Port Clinton. He gives me a nod, briefly scans the view, and moves on.

I meet up with him again at Delaware Water Gap. His name is Tunnel Vision, and he has an incredible past. His scar is from an auto accident. He fell asleep at the wheel and crashed head-on into a truck. Three times the emergency room doctor noted a time of death, but Tunnel Vision came back. One knee was completely shattered, and doctors said he would be consigned to walk with crutches, if he could walk at all. Almost immediately, rebelliously, he hatched a plan to walk the AT. In addition to his injuries, he was dangerously overweight. He lost fifty pounds getting ready to hike the AT, and he has lost another sixty-five since being on the trail.

Delaware Water Gap is an inviting town on the bank of the Delaware River, the last stop for thru-hikers in

Pennsylvania. The Delaware lies between Pennsylvania and New Jersey. This is an ideal town for hikers since there is a hostel where the trail enters town; there is also a post office nearby and a handful of restaurants. I stay at the hostel with a full house of hikers, including most of the ones I was with yesterday on the climb up from Lehigh Gap. The hostel is run by a Presbyterian church and is set up in two adjacent rooms in one wing of the church. The setup is familiar. There is one sitting room with a dusty old couch and a few chairs with duct-taped upholstery. There is a table with goods left behind by other hikers. A donation box is bolted to the wall; the cost for a night's stay is whatever you can spare. The other room is a bunkroom with two levels of plywood platforms. Hikers stake out a bunk by laying out their sleeping pads and bags, just like they would in a shelter. A makeshift shower stall is erected immodestly in the center of the bunkroom.

Thru-hiker Hopeful landed here at a critical juncture in his hike. He was hiking fifty miles south of here and had bottomed out, vexed by the heat and the rocks and the rain. He sat despairing at a road crossing when a driver stopped and offered to bring him to this hostel for a much-needed rest. Now he is distraught over driving past fifty miles of the trail.[28]

The rest of us are upbeat and fraternal, as is typical for hikers in town. One-Third's parents visit the hostel and take all of our laundry for a collective washing. Hikers take turns cycling through the shower, except for one hiker who is emitting an odor noxious enough to stand out even before showering began. People leaving the shower pointedly begin to broadcast "I am finished with the shower" and "the

---

28   Hopeful was rejuvenated after a few days off and got a ride back to the point where he left the trail. He would go on to complete the trail in its entirety.

shower is available" in his presence, but the suggestion goes unheeded.

Stretch and I go to Doughboy's, and we each eat half of a huge pizza. We stroll across the street, where the Village Farmer market has a deal too good to pass up: a hot dog, a slice of apple pie, and a doughnut for $1.50.

In the cool early evening, after showering, I wander across the street where there is a restaurant and a curio shop. In front, there is a pay phone and a park bench under the dim yellow glow of a street lamp. Here I do my most eagerly anticipated errands of every town stop, checking e-mail and calling home.

I've sped through Pennsylvania, 226 miles in the first eleven days following recovery from my ankle sprain. I've made hiking somewhat easier on myself by town-hopping through the state. My right ankle feels weak without support. I will continue to wear the Aircast for the remainder of the hike. My ankle would not return to full strength until long after the hike was over.

10
Delaware Water Gap to Kent

My entry into New Jersey is on the Interstate 80 Bridge, over the Delaware River. A concrete rampart separates foot traffic (me) from four lanes of vehicles. Trucks ramble past and shake the bridge. The trail hooks under the north end of the bridge and passes through a parking area on the Jersey side. The trail reenters the woods and rises steadily on a wide, rocky path. New Jersey immediately has a woodsier feel than Pennsylvania. The trees seem larger and more densely packed, there is more slope to the land, and more separation from the sounds of civilization.

It is a good day. Entering another state is always uplifting. From now on, I am breaking new ground. I have never hiked in a state north of Pennsylvania. I've only been to New York once, and I've never been in a state that is north of New York.

Ahead, a man is out for a walk with his son. I catch up and talk with them for a moment before grinding past. The man knows enough about the trail to guess that I am a thru-hiker, and he tries to impress upon his son the magnitude of my trek. He says he'd like to hike the trail someday, maybe when his boy grows older. Each encounter like this is a happy reminder that I am on a grand adventure, which evokes memories of reading the online journal entries of hikers who started before me. Bono was one of the first hikers (if not the first) to start the trail this season, with a chilly January 1 start date. I eagerly followed his journal for nearly four months before leaving home, looking for the most current insight to what lies ahead. Each new entry of Bono's journal exposed me to new sections of the trail, new places I longed to see for myself, and the emotional ups and downs of life on the trail. Bono was progressing slowly, by design, in an attempt to fully absorb the experience. When I started, he was a thousand miles ahead of me, approaching the halfway point. Now, I am the expert, relating thru-hiking anecdotes to those who dream to do the same.

Be quiet. I lift my trekking poles and carry them both in one hand, slow my pace so I can land my feet softly, and start scanning the woods for whatever it was that put my subconscious on alert. Not long after I start this prowl, maybe a hundred yards later, a bear takes off running through the woods. There are two. The second is a cub, and he doesn't go far before treeing himself. This scenario makes my heart race, because I know the mother won't go far. She has stopped and is out there somewhere unseen, trying to decide what to do about the threat posed to her cub.

I get my camera out and try to get a picture of the big cub up in a tree. Clawing and scratching at the bark, he circles the tree trunk, trying to keep me out of sight. Failing to make himself invisible, he climbs down and runs away. The mother bear had snuck back to within ten yards of the cub and was hidden behind a bush. When the cub runs by, she steps out and escorts him away.

More often than not, I sensed an animal's presence before seeing it, as was the case in this sighting. Something about the surroundings, possibly an unconsciously registered smell or sound, made me think, "A bear might be around here." My experience with moose was the exception. Further north, I had similar feelings of being in the presence of a moose—feelings that were not followed by moose sightings. The only moose I did encounter was in plain view, and I nearly failed to recognize it.

I eat my lunch on the rocky shore of Sunfish Pond under beautiful clear blue skies. The pond is huge, covering forty-one acres, anomalously located 1,380 feet above sea level where it was gouged into the land when glaciers receded from North America. There is an abundant supply of rocks at one point on the shore, which has inspired hikers to stack the stones into works of art. The most common arrangement is to balance a cylinder-shaped stone on one end, capped with as many disk-shaped stones as balance will allow. Some of the rock art is constructed with two columns supporting a beam, like miniature Stonehenge replicas. Dozens of sculptures adorn the shoreline, most of them two to three feet tall.

The trail follows the rocky west edge of the pond and then eases out into rolling terrain, where I pick up speed. About a mile after leaving the pond, I realize it's been a while since I've seen a blaze. I look behind me and can see no blazes on the north side of the trees, either. This is not too unusual, possibly just an undermarked segment of trail. I walk on until I am convinced I am off the trail. Backtracking is always the least appealing option. I retrace my steps for about one-half of a mile before I find a fork in the trail that I had missed. The AT veers to the right, and there is a small pile of twigs across the erroneous "straight ahead" path I had taken, obviously placed there to keep me from getting sidetracked. I had no recollection of this pile of twigs. I had stepped over them automatically, as I would any other obstacle on the trail, just like eyes will skim over missing or duplicate words in a sentence.

I traverse a series of gentle hillocks. The tops are open and grassy, reminiscent of the balds in North Carolina and Tennessee, but much lower. And instead of looking out to other mountains, the view is to the flat interior of the state, which is speckled with crisp blue ponds.

Awol hiking along a low, open ridge in New Jersey.

After walking only ten miles, I take a short walk down a dirt road to the Mohican Outdoor Center. There are multiple buildings on the property. The first one serves as the main lodge and contains a camp store. The lodge is a large, rustic building nestled among the trees. Two workers are on the shingle roof. About a third of the roof has been stripped down to the plywood decking, and the roofers are discussing their next move. I get a soda and a snack from the camp store and sit on a bench in front of the lodge, watching the roofers as I eat.

When I was in middle school, my dad decided to reroof our home. He wasn't a roofer, or even a laborer, and my brother and I were his helpers. The job ran past the weekend, and my mom and dad had a disagreement about us kids continuing to help. Mom didn't want us to miss school. So Dad had us get dressed for school, walk around the block, and wait until we saw Mom leave for work. Then we came home to roof and we were all happy. A couple of years later, a neighbor hired me to reroof his home. Before even having a driver's license, I was directing a roofing crew composed of the neighborhood kids.

The two roofers on the lodge haven't made any progress. They are still talking, pointing to different locations on the roof as if they are debating where to begin reshingling the area they have exposed.

One of them takes notice of me and asks, "Do you know anything about roofing?"

"A little." I've worked on a hundred roofs since middle school, but I'm not sure I'm ready to commit. I'm on a hike. I climb up the ladder to see how it's going. The two men are employees of the Mohican Outdoor Center, not roofers, and they introduce themselves. Scott is assistant manager of the facility, and the other is Bono, the thru-hiker who started January 1. It is now July 17.

Bono has taken a respite from his hike to spend the summer working as a cook and gofer. "I want to be the first one to start and the last one to finish," he now says of his hiking plans.

"We're not sure if we should start here...or here," they say, pointing to the locations under deliberation. But this is not their only concern. They haven't had experience weaving the replacement shingles with the shingles that are still on the roof. I won't be doing any more hiking today.

Roofing fills my afternoon and the better part of the next day. Many hikers flow through during my stint at the Mohican Outdoor Center—Stretch, Tipperary, Shelton and Jason, Leaf, Indiana Slim, Skittles, Dutch, and more. They are as surprised as I was to find Bono here. They had also read his journal and greet Bono like a celebrity for being the one breaking trail ahead of us all. I spend two nights at the hostel, both nights free as compensation for my work. Dave, the manager, also sees to it that I have free meals, drinks, and a new Appalachian Mountain Club T-shirt. On my second night, Bono cooks up a feast of grilled swordfish. I have decided to pitch in without asking for anything in return. Feeling useful and receiving gratitude is inherently rewarding.

Back at my workplace, at least once a year we would have an "all-hands" meeting. At that meeting, we are always reminded that the company would not be what it is without us; we of the all-hand class are important. Employees who are important don't need to be told, and if they are not important, being told doesn't make them so. On many days, it would've been possible for me to not report to work and have my absence go unnoticed. The company is huge. The company and the project I worked on could carry on—are now carrying on—without me.

Since leaving my job for the trail, I have received overwhelming support from former coworkers and from friends who hold similar jobs. They are intrigued by the adventure, but what they can most relate to is the desire to abandon the cubicle, to walk away from unfulfilling employment. In some ways I feel like a surrogate for their unrealized desire to escape, an escapee cheered on by the prisoners.

On the trail again, my hamstrings are sore from roofing, but they don't slow me down. The trail ranges from eight hundred to sixteen hundred feet in elevation, often open to views from the ridgeline. Below I can see a lake with a scattering of homes on the wooded shoreline. Boats stream long white tails in their wake. Rivers, ponds, and lakes are plentiful in the landscape below, but water continues to be sparse on the trail itself. When I bring my attention back to the trail, I discover that I have strayed from the white blazes. This is clearly a footpath, but it is not the AT. Backtracking, I learn that once again I had stepped over a pile of twigs that was meant to deter hikers from continuing along the ridgeline. The AT dips off the ridge and descends to Culvers Gap. I would repeat this frustrating error half a dozen times in New Jersey and New York, more than on any other section of trail.

Worthington's Bakery is right on the trail at Culvers Gap. The store is a heralded trail stop but has an insolvent aura, as if the owners are no longer restocking. There is a foot-long gap between the lone bottle of ketchup and a few loaves of bread. I browse the sparse shelves and cobble together a lunch. The young pierced-navel girl behind the counter, talking on a cell phone, probably would have been happier if I didn't bother her to buy food. She rings me up without saying a word to me, and without interrupting her phone conversation.

I sit out front eating, disappointed. A car pulls up; a man jumps out, addresses me as "hiker trash," and gives me a beer. He introduces himself as Gray Ghost, a former thru-hiker. "Hiker trash" is a compliment. He lives nearby, and when he sees hikers at the store, he stops to chat and help if he can.

I've noticed how other hikers now have untrimmed mustaches long enough to collect beer foam and sometimes food, so I've become compulsive about wiping mine after eating or drinking. Hiking along, I continue to be distracted by the length of my mustache. I can feel it when I wet my lips with my tongue. I decide I will keep the "no trim" policy for my beard and hair, but the mustache has to be shortened. Now. My knife is in my belt pouch, and there is a tiny pair of scissors on the knife. Stopping in midtrail without even taking off my pack, I take a hack at the right side of my mustache with no mirror to guide me. Immediately I can tell that my snip is too deep and crooked, so I abort the attempt. This ill-conceived bit of trimming jolts me into recognition of how indifferent I've become about my grooming. I hardly ever run a comb through my hair. I regularly go a week without changing or washing clothes, and almost as long without bathing, and now this.

I stay at Mashipacong Shelter with two college-age girls who are out for the weekend. They hug the far side of the shelter, put off, I'm sure, by this unkempt hiker who looks like he just took a bite out of his own mustache.

High Point State Park is so named because it contains the highest peak in New Jersey, which is only eighteen hundred feet. A monument is built on top, extending the height of the mountain another two hundred feet. The AT gets close enough for a view of the monument jutting out from the trees, but does not go over the peak. The terrain is mild with rolling hills, modest trees, and very little undergrowth. I have good visibility between the thin trunks of trees. Twice I spot bears strolling parallel to the trail. Neither bothers to run away; they pause apathetically to watch me pass. One is tagged on the ear.

By midday, I have moved out of the park into low ground, passing through swampy woodland and pasture-land. Former thru-hiker Jim Murray owns a farm here which is dubbed the "Secret Shelter," although its existence is no secret to thru-hikers. Trace, One-Third, Orbit, and Soul Train are lounging on a shady porch when I arrive. We entertain ourselves with trail stories, resulting in side-splitting laughter. Objectively, it would be hard to quantify why any of the stories are so hysterical. Mostly we laugh because we are elated about our experience and are happy to share it with one another.

Jim Murray pulls up in a jeep just after the other hikers have left. I thank him for access to his property and tell him of my plans to reach the town of Vernon, New Jersey, tonight.

"You have a long afternoon," he warns, and then he proceeds to ask rhetorically, "Have you ever heard about the Mahoosuc Notch being the most difficult mile on the trail? Well, some people say that the mile near the preserve is more difficult than that."

He doesn't elaborate, leaving me to ponder what could be so difficult about these lowlands. I have noticed the heat. All of the thru-hikers who rested here were soaked with sweat and left outlines of their backs or butts where they lay or sat on the dusty porch. The trail gets muckier as I progress. I startle a family of turkeys, which trot down the trail ahead of me. Bog bridges lie in long spans over the trail, which now has some standing water.

The trail exits onto a rural road, crosses a bridge, and then runs parallel to a steamy shallow swamp that was formerly a sod farm. This area is called Wallkill National Wildlife Preserve. The preserve ostensibly exists to promote waterfowl, but it truly excels as a haven for mosquito breeding. They swarm me mercilessly, stinging my exposed arms, legs, neck, and biting through my shirt to draw blood from my chest and back. They also drill unproductively into my pack straps. I dab on some Deet, but it does nothing to deter them. I collapse my trekking poles and stuff them into my pack so I have both hands free to defend myself, developing a constant, preemptive pattern of swatting my face, shoulders, and arms, often scoring multiple mosquitoes in a single slap. Damn the national park's preservation efforts. The end isn't even in sight before welts redden and itch, so I add scratching to my spastic slapping routine. There is a park bench located on this path through the breeding grounds. Never have I seen a bench look less inviting. I'm running this gauntlet.

The trail hits the woods and heads steeply up a hill. Most of my attackers fall back. The only ones still with me are the dolts who are sucking on my pack straps. I quickly tire of sustaining my joglike pace uphill. I collapse on the trail, sapped by the ordeal. I'm tired, hot, irritable, and feel like shedding my itchy skin. I've come twenty miles today, and I need to conjure the energy for six more. I take off my shirt, shoes, and socks and air out for nearly a half hour. I put on my new AMC shirt and a fresh coat of Deet and finish the day with renewed vigor. In the late afternoon, I cross another long patch of cattail-laden swamp. There are no mosquitoes to pester me, and a luxurious boardwalk cuts a path for me through the head-high cattails.

I easily hitch a ride to the Church of the Mountain Hostel in Vernon, New Jersey. The hostel occupies the clean and spacious basement of the St. Thomas Episcopal Church and is as thoroughly equipped as any hostel I would see. There are showers, laundry, TV, Internet, and a kitchen. And so, of course, the hostel is massively popular with thru-hikers;

at least three dozen are here. A few hours after dinner, Stretch, Tipperary, and I walk a couple of blocks to Burger King for a dessert of milkshakes and fries. I sense, correctly it turns out, that this would be my last chance to spend trail time with Tipperary. I try to walk slowly on our return, to keep a distance from a gruff-looking character ahead of us. Tipperary, with his unfailing congeniality, catches up with the man so he can introduce himself. I wonder if Tipperary has forgotten that people in the real world aren't used to introductions from strangers. I brace myself, not wanting Tip to be exposed to the rudeness I expect him to receive. Tip asks, "Are you a hiker, too?"

Initially the man's expression is defensive, and then his face is softened by Tip's sincerity. "Yeah. I'm a *hitch*-hiker."

Many hikers are still at the hostel when I leave in the morning. They are opting for a zero day, and I envy them. Too recently I took a day and a half off at the Mohican Outdoor Center. A man has offered Trace and One-Third a ride to the outfitter, and the three of them are stuffed into the cab of a pickup truck. I jump in the bed of the truck with my pack and bum a ride back to the trailhead.

With a pack full of food and weary legs, I trudge up the trail. Bono had told about sneaking rocks into the pack of his hiking partner, Rocket. Rocket suspected that his pack was heavier, but he did not find the rocks until the end of the day. Am I the victim of a cruel practical joke? My pack feels heavier than it should. It was unattended for most of my stay at the hostel, and there were plenty of thru-hikers, all potential suspects. I feel foolish and paranoid, but I know I will feel more foolish if I walk all day with ten pounds of rocks, so I stop and unload my pack. There is nothing there other than the same stuff that I always carry. Somehow it feels heavier.

A tree lies fallen next to the trail. The top points away, and the underside of the roots face me. A disk of earth ten feet tall was pried up when the tree toppled. I hear digging and then a grunt of recognition. A bear is on the other side of the root disk, and we've both just realized how dangerously close we are to one another. I back away and peek around the roots. To make matters worse, it is a mother bear with her cub. The cub scampers away, and the mom hops up on the trunk of the fallen tree and walks away, sneering back over her shoulder. I fumble with camera settings, hoping to get a shot before she gets too far, when she turns around to have a word with me. I get one picture as she growls and advances toward me. The growl sounds like that of a horse expelling air through its jowls, but much more effective at communicating a threat. I backpedal as fast as I can without turning to run, still trying to click pictures.

When I distance myself, the bear follows her cub. I review the pictures to see what I've captured. The last two pictures show nothing but tree limbs and patches of blue, as I had my camera skewed skyward during my frantic retreat. These two bears bring the total count to sixteen. I'm content to have seen a good number of bears, but I am no longer eager to see more.

I've definitely seen enough rocks. This day is as rocky as any day in Pennsylvania. About nine miles into the day, I hit the top of a ridge capped with a jumble of stones. "NJ/NY" is painted on a boulder, marking the border. Continuing along the ridge, there are many bulging slabs of stone, some as long as seventy-five yards, like concrete whales surfacing in a sea of shrubbery. I navigate this boulder-strewn ridge for five tiresome miles. Many times I need to pull myself up or lower myself down using my hands. At one juncture, trail builders have made a wooden ladder to manage a sheer rock face. I take a break and lie exhausted on one of the whale backs. I could sleep here, but I open my eyes when I hear Tunnel Vision and his brother Bull pass by. "We were ready to draw white chalk lines around your body."

Near the intersection of the trail with NY 17A, I spot a new ice cream stand. This more than compensates for my disappointing progress. While I am gulping down a milkshake, a customer offers me a ride to the town of Greenwood Lake. It is a tiny town clustered along the shore-line of the lake that does not draw in many thru-hikers. I stay at an old eight-room motel in a musty room with no phone. But it is cheap, and I am happy to be inside when an early evening thunderstorm rolls through, dense with lightning.

Hitching a ride back to the trail is tougher than most hitches. I stake out a spot where it will be easy for drivers to pull off the road. A steady stream of morning traffic passes without slowing, and then a police car pulls past my withdrawn thumb and coasts to a stop thirty yards beyond. Hitching is illegal in New York, so maybe this is his way of warning me to move on. Or maybe he watches for the reap-pearance of my offending thumb.

I go knock on his window and ask with affected naiveté, "Is hitching allowed here?" He tells me that hitching is ille-gal, but if I'm standing behind his car, he wouldn't be able to see anything. It's his abstruse way of giving me the go-ahead. Good intentions aside, my hitching is still spoiled because no driver is going to pull over next to the police car. I head down the road, dreading the possibility of a two-mile road walk just to get back to the trail. As soon as I am out of sight of the police car, I start thumbing each car that passes. Only a few pass before I have a ride.

With all I've read about the trail, I am surprised by the dearth of accounts about the difficulty of this section. The hills are low, but the trail goes steeply up and down, and there is a rock scramble at the top of many hills. This day is harder than the Roller Coaster in Virginia. Taken together, the last two days have been harder than anything since Tennessee.

New York City is sometimes visible from a few of these summits, but I walk this stretch of southern New York in perpetually overcast skies and intermittent light rain. A United States flag is painted on a slab of rock at one of these overlooks. "Remember 9/11" and a number of similar messages have been scrawled near the flag. The attacks of September 11, 2001, and the subsequent invasion of Afghanistan took place during the time I was contemplating my hike. The second war in Iraq began less than a month before I quit my job. From a national perspective, this was the most tumultuous era of my lifetime, and I was about to go on leave from the world. These events trivialized my selfish plans and added to my reservations about being away from my family, my job, and the world. There is no objective importance in walking the range of mountains in the Eastern United States. As my departure date neared, my unease faded. The news won't change because I'm not watching it. I had dismissed those thoughts, and they did not reenter my mind until seeing this memorial. I am doing the right thing.

The trail enters Harriman State Park, and I have a short reprieve from the rocky ups and downs in southern New York. The terrain in the park is grassy and open. Snakes like it here. I pause while a black snake slithers across the trail ahead of me. Snakes have been abundant over the past few weeks, so they no longer take me by surprise. I've seen a handful of them already today and hardly give them a second thought. I take note of this one because it is exceptionally large, at least six feet long and as thick as my wrist.

Before my day is done, there are more clusters of boulders. The trail passes though a crevasse in a huge slab of bedrock. The crevasse is chest-deep and barely wide enough for a person. The formation is known as the "lemon squeezer." My pack scrapes both sides as I squeeze through. A little later, at Fingerboard Shelter, Tunnel Vision tells me he had to carry his pack over his head. Bull and Stretch are also at the shelter, along with a section-hiking father with two young kids.

The father and kids have claimed one end of the Fingerboard Shelter, probably a bit worried about our shabby appearance. Stretch, Tunnel Vision, and Bull are all young men, but trail wear makes them all look older, especially Tunnel Vision with his scars. I am happy that the three of them are still young enough to act like kids. They imitate their favorite animated shows and giggle at their own humor. They are puerile in the best sense of the word, and they make me think better of the world. Tunnel Vision looks up at a wet sock hanging from a rafter overhead and asks, "Is that going to drip on my head all night?"

"Not if you sleep with your mouth open."

Later he performs a mock distress call: "I'm lost."

"Where are you?"

"I'm on a mountain surrounded by things that are tall and green…yes, they appear to be trees. I am directly under the sun right…about…hold on…right about…now!"

This shelter is made of stone and planted on a huge slab of smooth rock, giving it a wonderful, earthy feel. Thunderstorms rage much of the night, making for a restless night of sleep. Bats fly in and out of the shelter between bursts of the storm.

Everything is wet the next morning. My shoes get soaked from grass and undergrowth that are wet from last night's rain. More rock scrambles slow me down. The day is hot and humid, and the trail is demanding. I'm sweating more than I have anywhere on this hike. My clothes look like they would if I had jumped into a swimming pool. I reach the Palisades Parkway and see a road sign, unbelievably stating it is only thirty-four miles by highway to New York City. Four lanes of traffic zoom by at seventy miles per hour. I question my ability to reconcile this speed with my slow-moving world, and I wait for a spacious gap between vehicles before crossing.

Six miles later I reach Bear Mountain, New York. Bear Mountain is the name given to the city, a park, an inn, and a bridge. The park has vast mown lawns and a pond. Dozens of people are out picnicking, strolling the path around the pond, and feeding ducks. The Bear Mountain Inn is a sprawling rustic resort with a fancy restaurant, where the waiters wear white shirts and vests. My sleeveless shirt and shorts are wet rags, but unabashedly I plop down in a booth to eat lunch and dry out in the air-conditioned room. Beyond the inn, the trail passes through the Trailside Museum and Wildlife Center, along the same asphalt path where parents show their children a small assortment of zoo animals. A boy climbing on the Walt Whitman statue asks me, "Why do you have those ski poles?"

Then the AT crosses the Hudson River on the catwalk of the Bear Mountain Bridge, a four-lane suspension bridge. This is the lowest point on the Appalachian Trail: 124 feet above sea level. I carry my pack east over the bridge. Directly below, a tug pushes a barge north up the Hudson.

Stretch, Tunnel Vision, and Bull had told me of their plan to stop here and take a day off to meet friends in New York, so this is the last I will see of them on the trail. Crossroads left the trail in New York to return to work before losing his job. Tipperary is behind; Crash and Patience are hopelessly ahead. I am sobered by my separation from thru-hikers I was most connected with in the southern part of my hike. Where are Ken and Marcia?

In the restaurant my clothes had dried from soaked to merely damp. Back in the woods, they are quickly drenched once again. A southbound hiker greets me. He is wearing a full sweat suit, hood plastered to his head by a baseball cap, and gloves. He tells me he is out just for the day. A couple of years ago he suffered through Lyme disease, so he hikes in ninety-degree weather wearing stifling attire to ward off ticks.

Bear Mountain Bridge over the Hudson River in New York.

My next stop is the Graymoor Spiritual Life Center. The brothers who live at Graymoor are known for their hospitality towards thru-hikers. They invite hikers to a free meal, but I have arrived after dinner is finished. Odwalla, the hiker I met in Pennsylvania, is here. He thinks that the southern section of New York has been the hardest section of the hike.

It is reassuring to have his concurrence about the trail's difficulty. I'm not alone in my struggles. We lay our sleeping
bags out on top of picnic tables under a covered pavilion.
Wind-blown rain commences at nightfall. If I was not elevated, I'd be getting wet. Mosquito sorties persist all night
long. My body is filmy and sticky from a few sweaty days, and
my clothes are damp. Sleeping in the wet clothes no longer
dries them because of the humidity. I cannot sleep outside
of my bag because of the mosquitoes. I dab smelly repellant
on my forehead, neck, and arms because they will bite any
piece of exposed flesh.

I wake up with a plan to beeline twelve miles to Canopus
Lake Camp to get a shower. That would make me feel better, even though it would be a few more days before I could
wash these stinking clothes. I get to the road where the
campground is and stick out my thumb to hitch a mile down
the road. The first car to pass is a police car. He continues
past, ignoring my breach of the law. Two cars later, Margaret
DeVries, a youthful sixty-eight-year-old woman, stops to give
me a ride. "I just read about thru-hiking the Appalachian
Trail, and I thought I might meet a hiker," she says. When
I tell her of my plan to clean up at the campground, she
offers to take me to her house instead, where I can shower,
eat, and do laundry.

Margaret is an interesting lady; she fled Communist
Hungary in 1956. She has flown a hang glider and still takes
solo kayak trips on the Hudson River (a boat is strapped to
the roof of the car in which we are riding). She spends a
month each year at a youth hostel in South Beach. Margaret
is quick to express her appreciation for life in the United
States and her dislike for Communist rule. She tells of returning to Hungary after becoming a U.S. citizen to visit
her ailing father. Since the Communists believed that they

educated her and she had no right to leave and use her talents elsewhere, she was apprehensive about being detained.

Politicians will always offer to handle education, health care, retirement, and so forth, as if they come at no cost. But there are caveats. If the government is the provider of "free" education, then the government will also decide what is taught and, potentially, how it is used. The fewer responsibilities we have, the less free we are. Communism and democracy differ in this only by a matter of degree. We can vote away freedom as easily as it can be taken away.

"Hike your own hike" is a trail mantra. Thru-hiking seems to work out best when each hiker is attuned to his own interests. Perhaps counterintuitively, this attitude somehow fosters cooperation and generosity. This trail full of hike-your-own-hikers is as nice as any group with whom I've ever been associated.

Margaret returns me to the trail at 6:15 p.m. I am uplifted once again by trail magic received at a most opportune moment. Twilight is a wonderful time to be on the trail in this hot season. It is a time when there is a truce between nature and man. The afternoon heat has relented, storms have passed, the wind has died down, and activity is nil. I walk seven buoyant miles to the RPH Shelter, finishing in the dark under the guidance of my headlamp.

North of the RPH Shelter, the trail is much less difficult than it had been in the southern part of the state. There is less rock on the footpath and more packed dirt and grass. The trail rolls over small hills and cuts through pastureland.

A small stream, easy enough to step over, lies across the trail. The land hardly has enough slope to move the water. It is stagnant like a tiny canal, with thick green algae on the bottom. I only have a few sips of water left but skip this opportunity to refill, hoping against reason that I'll find better water later. Most of the streams these past few days have been similarly unappealing. Getting water in Pennsylvania was a hardship because of the scarcity of streams. In New York there have been streams, but they are the least appealing water sources on the trail.

I descend from the hills to a railroad crossing. The rails are elevated by fill, and a drainage ditch runs parallel to the hump of the fill. A foot of water is in the ditch; it is runoff water with an oily rainbow sheen. A fragment of a Styrofoam cup floats on the water. This sludge is much less appealing than the stream I passed, but now I've traveled miles without water and have no choice. I reach the Wiley Shelter at dark after a long and hot twenty-five-mile day. I have seen few hikers on the trail, and there are no other hikers here tonight. The water source for the shelter is a hand pump.

White blazes receding into Connecticut.

Today is a Saturday. I plan to walk only thirteen miles to reach the town of Kent, Connecticut, but I'd like to finish the miles by noon so I can pick up mail. Halfway to Kent, the trail crosses from New York to Connecticut. The trail in Connecticut begins auspiciously with an elegant hemlock forest. I reach the Kent Post Office just minutes before it closes. The town is very nice and manicured, with many shops and restaurants that cater to well-heeled tourists. There are no hotels or hostels, so the only lodging options are expensive bed and breakfast establishments. I make my way to the laundromat so I can get my clothes clean while I ponder my options. Doing laundry is inefficient for a single hiker. Many times I've washed a load of clothes containing only a lightweight shirt, shorts, and socks. Now that I'm done with muggy New Jersey and New York, I want to throw everything washable in the machine to exorcise the dirt and sweat and bug spray. The only item I keep out is my rain jacket, which I wear like a skirt, causing me to catch curious glances.

There is a small hotel in Cornwall Bridge about eight miles north of Kent that is less expensive than any place in Kent. I hitch a ride and make arrangements with the motel owner to stay two nights. Tomorrow he will drive me back to the trailhead near Kent, and I will be able to walk the trail from where I left off, back up to Cornwall Bridge. I can leave most of my gear in the room and have an easy walk tomorrow. I need it. Here is my journal entry for the night:

If I had to do it again I wouldn't. As of today that's how I feel about this AT hike. I don't say that because I'm having a bad day. I'm not going to quit, and I'm not disappointed that I am here. Doing this hike is too much hard work, too much pain, too much time away from my family, too many bugs, too much hot weather, too much cold weather, and too much rain.

11
Kent to West Hartford

My day of hiking without a pack from Kent to Cornwall Bridge is a transitional day. It is more like a day off than another day hiking, although I do cover eleven more miles of the Appalachian Trail. I walk an easy pace and pause whenever I have the urge to write, to take photos, or simply to contemplate my thoughts about this trip. The trail is a conduit, humming with memories from the miles behind me and electric with the possibilities still ahead. Despite my recent woes, I am certain that I will complete this hike. Nothing short of a debilitating injury or a dire situation at home would cause me to quit before reaching Katahdin.

My tendency is to stretch my days. Too often I'll pass up a side trail to a waterfall or overlook. I set an arbitrary goal to reach the next milestone in x number of days, racing to what is ahead at the expense of the present. I do not have an open timeline, but my restlessness is sure to move me along at a good clip. Completing the trail is a foregone conclusion, so I should feel free to enjoy myself. What I need to work on is a better balance of leisure time.

A huge slab of rock juts up from the ground, rising thirty feet at an angle of sixty degrees. Improbably, trees grow clinging to the surface of the rock, roots clinging to fissures in the surface. A flock of Canada geese drift downstream on the Housatonic River. I stop to write at a nondescript location, choosing to sit on a knee-high boulder under a canopy of lime green leaves.

It is easiest to characterize the AT in terms of its most challenging and spectacular features. Most people have experienced the difficulty of steep uphill climbs, rocky terrain, and pestering bugs. Likewise, spectacular overlooks and scenic waterfalls have universal appeal. But I have come to recognize that most of what is memorable and pleasing about my time on the trail is ordinary moments in the outdoors. Simply sitting unhurried in the shade of leaves is an irreplaceable moment. It is a joy in itself to amble through the woods for hours, even when views are limited to the dense trees surrounding me. It is fulfilling to be saturated with the sights, sounds, and smells of the outdoors. My fond recollections of my hike are full of unremarkable moments, like the smell of a dewy morning, the crunch of leaves underfoot, the blaze of a campfire, the soothing trickle of a stream, or rays of sun through a maze of trees.

Humans are creatures with a longer history of living in the outdoors than of living within the confines of concrete and artificial light. We have an atavistic sense of well-being when immersed in the natural world.

I take a break at Stewart Hollow Brook Lean-to and meet Lion King. He is a big bear of a man who is carrying a camera and filming a documentary on thru-hiking the AT.[29] He is groggy, struggling with insomnia and an ailing knee. "Why can't they make more trail like this?" he asks, referring

---

[29]   Lion King's excellent documentary is available through www.walkingwithfreedom.com.

to the five miles of beautiful, nearly level trail paralleling the Housatonic River.

Back in Cornwall Bridge, I stop at a small store with a couple of gas pumps out front and spend half an hour ogling the food. Before hiking, I had never considered convenience stores places for culinary adventure.

Leaving Cornwall Bridge the next morning, the weather is wonderful, clear and about seventy-five degrees. There are no significant rocky areas. Large hemlocks dominate the landscape, and often there is soft, pine-needle-covered trail. Midday, I reach Falls Village, Connecticut, a town built along the banks of the rumbling Housatonic River. The trail passes through the residential section of town, so there are no stores or restaurants to visit. I pass pretty homes on quiet, hilly streets. Between Falls Village and Salisbury, the trail is varied, with some hills, some rocks, and some grassy fields.

Like Falls Village, Salisbury is an idyllic New England community with homes that look like dollhouses with white picket fences. The downtown area has an inn, a few souvenir shops, candy stores, and nice restaurants. It is a town lived in by people who must do their real work elsewhere. My destination is a boarding house run by Maria McCabe, but the only direction that I have is "left from the trail on CT 41," and a house number. Near downtown there is a house with the right number, but all is dark. I knock on the front door and get no answer. I walk completely around the house looking for a sign. There is no sign, but that is not unusual for places that accommodate hikers. "Let yourself in" is a common policy, so I try the front and side doors.

I go to an ice cream store downtown for a treat, figuring I will return to the home later. Odwalla walks by as I sit outside with my ice cream cone. He says he is staying at the same boarding house that I am waiting to get into. "I just tried to get in. Were you just there?" I ask.

"Yes."

"That place right there?" I ask, pointing to the home where I was just prowling about and testing the doors.

"That's not the boarding house. McCabe's place is a few blocks away."

I follow Odwalla back to the right house, and we share a room. I call Juli and finalize plans to meet tomorrow. Weeks ago, she made arrangements to fly to Albany, New York, based on my projection of where I would be at this time. Our plan is to meet at a road intersection eighteen miles from here. Our girls are staying with my parents so Juli and I can hike together.

In Harpers Ferry there is a three-dimensional map of the entire AT. The midsection of the trail—from West Virginia through Connecticut—has the lowest mountains. The rougher sections are at the ends of the trail, peaking with the Smokies in the south and the Whites in the north. Today I enter Massachusetts, the eleventh state on the trail, and the elevations are ramping up. Bear Mountain, Race Mountain, and Mount Everett are all near twenty-five hundred feet, higher than any mountains in the last 550 miles.

Bear Mountain has the feel of a mountain much taller. The incline is long, and the descent is steep. Much of the summit area is open, rocky, and weathered. There are krummholtz: stunted evergreens ranging from three to six feet tall. At the bottom of Bear Mountain, the trail runs parallel to Sages Ravine, a powerful, tumbling creek cascading through a rocky ravine. I am tempted by a number of pristine swimming holes, but the water is icy cold.

Sages Ravine, near the Connecticut-Massachusetts border.

Race Mountain and Mount Everett are similar to Bear Mountain, having sparse krummholtz scattered among stony peaks. The walk between the peaks is particularly pleasurable since the traverse is made on a high, open ridge. I startle Jerry Springer on this ridge. He is filling a water bottle with harvested blueberries. So far he has about one-third of a quart. Jerry is a thru-hiker who is quick to explain that his trail name comes not from the talk show host, but from combining the first name of his favorite musician (Jerry Garcia) with "Springer" from the mountain where the trail begins. I take multiple breaks along this ridge, picking blueberries, taking photos, and eating lunch, believing that I am ahead of schedule to make my rendezvous with Juli.

After summiting Mount Everett, the trail stays on the ridge longer than I expect. Suddenly, I feel as though I've dawdled too long, and I'm ready to get off this ridge and see Juli again. My progress is slow through a jumble of rocks. The trail begins to descend, then levels off, and then ascends again. I need to go down to the valley where the road passes, but the trail goes through a series of exasperating ups and downs before finally releasing me to the lush vegetation of the valley. A half mile before the road, the trail passes through an overgrown pasture. I can make out the road through the head-high grasses. Ahead, Juli is hustling out onto the trail to meet me. She's walking just slower than a run, and she lowers her head, trying to hold back tears.

We drive north to the town of Lee, Massachusetts. The next morning we get a ride back to the trailhead where Juli picked me up.[30] It will take us two or three days to hike north to Lee, where we left our car.

Initially, the trail that we walk together is mild, continuing through pastureland for about four miles before reaching U.S. 7. At the road, there is a nursery that sells a small assortment of snack items. We stop and buy cold drinks, ice cream, and fruit. Juli must be thinking the trail really isn't as tough as I've made it out to be. I've already begun to wonder if we will finish our hike to Lee in two days instead of three. It is only thirty-three miles.

There are advantages to hiking with another person. We only need to carry one tent, one stove, one water filter, and

---

30   We got a ride from avid hiker Bluejay Lafey. Bluejay had been reading my Internet journal, and we exchanged e-mails. In planning my visit, I asked Bluejay about the region, and he not only offered us a ride, he bought us breakfast, too. He says doing trail magic is his way of banking karma for when he does his hiking.

so forth. Even though I carry the bulk of the load, my pack is pounds lighter than it would be if I was alone. Also, we finish chores more quickly. Many tasks, like filtering water, cooking, and setting up a tent, require nearly the same effort for one person as they do for two.

It is a hot day, but for me it is a reprieve from the heat of Pennsylvania, New Jersey, and New York. Gradually we gain elevation and stop to have a nice lunch on June Mountain at a clearing with a view to the north. The trail continues over a series of hills, but the terrain is good—more soil than rock—and the slope is gentle on both the uphill and downhill. Juli walks slower than I do, but I do not imagine that she is struggling. I stay behind and walk at her pace. The longest stretch of uphill trail we encounter is a gain of about eight hundred feet up an unnamed peak. Juli slows and eventually comes to a complete stop, standing still on the trail and leaning forward on her hiking poles. I pull up alongside her and see that she is not only exhausted, but in tears.

She feels defeated, her legs are sore, it is hot, and bugs are pestering her. She had not said anything to me about the difficulty, hoping that she could come and hike without slowing me down. We have already walked fourteen miles, which is a solid day for any hiker. Even though she is in excellent shape, Juli is fifteen years and three kids removed from her last backpacking experience.

A few miles later, we break at Mount Wilcox Lean-to. We have been walking at an easy pace, and Juli is in better spirits. We decide to move on. Juli's legs have stiffened, and now she is feeling pain on the outside of her knee. Her knee hurts more on the downhill sections of trail. I am certain that she's experiencing the iliotibial band friction syndrome that bothered me the first weeks of my hike.[31] It was negligent of me to have her walk so far on her first day, especially since I also had knee pain after walking only eight miles on my first day—eight miles that I didn't think were very hard at the time. We end our day at Shaker Campsite near dark after twenty-one miles, an absurd distance for anyone's first day on the AT.

Shaker Campsite is a small clearing with three tent platforms and a stream nearby. I still have hopes of making this a positive camping experience for Juli. We've made lasagna, the best of the freeze-dried meals. Twilight in camp is generally a wonderful part of the day, but this site is overwhelmed with mosquitoes. Juli drenches herself with bug spray. Deet from her hands melts away the measuring lines that are painted on my water bottle. But still the mosquitoes are little deterred. We retreat to the tent.

Our second day hiking together begins roughly. Juli's legs are sore from our long day yesterday, and the pain on the outside of her knee flares up soon after we get started. About a mile from camp, Juli is ready for a break. Since I am hiking the entire trail, a couple of hot and bug-ridden days are a segue to better times. Juli is only out for a few days, so this is not part of a larger experience; it is simply unpleasant.

"I don't know how it's fun for you to do this," she says.

Juli is trying to be a good sport. This is probably the most tactful thing she can think to say given her current circumstance, but still it hurts for me to hear this. I am having the adventure of my life, and I want to share it with her more than anyone else. I want her to experience firsthand the fulfillment that I feel out here. Worse, I worry that she

---

31   I suspect that IT band friction syndrome is a common, but undiagnosed, overuse ailment among hikers. Anyone planning to backpack should learn about this injury and how to prevent and alleviate the problem by gradually increasing the number of miles walked, and by using stretching exercises that target the tendon.

is thinking, *You are away from home, from me, for months—to do this?* Juli's sore legs won't get better with more hiking today, so we get out trail maps to see if there is a way to end this hike sooner. There is a road only two miles away, Main Street in Tyringham, Massachusetts, that also leads into Lee. From there, we hitch a ride back to town.

We spend the next two days like a normal couple on vacation. We go out to eat, sightsee, shop, and go to a movie. Juli has brought some of my clothes from home, and it is a treat to wear jeans and a cotton shirt after months of wearing the same shorts and polyester shirt.

Each morning, Juli drops me off on the trail and picks me up a few hours later so I can slack-pack (walk some of the trail without a full pack). Conveniently, there are two road crossings about nine miles apart. Slack-packing at this stage is effortless. Each of my nine-mile walks takes less than three hours. On the first day it rains most of the way, but rain is not such a nuisance when I can change into dry clothes at day's end.

At lunchtime after my second day of slack-packing, it is time for Juli to return to the airport. Her visit has been a success after all. She is sincerely happy for me to be hiking the trail. Juli is willing to hike with me again in Maine. We'll keep it shorter than twenty-one miles.

❈ ❈ ❈

Today is August 2, and I have been on the trail for one hundred days. My hike continues over mild ups and downs with few rocks. Even carrying a full pack once again, I cover ground with little effort, mostly daydreaming about the time I just spent with Juli. The trail is damp and spongy. Much of the deadwood is covered with wood ear fungus. Red-spotted newts are abundant. They are smaller than lizards, but slothlike in their movements. I worry about stepping on them. Hmm…no wonder the trail feels spongy.

Late in the afternoon, the trail deposits me onto Depot Street in the town of Dalton, Massachusetts. The AT passes through the middle of the small town on three different streets. I walk through town and look around before returning to Tom Levardi's home on Depot Street. Dalton is less spiffy than the other towns I've recently seen, but by no means run down. It is a town intended for use by residents rather than visits by tourists. Tom is a bachelor who has accommodated hikers for years. His place is not a hostel. He invites hikers to stay if it is convenient for him, and he does not charge for the favor. From the looks of his home, there are probably few times when it is not convenient. The house looks as if it has been commandeered by deadbeat relatives. More than a dozen hikers are here, a few lounging in front of the television, a few setting up tents outside, a couple laying out sleeping bags on the porch, and one is using Tom's computer. I sit outside at a picnic table with Dharma Bum, who is now joined on the trail by his girlfriend Suds. The three of us are cooking trail food for dinner. Just as we finish eating, Tom comes outside, offering pies and ice cream. Lion King stops to say hello. He and Dharma Bum are the only hikers staying here that I know.

At least four of the hikers here are southbound thruhikers: Fisher King, Squirrel Meat, Snail, and 3-ounce. Snail is not the same Snail that I met in the Smokies. For the past week I have seen a few southbounders daily, and I will continue to see about the same number of them all the way through the next two states. At this time and region it is common for the hikers who started at opposite ends of the trail to meet. Southbounders generally start the trail later, so they have not come as far: Dalton is 1,553 miles from Springer and 619 miles from Katahdin.

That night, most of the hikers staying at Tom's walk down to a pool hall and stay until closing at 1:00 a.m. Lion King uses his camera to his best advantage, getting "interviews" from the local women. The bar is filled with coin-operated pool tables. All the hikers congregate around one table and play games of 8-ball as two-man teams, everyone taking turns buying pitchers of beer. The winning team keeps playing. Lion King and I are lucky enough to win a handful of games against the other hikers. Two nonhikers put coins on the table; this is pool hall protocol for getting a turn to play against the winners of the game. Lion King walks around the table to talk with the newcomers, but I can't hear the conversation in the noisy bar. He returns to tell me, "We'll be playing for shots of Jagermeister."

Pausing to read a shelter register. Strings from the rafters are for hanging food bags. The tuna cans purportedly obstruct mice.

It's muggy-humid today, and the incline out of Dalton is harder on me than it should be. The drinks that had seemed like a good idea last night don't seem so smart in hindsight. The beer is sweating out of me like a shower, and the Jagermeister is playing ping-pong in my head. I traverse nine miles through a pocket of woods between Dalton and Cheshire by lunchtime. The woods are higher and drier than the woods south of Dalton. There are oaks, pines, and some birch trees. It is a fresh, young forest, and the trees are modestly sized, with ample sunlight shining through. The path cuts through stringy, ankle-deep, bright green grass.

Rain begins to fall when I arrive at Cheshire, so I duck into an ice cream store and sit out a heavy but quickly passing shower. The AT crosses town through a cornfield, and then crosses the highway before heading up Mount Greylock. I stop at a gas station at the road and make a lunch of sodas and junk food.

At the start of the ascent, Kane-son is adjusting his pack. I wait and hike along with him. Kane-son was in Dalton, exhibiting his mini-crossbow and telling of his plans to supplement meals by hunting small game. He wears cutoff pants, a western shirt with cutoff sleeves, a cowboy hat, and homemade Indian-style moccasin boots. "I have to restitch them at least once a week," he says. From first appearances Kane-son is eccentric—maybe even dangerous—someone I would have avoided if I had not ended up hiking alongside him. By the end of our jaunt together, I would be happy to have made his acquaintance, and Kane-son would have reason to wish he had not met me.

Kane-son is in his early twenties, hiking for a few weeks before leaving for the Merchant Marine Academy. His inspiration for hiking some of the AT, and his self-reliant style, came from reading about the life of Eustace Conway in

The Last American Man.[32] He speaks of reading other books with diverse views on the philosophy of living. Kane-son is willing to express openness, and he seems self-aware enough to know that he is too young to entrench his opinions. He is gathering ideas, trying to find his place. He has most of his life ahead of him and wants to live it in a unique and meaningful way.

In more practical matters, Kane-son is planning to stay at a shelter tonight but does not carry a guidebook, and so all that he knows is, "It should be around here somewhere."

I do have my guidebook, so I try to help. "The Mark Noepal Lean-to is 4.4 miles from Cheshire. We should be there soon," I say, judging by the time we have spent together hiking. We have been working our way up the most demanding climb since Bear Mountain. Within the next mile, we cross the Jones Nose Trail. This intersection of trails is supposed to occur *north* of the Mark Noepal Lean-to. Somehow we must have passed the lean-to. I read the guidebook twice to be sure, and even let Kane-son read the page for himself. "I think we missed it," I tell him.

Kane-son turns around to backtrack south to the missed shelter. We say our goodbyes, and that would be the last I saw him. Fifteen minutes after our parting, I pass a lean-to. The Mark Noepal Lean-to.

Still long before reaching the summit, I catch up to Ken and Marcia. Fog descends abruptly as the three of us walk together toward the summit. We intend to stay at the Bascom Lodge Hostel. Bascom Lodge is a cozy rustic stone retreat on top of Mount Greylock, the highest point in Massachusetts. The hostel is in a detached building that is separated

---

32   Elizabeth Gilbert, *The Last American Man* (New York: Penguin Publishing, 2002). Eustace has lived all of his adult life in the woods, without modern conveniences. He hiked the Appalachian Trail and made a transcontinental horseback ride from the Atlantic to the Pacific. He lectures about the merits of living off the land.

into bays, each with roll-up, overhead garage doors, clearly designed to store things other than people. Ken, Marcia, and I set up to sleep in one of these bays, next to a bay full of kitchen supplies.

I wander back to the lobby of the lodge, where a few hikers are mixing with the drive-in guests. There is a road to the top of the mountain. The lodge is larger than it appears from the front, since a lower floor is buried in the mountain. The land slopes away on the backside, exposing the underground portion of the building. From the balcony at the rear of the lobby, I look down on the mountain falling away downhill. Only the peaks of the evergreens rise above the milky fog, as if they have been submerged in a cauldron of dry ice. It is too chilly to linger. It is only August 3, but it seems as though my summer has come to a close as abruptly as the fog arrived. There would be more hot times on the trail, but they would be ephemeral. From here on, keeping warm would be more of an issue than keeping cool.

I take my time getting on the trail this morning, knowing that there is a pizza buffet in town six miles down from Mount Greylock and trying to schedule my day accordingly. But the godless people of North Adams have allowed their Pizza Hut to go out of business. I waste more time, making about a mile-and-a-half round trip to eat a consolation lunch at another restaurant and to make phone calls. I get back on the trail at 2:00 p.m., still hoping to do fourteen miles.

On the ground there is a grayish mass the shape of a deflated football. As I pass, a sting on the back of my calf helps me to realize that what I am looking at is a fallen wasp nest. I do a wasp-bite dance ten yards up the trail, where I see a note with a warning: "Watch out for wasps!"

The trail ascends about two thousand feet in four miles from North Adams up to the Vermont border. I'm worn out by the climb, soaked in sweat, probably by rushing up the mountain too fast. I sit and stare at the Massachusetts/Vermont sign, trying to recall why I thought I needed to walk fourteen miles after leaving North Adams. There is also a sign for the Long Trail. The Appalachian Trail and the Long Trail are one and the same for the next 105 miles, and then the trails diverge. The AT turns east to New Hampshire, and the Long Trail continues north through Vermont to the Canadian border.[33]

By the time I reach the Seth Warner Shelter, I hear the distant rumble of thunder. I am far short of my fourteen-mile goal, but I decide to end my day of hiking. One hiker is already in the shelter, laying out his sleeping bag. Four others sit cooking dinner at the table directly in front of the shelter. The four of them are all relatively clean and shaven, probably just out for the weekend. "Are you staying in the shelter?" I ask the group of cooking hikers.

"No, we're setting up a tent over there," one of them replies, pointing to a clearing twenty yards away.

Under the conditions—imminent rain—I'm elated to have shelter space. More hikers arrive and fill the small shelter. Just after the day hikers finish their dinner and set up their tent, rain comes down in a deluge. Those of us in the shelter edge away from the leaks dripping from the roof and lie on our bags staring out at the rainfall. Rain can be as mesmerizing as a campfire. It splatters off the table, frees pebbles from the earth, showers the trees, and drums on the

---

33   Calling my bearing on the trail "north" has always been a generalization, and the generalization is less accurate the further I travel up the East Coast. My direction is nearly northeast. Even my compass gets confused this far up the coast. Magnetic declination: In North America, the earth's magnetic field pulls a compass to a point more near the top center of Canada than the North Pole. On Springer, a compass points four degrees too far west; on Katahdin it is off by more than seventeen degrees.

roof. Puddles form, and muddy little streams snake down-hill.

One of the day hikers sprints up to the shelter and looks inside to assess the free space; there is none. Water pours off the bill of his ball cap. He returns to help his companions, who are trying to raise their collapsed tent. We hear them shouting at each other over the rain, and yet there is laughter mixed with the shouts: "Whose dumb-ass idea was this!"

My clothes are not a drop drier than when I hung them up last night. It is still raining in the morning, and light, misty rain comes like breezes during the day. Everything is wet. I am wet from contact with the underbrush and from sweating in the humid air. The first eight miles of my hike are fairly level, bumping only slightly up and down along the ridge. The spongy wet soil tugs at my shoes.

Privies are much more common here than they are in the south. There is one at every shelter, and they are more uniform. Most have the time-honored outhouse design with four wooden walls, a slant of a roof, and a crescent moon cut into the door. Many have chicken wire wrapped around the bottom three feet of the walls to keep porcupines from eating the wood. The privy at Congdon Shelter is one of these. Poems and jokes are written on the interior walls. Among them is this truism: "Spam is even harder and heavier to carry in your belly than in your pack."

The descent to Vermont Route 9 is a hazardous, steep, and wet field of rocks. There is a concession trailer parked at the trailhead. I plop down in a folding chair and eat three hamburgers. The woman who owns and operates the lunch wagon sits with me and tells me how the rules of operation are ambiguous. Sometimes she is here; sometimes the police come and run her off. I am not much for conversation, sitting idle, enervated by the rain, my mud-soaked shoes, the general filth of my person and all my gear. It is not often that I am so bothered by being "dirty" on this trip. Most of the time I wash myself and my clothes when I have the opportunity, not because I am compelled by discomfort. Now I decide to create the opportunity to get clean. The road where I sit leads into the town of Bennington. I stick out my thumb, and in moments a pickup truck pulls over.

Buckeye arrives shortly after I do, and we share a motel room. He hiked the southern half of the trail in 2002 and is doing the northern half this year. Buckeye is also in town to escape the bad weather. "If we were paid to do this, we would have quit by now," he says. Obviously his joke rests on the fundamental enigma of the trail: why do we voluntarily, happily (mostly), submit ourselves to tribulation? Aside from the spectacular moments, aside from the gratification of working to accomplish a goal, there is ownership. This endeavor is much more endurable because we "own" it. We are here by choice, and we are going about it in the way of our own choosing.

My inevitable return to work has crept into my mind, and I mingle my thoughts. In *The Snow Leopard*, Peter Matthiessen notices that sherpas are cheerful in their work and often do more work than they are paid for, even though they earn a pittance. He observes the sherpa belief that "it is the task, not the employer, that is served" and that "the doing matters more than the attainment or reward."[34]

This seems to be an attitude worth striving for when I return to work, to perform my job as if I was doing it under my own guidance—as I would want it done myself—not to limit myself to the role of employee, and not to refrain from giving more of myself to the job than is warranted by my pay.

---

34   Peter Matthiessen, *The Snow Leopard* (New York: Penguin Books, 1978).

It is I who would benefit. Time is most enriching when spent industriously.

The motel clerk drives me back to the trail in the morning. The walk up from the road is gradual, with a manageable amount of mud. I arrive at the Goddard Shelter a little after 2:00 p.m. This shelter is at an elevation of 3,540 feet. Early into Vermont, the trail is already at a higher elevation than at any point in the past four states. There is a clearing in front of the shelter and I look out to tall and spindly pines, but the sky is too overcast to see the horizon. Vermont is the twelfth state on the trail, and I have less than six hundred miles to go. For more than half of my hike I viewed my overall progress as the number of miles I had under my boots. I remember noticing when I had completed one hundred, five hundred, and one thousand miles. Now the important number is the number of miles remaining. I am in countdown mode. I've averaged over one hundred miles per week, so for the first time I have a firm grip on my finish date; six weeks from now will be the middle of September.

There are already a handful of hikers in the shelter, including Odwalla, Buckeye, and Jerry Springer. Raindrops spot the dusty porch of the shelter. More hikers arrive. I am torn between claiming a spot in the shelter or moving out in the drizzle. I've only traveled ten miles. Rainfall intensifies, blowing so hard that we string ponchos and tarps across the shelter front to keep the sleeping platform dry. I'm staying put.

There are five more hours of daylight. For the eight of us holed up in the shelter, it is a restless time. When conversations lull, I write letters and catch up on my journal. Jerry Springer has a filter for brewing coffee on a camp stove. He shares, and it is excellent. I spend some time looking over my guidebook and making plans for the next few days.

Odwalla has trail maps, and I take a look at the profile of the trail ahead. The town of Manchester Center is exactly thirty miles away. I've already hiked over twenty miles on thirty-seven days of this journey, but I've yet to do thirty miles, and the idea is enticing. The days over twenty miles are always trying, but a thirty-mile day is a challenge. It would be a new experience to add to my adventure. I try to recruit Odwalla, but he is not interested. From the look of the map, I can see why. Stratton Mountain is an imposing obstacle in the middle of the stretch. It is four thousand feet high, and I will have to walk twelve miles before even starting the climb. It would've been wiser to do my long day in the midsection of the trail, but it is too late for that. The days are already getting shorter, and further north the terrain will only get harder. I will try for thirty tomorrow.

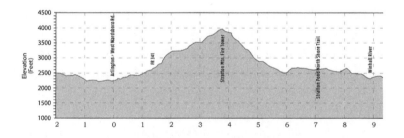

Profile map showing eleven miles of the
AT encompassing Stratton Mountain.

I am off early in the morning in a damp fog. Even if I was able to backpack at three miles per hour without stopping, I would be in for a ten-hour day. I can't sustain that speed, and I'll have to take breaks. I am in for at least twelve hours of intense hiking, and there is hardly that much daylight.

This part of Vermont has a deep forest look to it. Ferns cover the ground, streams cut across the trail, and spongy green moss covers the rocks and creeps up the tree trunks. Wet pines are wonderfully aromatic. And there is mud— mud stamped with hundreds of deep, water-filled shoe prints. Stratton Mountain won't be the only thing slowing me down. The trail is concave from wear down the center, and so it is an incubator for mud. I try to walk on the outer edges, but trees and dense undergrowth prohibit it. Where there is leeway it gets trampled as well, so the muddy trail bed bulges out like a recently fed snake. Hikers before me have thrown branches and stones onto the path, trying to bridge the muck. Shelter registers are full of entries by hikers complaining about the conditions, referring to the state as "Vermud."

There are heady moments when I strut down the trail, strong and untiring. I'd like to convince myself that I am in perfect equilibrium and can go on indefinitely. It is just walking—it can't be that hard. But I've been at it long enough to know it doesn't work that way. Changes creep in with the stress of miles. A hot spot flares up on my foot, the pack belt cuts into my hipbone, rain pesters me, my knee tightens, and hunger suddenly makes me feel weak. Heavy legs tell me to put my weight on my butt for a while.

I'm up and over Stratton Mountain by 3:30 p.m. I've made good time under the circumstances. I have twelve miles to go and about four hours of daylight. The trail is relatively level the rest of the way. At 7:30 it's getting dark and I'm racing for the road. I worry about trying to hitch in the dark. I scramble out to the road at dusk. To my relief, it's lighter than in the woods, and the first car to pass gives me a ride to town.

I stay at a boarding house in the center of town. It is more like a hostel, and the only guests are hikers. I will stay in town tomorrow.

I spend my zero day walking all over town. I do laundry, eat breakfast and lunch at restaurants, and visit the library. An immense Orvis fishing store, their flagship store, is on the same road as the library. There is a pond on the grounds where fly-casting practice is taking place. Students are flicking the flies down with a splat, their teacher alongside them unrolling lazy loops of line across the surface.

Dharma Bum and Suds are on a curb looking over a map. As I approach I see that the map is not a trail map, it is of the state. Frustrated by the wet weather, they are looking for someplace other than the trail to spend the next few days.

Manchester Center is a pretty town, a little larger than other trail towns, and it's swollen in the center with brightly advertised factory outlet stores. The stores are dispersed, many having their own buildings. There are more high-end stores than would seem supportable in this rural location: Armani, Ralph Lauren, Coldwater Creek, and Timberland are among the offerings. The stores have no draw at all for me. Months of scrutinizing everything that I carry have conditioned me to view possessions as burdens. I do spend time at two of the outfitters. I am unhappy with my pack and my shoes are coming apart, but I do not find suitable replacements. The outfitter tells me of a family who will let thruhikers stay overnight.

I hitch out to the home, which is on the edge of town near the trail crossing. It is a nice piece of property with a house and a barn. The couple who own the home have hiked the entire trail and still do maintenance work on the trail. Their basement is set up for hikers, with a few beds, an assortment of trail books, and a refrigerator. I am the only hiker staying tonight. I use the evening to work on my pack.

The "internal frame" of my backpack is two aluminum bars on the opposite side of the pad that rests against my back. The top of the bars tuck into a plastic flap near the top opening of the pack. The bars help to transfer the weight of the load down to my hip belt. After a thousand miles of bouncing, the bars have worked loose from the plastic flap. The weight of the pack falls on my shoulders, like an old-fashioned knapsack, instead of being distributed by the frame. Also, the plastic flap wedges awkwardly between the bars, tilting the load to one side. I stab holes through the plastic, wrap string around the supports, and cauterize the whole mess with my stove. While I am at it, I cut out the internal compartment intended for water bottle storage, a feature that I quickly found to be impractical. I clip off all unused straps and trim excess length from straps I use. I had refrained from these customizations, thinking that I may sell the pack later. But no one, including me, is going to want the pack after this trip is over. With my pack thus MacGyvered, I'm ready for the AT once again.

Acquaintances and strangers who have read my journal and sent messages of encouragement tell me how thrilling it sounds to thru-hike the AT. I don't think I've put an unduly positive slant on my journal, but they are more inclined to relate to the pretty pictures and good times than the everyday effort of carrying a pack. "I am totally engrossed and so envious!" "WOW! What a great adventure." Today, I feel it perhaps as they do, looking at my environment with fresh eyes and seeing the wonder of it anew. I'm a lifelong resident of Florida. I recall coming to the Appalachians as a kid on family vacations, awed by the expanse of mountains, the trees, the fresh air, and the cascading streams. These are my thoughts as I make my climb up Bromley Mountain.

The trail leads into a grassy clearing about ten yards wide. The clearing looks like it continues all the way to the top; this must be a ski slope. At the top, I can see the lift cables, a warming shack, and a sign pointing to my ski slope, the "Run Around." Looking north, I can see that I have a bit of up-and-down trail ahead of me. The trail descends from Bromley on a moderate to steep decline through a mix of moss, mud, and boulders. I pull out a Pop-Tart and eat as I descend, knowing that I should be attentive to footing on this slippery trail. The mountains are waterlogged from days of rain. I even pause before one fateful step across the slippery rock slope. Sure enough, I go down, still clutching at my Pop-Tart. I'm able to hold on to it through my long backslide, but I crush it in my clenched left hand. I watch longingly as one large crumb of my fractured meal bounds into the bushes. The whole thing happens in slow motion.

I've put a deep scratch in the face of my watch, but I still have some of my precious Pop-Tart. I couldn't care less about my backside; I don't even bother to brush off. Instead I stand and start funneling the crushed tart into my mouth, shuffling forward like a food-obsessed idiot. A few feet later I slide again, resuming my luge downhill. This time I lean right to keep my food hand airborne. At times like this it's good not to have a hiking partner.

Rain falls lightly and intermittently throughout the day, but overall it is a pleasant and scenic day. Jerry Springer is resting in a stately hemlock forest. The forest floor is matted with needles, and there are also a number of stones. Hikers have stacked the stones to build temples befitting the land-scape. Jerry is just standing idle with his pack off, taking in the solemnity of the scene. I see a couple that I've not seen on the trail before. They pick up their pace when I come up behind them, and they seem perturbed when they finally pull aside to let me walk past, too perturbed to respond to my "Thanks."

I have lunch at the well-engineered Peru Peak Shelter. The roof extends far beyond the sleeping platform. No rain will be blowing in here, as it did at Goddard Shelter. The couple I passed earlier arrive, and they pause for a minute and run their eyes over the shelter. They still have said nothing to me. "What do you think of this one? One to ten?" the man asks of his partner.

"Five," she says definitively, the man nods in agreement, and they turn to walk on. They couldn't be talking about me; a five out of ten rating would be too generous. They are insulting the shelter! I've seen enough shelters to know this is a good one. Their aloofness I can handle, but a poor assessment of this fine shelter has me cursing muddy trail slippages upon them.

I stop for the night at Big Branch Shelter. The Big Branch River runs in front, cascading over boulders and making a soothing racket. I am the only guest, and I fall asleep reading a dog-eared paperback copy of *Shane* that was left in the shelter. I am awakened at 11:00 p.m. when two hikers arrive by headlamp and settle in.

When I am ready to leave in the morning, the hikers are just getting up. They are Nooge and Tucker, college-aged thru-hikers who started the trail over a month before I did. I had passed them a few weeks ago without meeting them. They are in great shape, but they had been dawdling. Now, they have to average thirty miles a day to finish before college starts, sometimes hiking into the night.

The trail briefly runs tangent to Little Rock Pond. I am sluggish, so maybe the cold water will wake me up. I strip and jump in. Only feet from the trail, I'm risking an audience, but no one passes. The water is refreshing, but the rocky bottom of the pond is torture on my tender feet. My feet hurt when I walk barefoot, even on smooth ground. The rain has been hard on my feet. They are soggy and wrinkled, and sloughing dead skin from calluses. I have another cracked toenail—it will be the sixth one I've lost—and it is in the painful stage of working itself loose.

Six miles further, I sit for a break at a parking area that is empty but for one car. Two people are waiting at the car. The shelter-rating couple arrives, and they are relatively mud-free. Apparently they've escaped my vexing. The car couple has brought lunch, and the four of them pull out coolers and set up a picnic. They don't offer me a thing, not even a word.

It is raining and my toe is throbbing when I reach Clarendon Road. I walk west on the road a half mile and eat at the Whistle Stop restaurant, a small diner built into a train car. Further down the road, I visit a convenience store to get food to take with me. When I leave, I see thru-hiker Rain Crow in his truck. We've crossed paths on the trail a couple of times, and now I get an explanation of why I've twice seen him hiking southbound. Rain Crow will leave his truck at a trailhead, and hitch or catch a bus to another location on the trail a few days away. He hikes back to his truck and repeats the process. He will hike either north or south on each segment, whichever is more convenient, but overall his progress is northbound. Rain Crow offers to drive me around, looking for a place to stay. We pull up to a dilapidated motel with a gravel driveway and parking area. Ragged curtains blow behind the open jalousie windows. The rooms have no phones or air conditioning, so I am not enticed to stay. Rain Crow delivers me back to the trail.

With the rain stopped and with my hunger sated, I climb easily up to Clarendon Shelter. It is a leaky, broken-down shelter with a patchwork of repairs. String crisscrosses the front of the shelter, making an improvised clothesline. The line has more clothes than I've ever seen hung in a shelter. It's so weighted with wet clothes it impedes access. At a glance I count eight pairs of socks, and yet only one section hiker is in the shelter. "They all belong to those people," the hiker says, pointing to a tent twenty yards away. He tells me that there is a man and a woman, but they remain tent-bound during my stay and I never see them.

The next shelter I pass is the Governor Clement Shelter, a grubby, deep, dark shelter circled by tire tracks. There is trash in the fireplace, and offensive graffiti litters the walls. Shelters as a whole have been better than I anticipated. Collectively, AT shelters are my provisional home; to see any of them vandalized is disturbing.

I am much stronger today than yesterday. Some days I have more energy than others, with little correlation to sleep, diet, or conditions on the trail. I have not been sick on my hike. I haven't had a cold, or even a headache or upset stomach. My vigor is timely, for there is a climb of twenty-five hundred feet from Governor Clement Shelter to the top of Killington Peak. There are some rocky clearances on the south face of the mountain, and I can glimpse a view of the mountain range through the partially overcast skies. If there have been other overlooks in Vermont, I cannot recall; they would have been clouded over. There is intermittent rainfall again today.

My shoes are caked in mud, so I switch to camp shoes as soon as I reach Interstate 4. I don't want potential rides to pass me up for fear that I will track mud into their car. I intend to buy new shoes in the town of Rutland. My muddy, smelly shoes are falling apart. Still, I regret parting with them. These are the shoes that I purchased back in West

Virginia that may have saved my hike. It is impossible to know if I would have continued this far dealing with the foot pain I had before switching to these shoes.

I get a ride from Carrie, a gregarious twenty-year-old with a beat-up, muffler-dragging car. As we drive I stare at the hood in front of me, at the curious silver-gray color. The paint looks almost like it is pin-striped, but some of the "stripes" are flapping in the wind. Carrie explains. "I took it in for the inspection, and they failed it 'cause they said there was too much rust. I can't pay for a paint job. So I...me and my friend... we bought some duct tape and we taped it up bumper-to-bumper. Every inch of it. I took it back and it passed."

Carrie and her duct-taped car.

Carrie takes me to the post office, outfitter, and a shoe store. Upon leaving each location she asks, "Where do you want to go now?" She would have chauffeured me around more, but I didn't want to abuse her generosity. We part ways at the shoe store, where I buy my sixth and final pair of shoes. I walk to a nearby motel to stay for the night.

Rain is the dominant feature of my passage through Vermont. It has rained every day, but there have been few strong rains. Trees accumulate light precipitation and then drip on me. Today is again gray and humid. Every rock, branch, and leaf is drenched, as if the earth was dunked in a giant tub. Anywhere that the ground is level there is mud or standing water. Streams that cross the trail overflow and course down the footpath. One stream is swollen to a width of six feet, too wide to jump over, and inordinately deep. After failing to find a crossing, I wade through, surprised to have the gushing water rise nearly to my kneecaps.

The open ground in front of Stony Brook Shelter is pockmarked with puddles. A crowd of hikers is here; ten of us are in a shelter that would comfortably sleep six. Still more are tenting nearby. Eight hikers sleep packed side by side, conventionally arranged in the shelter with their feet toward the opening and their heads to the back. Since this shelter platform is slightly oversized, there is about eighteen inches of platform remaining at their feet. The last two hikers to arrive (Siesta and me) sleep clinging to this sliver of leftover space perpendicular to the other hikers.

These days on the muddy trail are little fun. I am just moving north while waiting for better days, reminiscent of the rainy days I trudged through in Virginia. Rainfall is heavy in the early afternoon. I welcome this decisive rain, taking it as a sign that this dreary front is finally pushing through. By the end of the day, the skies clear.

I approach a large but unnamed stream where a hiker is getting water, his pack leaning on a tree nearby. I've not seen him before, and without introduction he exclaims, "There he is! Can I get a picture?" I wait while he gets his camera and snaps my photo. "I'm Goggles. Surprised to see you here—you're going to make it!" Goggles is thru-hiking southbound. He used to live in the same county where I now live, and friends he left behind have been sending him my newspaper articles. In the last article he received, I had written about my sprained ankle.

The Rosewood Inn is my intended destination today, but when I arrive I find that the inn has been closed. I have already hiked seventeen miles, but I decide to push on for another nine to West Hartford. None of the days I have remaining will be this long. Goggles had told me that there is no lodging in town, but some families will take in thru-hikers. He stayed in someone's home, but I did not ask for details because at the time I did not plan to stop in West Hartford. I arrive after 7:00 p.m., exhausted. The only store is closed, so I wander down the street and talk to the first person I see. It is Kevin Kemmy, and when I ask him where I might stay, he replies, "You can pitch your tent in my yard."

"I don't have a tent." This is no lie. My tarp is at home; Juli is making modifications to it. My tarp hovers six inches off the ground, so it is not mosquito-proof. Juli visited during the peak of the buggy season, when I was intent on having this defect of my tarp corrected. I sent my tarp home with her and asked her to sew a skirt of netting around the perimeter. Mosquitoes have already become scarce. By the time she mails the modified tarp back to me (in Glencliff, New Hampshire), mosquitoes will no longer be a problem. Meanwhile, I have to use shelters, hostels, hotels, or sleep outside uncovered. The last option is particularly unappealing with the recent abundance of rain. In trying to fix a problem that went away on its own, I created a new situation to deal with. I should run for office.

Kevin bails me out. "Well, then, come and stay in the basement."

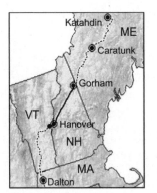

12
West Hartford
to Gorham

The only store I see in West Hartford is a convenience store with a gas pump out front. This morning the two cars parked at the store have "Take Vermont Back" bumper stickers. Inside, there are only two aisles, packed with everything people buy in convenience stores, only with less variety. In the back corner, there is an L-shaped counter with six barstools, and beyond the counter, the store clerk is doing double duty as a short-order cook. It is here that I have breakfast with four locals—thoroughly blue collar, big, weather-beaten men who leave none of their barstool seats unused.

Ten trail miles away is the Ivy League campus of Dartmouth College. In between here and there I walk through a peaceful, rolling forest of hemlock and white birch. A southbound hiker ambles by humming a tune, not missing a note as we pass.

I ease out of the woods onto a quiet residential street. Homes are nicely tucked away among the trees. This is the start of a three-mile road walk on the AT through the adjacent towns of Norwich, Vermont, and Hanover, New Hampshire. The towns and states are separated by the Connecticut River. I cross the river on a stately, four-lane bridge with "VT. | N.H." etched on a pillar in the middle. Passing over the bridge, I feel like I am entering a portal. My enthusiasm builds. Beyond this gateway are the final two states, which for the moment I imagine to be a lofty, remote, mountainous Shangri-la.

Hanover is a busy town. Bars and restaurants and ice cream shops and bookstores are bunched up close to campus. There are stores selling hats and green and white T-shirts that proudly and simply proclaim "DARTMOUTH." People fill the street, walking between shops; students tote books between classes and play hacky sack on the sidewalk. The wealth of the town is reflected in the architecture and upkeep of the area—and in the lack of affordable lodging. Still, thanks to the college kids, it is a place where a grungy hiker can feel comfortable. Most students still live on a budget, park on lawns, paint artwork on walls, play loud music, and hang banners from windows.

In the past, hikers were allowed to stay in fraternity houses on campus, but word on the trail is that the houses are now turning away hikers. On a tip, I try the Phi Tao house and get lucky. I am greeted by John, who shows me around the house and tells me the rules. There is a long list of them: no using the kitchen or laundry, no shoes indoors, shower only on the second floor, and sleep only on the floor in the basement. I don't mind; being allowed to stay for free is extremely hospitable.

"I thru-hiked last year," John tells me.

I know he has made the statement to put me at ease after presenting all the restrictions. "That's great," is all I can summon in reply.

John must have interpreted my simple response as skepticism, since he quickly adds, "I've gained sixty-five pounds since finishing the trail."

I truly am not skeptical of him completing the trail. He is a big guy, but I have seen plenty of overweight hikers stick with it and plenty of well-conditioned people quit. I have been considering how to transform my atrocious eating habits on my return to the real world. If I keep eating like I do, I will put weight back on faster than I lost it. I should ramp down my eating before I even finish the trail—but not yet. I walk down to the campus co-op grocery and bask in the wonderful display of food. The store is promoting corn by cooking it on a grill outside and giving it away to customers. I sneak in line twice to get two servings. I take home trail food and a box of eight doughnuts for breakfast, but I eat four of them on my walk back to the house.

The centerpiece of campus is Dartmouth Green, an expansive lawn with the library tower and clock as a backdrop. There are obligatory ivy-covered brick buildings, churches, and a contemporary student center. All the buildings have a style befitting the campus, yet they are not uniform. Some are brick, some are slate, some are sandstone, and some are whitewashed, but all are pleasing to the eye. Since there is no laundry in Phi Tao, I walk over to another set of dormitories. I chat with two girls, follow them into their dormitory, and find laundry machines down in the basement.

Arrow, the 2002 thru-hiker I met before the start of my hike, had told me that he makes many weekend trips to the trail in New Hampshire. I give him a call, and we arrange to meet at lunchtime the day after tomorrow. It gives me no pause to plan on walking thirty-six miles in a day and a half.

In the morning, I follow the trail across the town of Hanover, past the bookstores, past Dartmouth's football field, past the co-op grocery store, and back up into the hills alongside the ball fields.

For miles, the forest is dense with hemlocks and birch trees. Under cover of the trees, it is dark and damp, a breeding ground for mushrooms. They are as small as a pencil eraser and as big as a saucer. Most have the typical mushroom dome, but some are flat-topped; one is shaped like a funnel, and some are shaped like coral (and are predictably named coral mushrooms). I see mushrooms that are white, red, orange, yellow, blue, and purple. The more I eat, the more colorful they are.

The trail meanders over this fecund soil for twenty miles, with soft hills and valleys ranging between elevations of eight hundred and twenty-three hundred feet. After crossing Lyme-Dorchester Road, the trail takes on a different look. The terrain is higher and drier, and the mushrooms are replaced by rocks, hills by mountains. From the vantage point of a rocky ledge, I can see a mountain rising up ahead, slightly off to my right. The mountain is completely forested, but still a fire tower is visible above the trees at the summit. The fire tower identifies the peak as Smarts Mountain, my destination for the night.

I know from my guidebook, my watch, and dead reckoning that I am a little more than a mile from the tower. The path is predictable; I will dip into a saddle between here and Smarts Mountain, and then turn right and climb uphill on the ridge that I now see in profile.

Geometry adds to the allure of hiking. On the AT I never feel like I am traveling on a straight line. I weave through boulders, sweep along a side-hill curve, spiral around a mountain, roller coaster up and down, skirt along the precipice of a cliff, pass through a narrow gorge. There are limitless physical configurations, ever-changing, inviting me to walk, pulling me forward to feel myself traverse the arc of the trail through the transitions, navigate the obstacles, fight gravity in a climb, or ride the pitch downhill.

Locations are engraved in my memory with positional attributes based more on my own internal sense of direction than on any objective reference point. I think of the trail veering to the left or of myself being on the right side of a mountain when "left" and "right" could be north, south, east, or west. My mind's eye sees shelters I have visited from a chosen perspective, regardless of their actual orientation relative to the trail.

I have been on the trail for twelve hours, covering 23.4 miles. It is dark and I am too tired to cook, so I have a dinner of candy bars that John gave me when I left Phi Tao.

On top of Smarts Mountain, my shelter is a rickety fire warden's cabin, no longer in use, next to the fire tower. Viking, from Germany, is the only other hiker here. I chase a mouse off the doorstep as I enter. A broken window is covered with a plastic sheet. The plastic sheet is foggy and spotted with age, but the silhouette of a mouse climbing on the window sill is discernible. When I hang my food bag, I see a mouse peering down from the rafters. "For me?" he asks.

Between the cabin and my meeting point with Arrow at Atwell Hill Road, I cover twelve scenic and challenging miles. Climbs up Eastman Cliffs and Mount Cube are notable for the transition to rocky ground and scrub pines. Arrow has brought two friends, Wakapak and Giggler. They all did thru-hikes in 2002. They have brought a propane grill, a cooler, and an assortment of snacks. A gathering forms around Arrow's van to take in the burgers, chips, sodas, and beer. Northbounders and southbounders are here in roughly equal numbers. Northbounders, myself included, are eager to hear about the White Mountains. We solicit information from last year's thru-hikers and from southbound hikers who just exited the range.

The Appalachian Mountain Club (AMC) runs bunkhouses called "huts" in the White Mountains. They are large cabins that can sleep forty to ninety paying guests and have no road access. All guests have to hike in to the huts. The huts generate their own power from wind, solar, or hydroelectric generators. Each has a staff of about six that is responsible for cooking, cleaning, entertaining guests, and packing in supplies. The first few thru-hikers to arrive at a hut can do work-for-stay, and they cannot stay for more than one night. In exchange for menial tasks like setting tables and washing dishes, hikers are fed leftovers for dinner and breakfast, and sleep on the dining room floor.

One of the southbounders tells of his pass through the White Mountains. Work-for-stay at the AMC huts is such a generous deal that he stopped at every hut. Some days were short. For example, the distance from Mizpah Hut to Lakes of the Clouds Hut is less than five miles. He is fit, muscled, and proud of himself for slowing his pace in order to fully exploit the thru-hiker benefit. Is it a virtue to maximize your consumption of goodwill? It should be taken as it comes, rather than pursued. The southbounder is seemingly unaware that his indulgence likely deprives other hikers of this limited provision. Most huts only take in the first two thru-hikers. Hikers arriving after walking their normal day would be shut out by the southbounder who scampered between huts.

The southbound hikers experienced cloudy, drizzling weather through the Whites. I never visualized these treeless peaks with anything other than the blue sky that I've seen in pictures. I've been foolishly dreamy about where I am headed, and I swing toward pessimism. Of course

I could get rain in the Whites. Odds are I will, considering my AT experience to date.

In fact, dark clouds materialize as I rouse myself back to the trail. Arrow and friends pack up the van. I will meet them again at the next road crossing at Glencliff, eight miles north. Arrow assures me that it is an easy walk. I don't think I will mind getting wet. After being on the trail for only minutes, the rain comes. I don't bother with any rain-wear, and I had covered my pack before leaving. The rain quickly intensifies into a storm. Cold, heavy drops of rain pound on me, and furious bolts of lightning crash down among the trees. I feel exposed. I *should* be struck, since my water-filled body would be an excellent conductor to bridge the bolts from the sky to the ground. I haven't been caught walking in such a lightning-laden thunderstorm since the storm I experienced near the North Carolina border, and it refreshes my opinion that lightning is the most fearsome threat on the trail.

I hustle down a blue-blazed trail to Ore Hill Shelter, as happy as I have ever been to reach safety. Most of the group, who were just at the van enjoying a hot lunch, are now cowering from the elements.

From Glencliff, Arrow takes me to his parents' home for a shower and laundry. He returns me to the trailhead the next morning, and he will meet me again at the end of the day. All of the 9.5 miles I walk today will be spent going up and down one massive mountain, Mount Moosilauke. I am in the White Mountain National Forest.

At the foot of the mountain I see a porcupine. He is large with ungainly bristled armor, but he is agile enough to climb up a tree and cluck at me while I take his picture. The trail cuts through a dense forest of pines. Initially they are about twenty feet tall. As I go higher, they shrink down to perfect little three-foot-tall Christmas trees. Then they disappear altogether and the AT is above tree line for the first time. A naturalist is at the summit, speaking to a small group about the fragile nature of the alpine environment. Ken and Marcia are taking in the panorama. I say hello, but cannot linger in the cold breeze. I'm wearing shorts and a sleeveless shirt, which were barely warm enough at the foot of the mountain. At the peak it is at least ten degrees colder, and the unimpeded breeze makes it seem more so. Since Arrow is helping me to slack-pack today, I've left most of my gear, including my jacket, with him.

The descent on the north face of Moosilauke is the steepest I've experienced on the trail. The trail has no switchbacks, and most of the soil is washed away by erosion. Tree roots and bedrock lie exposed. The trail descends so sharply that I often turn to face the mountain and climb down backward so I can grab roots as handholds. A waterfall runs parallel to the path for much of the way, spraying mist onto the trail and making footing even more uncertain.

In some places, wooden steps are implanted into the bedrock. A notch is cut into the stone, and a railroad-tie-sized chunk of lumber is set into the notch, secured by spikes of rebar. These improvised steps are not uniformly spaced, being separated by a distance equivalent to two or three steps that would be placed in a building's stairwell. To get a feel for the difficulty, try taking stairwell steps two or three at a time without using the handrail. Spread some rocks and twigs on them, and then spray them down with water. If you still haven't been kicked out of the building, try it carrying a pack. On Moosilauke, a misstep would send me tumbling into a waterfall. Some of the timbers are loose and wobble when I land. Some are missing, giving me the unnerving visualization of one popping loose underfoot.

The descent ends at Kinsman Notch, where there is a road crossing and a parking area. Arrow is here, grilling more hamburgers and hotdogs. Hikers Duff, Ken, and Marcia stop to chat and eat. Arrow drives me to North Woodstock, which is situated at the intersection of two roads, the road that we are on and another road that crosses the trail sixteen miles north of here. Tomorrow I will slack-pack those sixteen miles and hitch a ride back into North Woodstock. I will repeat this slack-packing technique in the similarly situated towns of Gorham, Andover, and Rangeley.

I stay at the Cascade Lodge in North Woodstock. There are only a handful of rooms, and they are all upstairs and in desperate need of repairs. Downstairs is cluttered and yellowed by smoke. There is old furniture, tables mounded with papers, and overflowing hiker boxes. A computer is tucked into the disarray at the rear of the room, and the owner's teenage grandson is affixed to the screen, so immobile that I nearly overlook him. A hiker can feel at home here, and it is by far the cheapest lodging in town.

When the owner returns me to Kinsman Notch, I look up at Mount Moosilauke towering over the road to the south, and more mountains tower above the road to the north. The peaks are beautifully outlined by Windex-blue skies. The setting evokes spontaneous elation, a sudden feeling of overwhelming goodness, rightness, optimism, happiness, and eagerness for being where I am, involved in what I am doing. Partway up the first climb I pass southbound hikers who ask how far I am going.

"I'm a thru-hiker," I say, recalling the hesitancy with which I would have given that answer back in Georgia. This *is* what I am now; I belong.

Mount Kinsman is the main feature of the day. There is a long and steep incline up the mountain, so steep in places that trail builders have installed wooden ladders. The mountain has two peaks, and from the south peak, I can see that the north peak is the steeper of the two. The north peak looks so pointed that it is hard to imagine that there could be a walking path to its pinnacle. The sight makes me eager to go there. I have fun working my way up the second peak, using my hands nearly as much as my feet. Rain falls and makes the trail slick and muddy. The descent is every bit as steep, and much less fun.

A section-hiking family (a mom, a dad, an unwilling pre-teen daughter, and a reluctant dog) is headed up Kinsman. All are carrying full packs, and the dad is dragging the dog on a leash and yelling at it for nearly causing him to fall on this dangerous slope. The daughter is asking if they can turn around. They say they are headed for a shelter I had passed on the other side of the mountain, and gauging by the time it took me, they would arrive about an hour after dark. They are irritated, dispirited, and headed for a night hike on a wet trail on one of the most dangerous sections of the AT.

Lonesome Lake Hut, the first of the AMC huts on the AT, sits serenely next to Lonesome Lake, and Franconia Ridge rises like a wall on the far shore. My sixteen-mile day has been work, even though I slack-packed with less than twenty pounds. I hitch back to North Woodstock, satisfied with my two sorties into the White Mountains. Tomorrow I will take on the bulk of the Whites with a full pack, spending four nights before my next resupply.

I wake up sore and worried that I am getting sick. My soreness is status quo, and a big breakfast in town eliminates my malaise. Conditions, crisply cold around sixty degrees with clear skies, are perfect for a foray into the mountains. I'm eager to go, but I have a newspaper article to finish before leaving town.

When I finally leave North Woodstock, I walk toward the north end of town so I can hitch near the front of a convenience store. It looks like an easy spot for cars traveling down Main Street to pull over. Instead, my ride comes from a man who is leaving the store. His purchase, a twelve-pack of beer, is in the front seat between us. One is missing, because he's got it in his hand. "You want a beer?"

"No thanks." It is before 11:00 a.m., but there's no need to point that out to him. It is obvious he's the kind of guy who starts drinking even earlier than this on some days. Like today, for example. His eyes are squinty, and his tongue gets in the way of his words. His driving is erratic, and I wish we weren't talking because he looks at me and not the road when he talks. I've told him about my long-distance hike, and he figures I must be living off the land.

"You must have a nice hunting knife."

"No," I answer, "I haven't been hunting."

"You ain't carrying a fucking hunting knife?" he asks again. "What if you get attacked by a fucking bear? Fuck! You'd be fucked!" His cursing is not angry; "fucking" is just an all-purpose adjective, and sometimes a sentence.

"Here it is," I say, pointing to the trailhead where I've asked him to take me. "Thanks a lot for the ride."

"Okay, man. Good luck. Git yerself a fucking knife."

The trail begins a long ramp up Mount Lincoln. Most of the six miles I walk today will be uphill since I will end my day about four thousand feet higher than where I started. The bulk of the climb is uniformly inclined at the angle of an escalator. The terrain is rocky, and the trees are evergreens. Thru-hiker Sparky is on the path ahead of me, moving slowly, not feeling well. I stop and let her pick from a few over-the-counter medicines I carry, and then I walk with her for about a mile before feeling like I need to move on. We are headed above tree line, so I hope she is fairly judging her capabilities.

A couple of AMC workers are at Liberty Springs Campsite. I inquire about staying at Greenleaf Hut. The hut workers (they call themselves "croo") have some flexibility in how they implement the work-for-stay policy. They can turn anyone away, but usually their discretion works in favor of thru-hikers. Still, uncertainty about hut openings is unsettling, especially since Greenleaf is a mile off the trail. One of the AMC employees is a croo member at Greenleaf. "We hardly ever get more than two thru-hikers coming down to Greenleaf. And usually we'll take all that come, since it's such a long walk down."

The trail begins to level, trees become sparser, and again I hike out above the timberline. The AT stays above the trees for the next three miles. The upper slopes of the mountains are still green with ground-hugging alpine vegetation. Hikers are asked not to stray from the trail because of the fragile nature of growth at this elevation. Gray and rust-colored granite bulges out along the ridgeline, like the spine of an exoskeletal beast. When I summit Mount Lincoln, I can see the next mile of trail along the rocky spine of Franconia Ridge. It is an awesome site. It doesn't look like a mile to the next peak, Mount Lafayette, but moving specks—hikers on the trail—give scale to the scene that is before me.

From the top of Lafayette, views in all directions are bounded only by the limits of my vision. The enormous expanse of land evokes a powerful feeling of liberation. We spend an inordinate amount of time indoors, and the physical confinement limits the metaphorical bubble of our aspirations. Large rooms, like the vaulted interior of a church, are uplifting. Outdoors, we are free to reach for the sky.

Franconia Ridge leading to Mount Layfayette.

I leave the AT to take the path down to the hut. The trail is steep and rocky. Although it is only a mile long, it takes me forty minutes to traverse. Greenleaf Hut is on a flat shelf of land on the shoulder of the mountain. Beyond the hut, the mountain falls off steeply to Franconia Notch. From where I stand, I cannot see down into the notch, but I can see across the gap to Cannon Mountain. New Hampshire's state emblem is a facelike rock formation that was on the side of Cannon Mountain. A week after I started my hike, the Old Man of the Mountain broke loose and tumbled into Franconia Notch. Before his fall, he was staring at Greenleaf Hut.

Thru-hikers Dirty Bird and Fido are at the hut before me, but the croo allows me to do work-for-stay as well. Later Sparky arrives, and she is granted a spot in the hut, too. My task for the night is to organize a bookshelf full of books that they have available to guests. Dirty Bird and Fido get the somewhat less appealing task of turning the compost. We are treated to leftovers for dinner, and there is plenty of everything: ham, mashed potatoes, peas, and apple pie.

The AMC huts implement a number of environment-friendly features. They are lit by 24-volt battery systems charged by solar, wind, or hydro generators. Stoves run off propane. Food waste is composted. There are no napkins, and there are no paper towels in the bathrooms. There are no showers. The bathrooms have composting toilets, and they are as odorless as any public restroom I've ever used. Guests are expected to pack out their own trash. Twice a week the croos pack out garbage and return loaded with supplies. There is no road access.

In the morning, the last chore for us work-for-stay hikers is to sweep the rooms. It is not much of a task for four people, and the croo needs no help cooking. For breakfast, we again get leftovers. The only downside to the arrangement is waiting for the croo to finish with the guests before we can eat. After guests have eaten, the croo gives them a brief presentation, and one croo member offers to take all willing guests for a guided hike. We gather up the dishes, and the croo does the washing. Only then do we get to eat. I am accustomed to starting my hike around 7:00 a.m., but I would never leave the huts before 9:00. It is a setback that I gladly suffer for the meals and accommodations.

The trail in the White Mountains is everything I ever heard it would be. Here I see the most spectacular views of anywhere on the trail. And it is also as difficult as I have been warned. The terrain is as rocky as Pennsylvania, and the steepness of the climbs is unparalleled. Imagine a mountain range sculpted using beach sand, with mountains as tall and steep as the sand will allow. Wind and time would erode and soften the sculpture. The mountains would melt down; the peaks would become less pointed and the slopes more gradual. A week-old sculpture might be representative of the shape of the majority of the Appalachian Mountain Range. The White Mountains would be like the sculpture the moment it was completed, with the sharpness and steepness still intact. No other mountains on the AT are this austere. Only the Great Smoky Mountains come close; they may be equated to one- or two-day-old mountains of sand.

I've been doing less than two miles per hour on the days in the Whites, and fourteen miles is a full day. Most everywhere else on the trail I would plan to hike about twenty miles a day, and in a pinch I could hike faster than three miles per hour. My feet hurt with renewed intensity now that there is more rock walking and steep, toe-jamming descents.

There are a number of section hikers on this strenuous trail. Many take multiday vacations to hike hut to hut through the Whites. Three of them are coming uphill, and I watch them labor through the chaos of rock. We meet at the intersection of the AT and another side trail. One of the hikers points to the side trail and says, "That way is the campsite," and then, pointing down the trail he just climbed, "and that way is hell." I see no other thru-hikers northbound or southbound while I hike, which may be a good thing since we are vying for work-for-stay at the huts.

Near Galehead Hut, there is a respite of somewhat level and wooded trail. A furry brown animal scurries along the ground and then up a spruce tree. It is a marten, an animal looking somewhat like a cross between a fox and a squirrel. Martens are elusive, and rare in New Hampshire, so I feel fortunate to see him.

I am the first thru-hiker to arrive at Zealand Falls Hut. Biscuit arrives shortly after I do, and we both do work-for-stay. This croo takes a more literal view of work-for-stay, so we wash windows, sweep, and set tables. This hut, like all the rest, is fully booked with paying guests.

Pine marten.

The hut is situated on the side of a mountain, facing downhill. The waterfall after which the hut is named is only twenty yards away. After dinner it is dark and I sit out front looking across the valley. The sky is cobalt blue above the undulating black silhouette of the mountains. Mars is shining brightly, more prominent than any star. The red planet is closer than it has been to Earth in sixty thousand years.

The first five miles north from Zealand Falls Hut are excellent, easy and level, so I walk faster than I have in days. From the right a bear and cub are on a collision course with me, all of us moving too fast and getting ourselves too close to each other. I stop and the mother bear retreats, but the dummy cub trees itself so the mom has to come back and stand guard; it is approximately the same scenario I've had with all momma bears. The cub is in a tree close to the trail, and the mother bear is standing *on* the trail. I wait for a minute, impatient for them to allow me to proceed. The trailside vegetation is too dense for me to walk around. Will they run off if I get closer? That is an approach I've yet to try on bears. I advance a few cautious steps. The bear raises her head, extends her neck, and trains her ears on me. She is not intimidated. I think better of pushing her further. If I get mauled, surely the news team will interview the man who gave me a ride back in North Woodstock: "I told him to get a (bleeping) hunting knife."

I backtrack as far as I can, still keeping the bears in sight. Once I am at a distance, the cub climbs down, and they continue on their way across the trail. A half mile later I see hikers headed south, and I warn them of the bears. "That's okay, I have pepper spray," one of them replies, yanking loose a canister that was strapped to his shoulder pad. They hasten forward like a hunting party.

Eight miles of the trail pass quickly, mostly downhill to Crawford Notch where U.S. Route 302 passes through the White Mountains. Starting back into the woods, the forest is darkened by the dense trees and humidified by a stream. It is one of those places that I feel should be inhabited by a moose, but I don't see one.

The trail is much steeper heading north from the notch. Trees block all wind, and I sweat heavily as I strain up the mountain. The trail seems to dead-end into a slab of bedrock rising nearly vertical. I think I must be off the trail, but I look back and see a white blaze on a tree behind me. There is no way around. On closer inspection of the slab, there is a fissure that allows me to get foot- and handholds and make my way up fifteen feet to the top of the rock wall. I repeat this process of hand-over-hand climbing up short walls ten times on this single ascent. I am in disbelief that eighty-year-olds and at least one blind hiker have come this way.

My difficult climb is rewarded with a wonderful view from Webster Cliffs. From the rocky, open shelf of the cliff, I look south across the gulf of air between the mountain that I descended in the morning and the one I just climbed.

Down below in Crawford Notch, at the nadir of the V between the mountains, runs the road that I crossed just one hour ago. There is a parking area and a pond, and barely discernible people move about. The word "notch" is used in place of "gap" or "valley" in the White Mountains, and the word seems more appropriate. Notch sounds more descriptive of these chasms between mountains, where a giant might get his foot wedged.

The trail turns toward the northern front of the cliffs, still on rocky ground with weather-stunted trees. The temperature has dropped, and I can feel my sweat evaporating rapidly in the gentle breeze. From Mount Jackson I can see an expansive view of the Presidential Range, the subset of the White Mountains between Crawford Notch and Pinkham Notch. On the horizon, Mount Washington looms so bulking that it blocks from view all that lies beyond. A blanket of trees covers the saddle of land between the peaks. Among the trees down and to my left there is a dot of white that is Mizpah Hut, two miles away, my destination for the night.

At the hut, Biscuit says, "I saw a moose just after the road. He was young and didn't seem scared of me. He stared right at me and wouldn't go away. Moose don't see well, so maybe he didn't know what I was. Did you see him?"

Biscuit is a student at Boston College. She is slender but strong, and I like that she has not attached herself to a group, as young thru-hikers are more prone to do. We are doing work-for-stay again, and she is a good companion. Our tasks for the night and morning are simply to set the tables for dinner and breakfast.

The morning weather is as good as I can hope for when I leave the hut and head for Mount Washington. It is just below sixty degrees, and the wind gusts are up to thirty miles per hour. This is calm for the Presidential Range. Less than a mile from Mizpah Hut, I go above tree line again as I ascend Mount Pierce. I will stay above tree line for the next twelve miles.

The terrain is a mix of rocks and matted blue-green vegetation. Rocky pinnacles jut up along the ridge. Fortunately, the trail weaves around, rather than over, the peaks of Mounts Eisenhower, Franklin, and Monroe. As I bend around the right of Mount Monroe, the Lakes of the Clouds Hut comes into view.

Lakes of the Clouds Hut and Mount Washington.

The hut is perfectly nestled in the saddle between Monroe and Washington. Lakes of the Clouds is the largest of the huts and is a simple, solid, ranch-style structure. The architecture of the hut blends beautifully with the landscape, complementing, rather than detracting from, the picturesque austerity of the mountain. The same cannot be said of the spindly collection of weather antennae on the summit. From the northbound approach, Mount Washington rises to the right of the hut. The left shoulder forms a long, gradual slope. The cog railway, a steam-powered train that carries sightseers on a six-mile round trip ride to the top, travels along this slope.

A pair of southbound hikers, fit and young, are reading a pamphlet describing hikes on and around Mount Washington, noting the distances and time estimates for the walk from Lakes of the Clouds Hut to the summit. "Distance 1.5 miles, uphill one hour twenty-five minutes, downhill forty-five minutes," he scoffs. "We walked that in less than fifteen minutes, didn't we?" I note that neither has a watch. I am slow among these rocks. Even on the downhill, I lose time finding good foot placement. If I was to allow myself to speed downhill recklessly with the pull of gravity, I imagine I could manage a bit better than three miles per hour. The southbounder's claim puts their speed at a joglike six miles per hour, which would enable them to cover forty-eight miles per day, assuming they limit themselves to eight-hour hiking days.

Northbound hikers have heard such claims often enough to make inside jokes about time estimation. If we do many miles in a day, then we are hiking in "southbound time." To be fair, southbounders have undoubtedly heard the same exaggerations from northbounders.

The speed of the croo traveling between huts truly is amazing, and verifiable, since I have been passed by them. As I leave the hut, I see a long-legged croo member heading up Mount Washington ahead of me. I am determined to keep up, even though he's only carrying a day pack. He has a fifty-yard lead, and I cannot close the gap. His strides are longer, so I quicken my pace. I am not winded, but simply cannot place my feet fast enough. This side of the mountain is entirely composed of rocks, so there is no beaten path.

The trail is vaguely defined by cairns.[35] I meander, drifting to rocks that offer the flattest foot landing surfaces. I look up at the ever more distant croo member, who moves in a direct line, never seeming to shorten or extend his stride, letting his foot take hold wherever it lands.

I've lost sight of the hiker ahead and wonder why the trail has veered to the west of the summit. The trail is level now, as if circling the mountain. When will it turn back up-hill? The view ahead clears, and I can see that the path is headed slightly downhill toward the track of the cog rail-road. I am on the wrong trail. I cannot imagine how I got off the AT. There is no point on the path where I had any in-decision about where I was going. I hadn't seen signs or no-ticed anything that hinted of a fork in the trail. I had taken a long look at the map last night back at Mizpah Hut. I know the AT descends from Washington near the cog railroad tracks, so I continue on, hoping to reconnect with the AT. The trail passes under the tracks, which are dripping with black soot. Shortly beyond the tracks, there is a marked trail intersection, where I learn that I have skirted the mountain on the West Side Trail. I head southbound on the AT, back to the summit of Mount Washington. I leave my pack at the intersection since I will be coming back down the same way. Getting myself lost causes me to miss four-tenths of the AT on the north side of the mountain. I walked that much extra on the West Side Trail, and I walk the north spur of the AT twice.

In addition to the cog railway, there is a road that deliv-ers tourists to the summit of Mount Washington. For a fee, you can drive your car up the narrow, winding, car-sickness-inducing road and get a bumper sticker that says, "This car

---

35   A "cairn" in the Whites is a conical stack of stone, usually as tall as a man. In the absence of trees, this is the most effective way to mark the trail. White blazes are hard to spot on the rocks here since there is frequent fog, rain, and snow.

climbed Mount Washington." You have to stop at intervals on the way down to let your brakes cool. A handful of buildings are up here, including a weather observatory, a snack bar, and a gift shop. The whole scene seems oddly tranquil for a mountain known for extreme conditions.

"Mount Washington has a well-earned reputation as the most dangerous small mountain in the world," is just one of the warnings stated in AMC's White Mountain Guide. The wind exceeds hurricane force (75 mph) on more than one hundred days in an average year, and the highest surface wind speed ever recorded (231 mph) was taken at the weather observatory on the summit. There may be snowfall, even in the middle of the summer.[36]

The weather can change suddenly, and there is an extreme difference between the weather on the mountaintop and the weather in the valley four miles below. Over one hundred people have died on the mountain, mostly from hypothermia. Mount Washington is accessible and underestimated—factors that contribute to the death toll. It is not easy to understand how people can die on a mountain with a snack bar on top. The AMC guide doesn't mince words: "If you begin to experience difficulty from weather conditions, remember that the worst is yet to come, and turn back, without shame, before it is too late." The book goes on to suggest inexperienced hikers would be wise to get their experience elsewhere, and that most deaths are due to "the failure of robust but incautious hikers to realize that winterlike storms of incredible violence occur frequently, even during the summer months."[37]

---

36   Gene Daniell and Steven D. Smith, *White Mountain Guide* (Boston, MA: Appalachian Mountain Club Books, 2003). Mount Washington is 6,288 feet high, second only to Clingmans Dome on the AT. The term "small" is relative to the world's highest peaks. Mount Denali (aka McKinley, 20,320 feet) is the highest peak on the North American continent. There have been roughly the same number of deaths on Denali and Washington.
37   Ibid., 4.

Biscuit is in the snack bar. I left before she did this morning, but she is here first because of my diversion. When I arrived, I could see all the way down to Lakes of the Clouds. When I leave an hour later, thick clouds have blown in, and visibility is about thirty yards. The temperature has dropped fifteen degrees, and the wind is up to forty-five miles per hour, with some stronger gusts. The mountain is covered in a cold, damp fog. The howl of the wind makes it difficult to hear anyone more than an arm's length away. Despite warnings of the volatility and severity of the weather, the sudden change is a shock. Biscuit asks if we can hike together; I gladly accept.

On the plateau between Washington and Madison, I feel suspended, like walking on the canvas of a vast tent, whose poles form the mountain peaks. The ground is a jumble of suitcase-sized rocks, leopard-spotted with green lichen. Cairns look ghostly, shrouded by fog.

There are dozens of trails in the White Mountains. The length of the Appalachian Trail is comprised of segments of other trails. Today I have been on the Crawford Path Trail, the West Side Trail (though I wasn't supposed to be), and the Gulfside Trail. Signposts at trail intersections identify the choices, but "Appalachian Trail" is not always identified. A sign may point to the northbound Osgood Trail or westbound Gulf Trail, and we need to know which one is the AT. On some signs, hikers have helped by carving the AT symbol next to the right choice. This is the one section of the AT on which I would advise carrying maps. Unfortunately, I don't have any with me now. I do have Biscuit with me, and I am more confident in her directional choices than my own.

Our miles pass safely, and quickly, since we sustain a running conversation about Biscuit's time in India, books, and the Gulf War. Fog has lifted somewhat as we near the splendid sight of sanctuary, Madison Springs Hut, dwarfed by the pyramid of Mount Madison rising behind. We are doing work-for-stay again. I haven't seen another northbound thru-hiker since leaving Greenleaf Hut. Large, heavy wood tables and benches serve as dining tables at all the huts. At bedtime they are pushed to each side of the open dining area. I lay my sleeping bag underneath a table to avoid being stepped on in the darkness.

The sound of wind slapping into the hut rouses me from sleep in the middle of the night. The cold air penetrates the hut as if the walls are perforated. I sleep on the cold wood floor of the dining room, fully clothed and buried within my sleeping bag. I am fortunate to be housed in the hut; my tarp would stop much less of this cold wind. In the morning, I wake from a deep sleep to the sounds of the croo in the kitchen. Biscuit has already put away her sleeping gear. I hustle to get myself up before they start putting food on the table above me.

The hut croo does a skit during breakfast, a takeoff on *Star Wars*. The costume for the young man playing Princess Leia is a pair of bagels strapped to his head like earmuffs. Darth Vader has a colander for a helmet and wears a black graduation robe. "Come to the Dark Side, Luke. You won't have to pack out your trash."

"Well, it *is* kinda heavy..."

Also, a croo member reads the weather report from the Mount Washington Observatory. It is forty-two degrees, wind gusting up to sixty-six miles per hour, wind chill twenty-eight degrees, visibility one hundred feet. Biscuit and I agree that it's safer if we hike together, at least until we're over Mount Madison.

The trail heads directly up the rocky summit of Mount Madison, a pile of rocks that is tough enough to negotiate without steady forty-mile-per-hour winds. The air is crisp and cold, the wind growing stronger as we climb. Sparse clouds are in the sky, white and wispy, blowing past at surreal speed, like frames of time-lapse video. I wear every bit of clothing I have, including rain gear, and I still feel cold despite the exertion of hiking uphill. Two packless guests from the hut are ahead. They approach the summit crawling on all fours, unable to stand in the wind. Their jackets fill with wind and extend above their backs like parachutes. Near the peak the gusts are so strong I can't move safely, and so I stay put for a minute or more, bracing myself against the wind. When blown from behind, I lean into the boulders and crawl, following the example of the hikers before me.

Biscuit and Awol on the summit of Mount Madison.

After the summit, there are still a few miles of ridge above tree line. My hands are numb inside my gloves. The trail turns east and follows a long, narrow ridgeline on a gradual downhill slope. The wind, blowing strongly from our right, displaces me each time I lift a foot, yet I have to be careful to land on flat, stable rocks. It takes Biscuit and me three hours to travel three miles from Madison Hut. Biscuit's pack cover blows off her pack, saved by a cord snagging on her shoulder strap. She looks downwind, to the north where all the land we see is below us, and asks, "Where do you think that would have come down?"

"In Maine," I answer.

Below timberline, the weather warms quickly. Off come the jacket, long pants, and gloves. By the time we reach Pinkham Notch, I am in shorts and a T-shirt. Two hours ago the wind chill was below freezing. Pinkham Notch is a major trailhead on New Hampshire Route 16, about eleven miles from Gorham. AMC runs a resort at Pinkham Notch, and there is a large parking lot bustling with guests and day hikers. Arrow is here waiting for us; he takes me and Biscuit into Gorham.

We stay at the Barn Hostel, an inexpensive backpacker bunkroom adjacent to a bed and breakfast. The building is shaped like a barn, with real beds, not bunks. Twin beds and queen beds are lined up in the loft like a mattress showroom. There are at least a dozen thru-hikers. I recognize Spock, a thru-hiker I last saw in the Smokies. Spock and his wife had jumped up to Katahdin and started hiking south (flip-flopped). They were in the 100-Mile Wilderness when his wife took a frightening fall.[38] She sustained a laceration on her head and bruises everywhere. Spock said they were very fortunate to chance upon a ranger and get a ride out of the woods. His wife had to end her thru-hike.

Completion of the Presidential Range is a significant milestone for me. I am celebrating with a day off in Gorham. Since the start of my hike, I have told people, "I am headed for Maine," and now I am on the doorstep of the final state. I feel like I'm on the home stretch, even though I still have more than three hundred miles to go, and many

---

38   The 100-Mile Wilderness is the most remote stretch of the AT, spanning from Monson, Maine, to the southern boundary of Baxter State Park.

of them will be difficult. Arrow is in town again today, and he treats me to a lakeside grill of sausage, chicken, and corn on the cob at Jericho Lake just outside of town. Later, we go to see Glen Ellis Falls near Pinkham Notch. From there, we can see hikers traversing rock ledges on the way up Wildcat Mountain. That's where I go next.

Gorham reminds me of Hot Springs in that it is a town concentrated along Main Street. It is a tourist town, with more hotels and restaurants than would normally be supported by its meager resident population. Some stores and hotels have "Nous Parlons Francais" signs; we are only sixty miles from the Canadian border. There are gift shops with moose and bear sculptures on the lawns. High-peaked roofs, the six-foot-tall ice cream cone on the parlor, and the clock atop the red town hall stand out brilliantly against the vivid blue sky. Further in the distance, the White Mountains form a razor-sharp horizon. In the winter, the town fills with skiers. Now, in late August, hikers are everywhere.

On the streets I see Muktuk, a hiker I met in Erwin. He flip-flopped from Harpers Ferry and is getting off the trail after reaching Mount Washington. He is out of time and motivation and seems resigned to his decision to end it here. I recall the excited conversation Muktuk led back at Overmountain Shelter and am sad for how it contrasts with his somber mood today. Our time back then was analogous to college graduation; now we talk of retirement.

I think of what I am doing on the trail. What have I accomplished? My time on the trail has been fantastic, but there has been no epiphany. I've nearly used up my quota of time being Awol. I have to go back to the real world, earn a living, and support a family. I have no insight into how I can return and avoid the doldrums that brought me here.

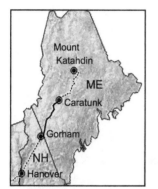

13
Gorham to
Caratunk

When my father took us hiking as kids, I was lukewarm about the trips. Yeah, the mountains looked neat and all, but couldn't we just drive around and look at them? Why'd we have to walk for miles and camp for nights on end and eat such nasty food? My dad's idea of good trail food was mincemeat and Vienna sausages. I couldn't discern how my older brother Chris felt about our trips; he was the least expressive person in our family.

In 1981 Chris spent a couple of weeks hiking in Florida, and then he hitched up to Georgia and started hiking on the AT. When he reached Damascus, he decided he would continue hiking all the way to Maine. In that year, only 140 thru-hikes were recorded. Gear and the trail itself have changed since then, and Chris was an iconoclast even in his own time. He hiked with no shelter, no stove, and very little money.

I was in college when Chris thru-hiked. I was hankering to join the workforce and little attuned to his adventure. For the next twenty years, until meeting the retiree thru-hiker in the Smokies, I would think of thru-hiking as something that

Chris Miller at the conclusion of his 1981 thru-hike.

free-spirited young people like Chris do instead of going to college.

When I was near thirty years old, I went for a short backpacking trip with Juli and a friend. It was even harder than I remembered from my trips as a child. I suffered from leg cramps; we got rained on and terrorized by lightning.

We cut our trip short. I concluded that age had rendered me unsuitable for carrying a backpack for any significant distance.

Coincident with my inspiration by the retiree, I had been taking better care of my health, and I began to rethink my suitability for the trail. I'm tolerant of physical discomfort, I travel well, and I don't have to shower every day. I have a strong, slow, runner's heartbeat, even though I've never been a dedicated runner.

Upon deciding that I would thru-hike, I spoke with Chris. He contributed to my feeling that thru-hiking is best done alone, but he couldn't convince me to take on his minimalist style.

"I think I'll take a tent. They make them nowadays that only weigh three or four pounds," I said.

"How much do they weigh when they're wet?" Chris asked pointedly.

❀ ❀ ❀

I get a late start from Gorham and worry about the long slack-pack that I am planning. Only a block down the road it rains hard enough for me to stop and put on my pack cover. Looking out to the mountains, the clouds collide with the peaks and twist into swirls of gray and white. I also decide to put on rain pants. It is an annoying task because I have to take my shoes off to put them on. My pack is falling apart; again the supports fall out of place and drop all the weight on my shoulders. Also, there are curved metal rods on each side of the pack that have worn loose from their cloth stays. The rods spin out of place and poke me in the rear. The pack spurs me like I'm carrying a little jockey.

The sum of my frustrations leads me to turn around and stay in Gorham for another day. I spend the day regrouping for the remainder of my hike. I find new rain pants with zippered legs, and I rig up my pack once more.

Juli and I speak on the phone. She has had a difficult day, too. She has been working, mothering three kids, posting my journal, and sending me packages, along with all of the other household chores. "I'm ready for it to be over," she says, referring to my hike and the situation it has put her in.

Before leaving for my hike, I needed to know that Juli was committed to staying the course at home. It would not have been wise to take on the AT if she had given only a half-hearted "if that's what you want to do" acceptance. If that had been the case, she would be too inclined to reproach me while I was away. I could imagine a nearly tangible band stretching back home, tugging with more resistance as I headed north. Juli has been supportive, never wanting me to quit, and up until now, sparing me any guilt over making her life more challenging. She only tells me now, knowing that it cannot be construed as calling me back home.

When I had told one friend, a married woman, about my plans for a four- to five-month. AT thru-hike she said, "Good thing you're not married to me." She was right, but it was best not to tell her so.

Juli and I also finalize plans for the end of the hike. Juli, our daughters, and Juli's two brothers will fly to Maine on September 16. My timeline is now fixed. I have twenty-one days to hike 314 miles.

I leave Gorham after my second night in town, planning to return after my slack-pack today. The AT from Pinkham Notch to Wildcat Mountain is rigorous, often inclined steeply enough for me to lean forward and touch the trail with my hands. Even after hiking over eighteen hundred miles, I sometimes feel winded and my thighs burn a short way into an uphill climb. Usually it means I'm going too fast. I slow down, find my pace, and think about something else. Next thing I know, I've gone another hundred yards and I'm no longer struggling.

A group of hikers ahead are having difficulty with the climb. As I pass they make comments: "Look at him, just waltzing up the trail." Of course they are unaware of how I have to manage my own struggle. If a person who has not had enough exercise attempts to backpack, then he will find the going difficult. He might think, "I sweat, I get out of breath, I'm out of shape." But he is wrong to think the tribulation is uniquely his. Everyone sweats; everyone pants for breath. The person who is in better shape will usually push himself to hike more quickly and bump into the same limitations. But when the fit person is stressed, he is less likely to attribute the difficulty to his shortcomings. Backpacking is hard—that's just the way it is. Obviously conditioning is advantageous, but the perception of disadvantage can be more debilitating than actual disadvantage.

It takes me two hours to cover the first three miles and reach the top of the ridge. At this rate, I would finish at 10:00 p.m. The remaining ridge walk is rather saw-toothed, with each mountain on it having secondary peaks. Wildcat Mountain has summits A, B, C, D, and E. Carter Mountain has South, Middle and North summits. The trail goes over every one. At 3:20 p.m. I stop at Imp Campsite to get water after traveling thirteen miles without taking my pack off. This is the farthest I've walked without a pack-off break. I'm back on the trail in fifteen minutes, needing to hike eight more miles before sunset.

A note on the side of the trail warns that a "4,000-pound moose chased a hiker" near this spot; four thousand pounds is about three times the weight of a large moose, so more than likely it was a fisherman who wrote the note. Moose tracks and droppings are everywhere. The AT is hemmed in by trees and underbrush. Occasionally a moose-trampled path cuts across the trail. Should an angry moose step onto the trail, there would be no easy exit.

The final four miles to Interstate 2 are easy and eventless, enabling me to reach the road before dark. I easily hitch a ride into town and spend my last night in New Hampshire.

I leave town in the morning and head down the road to find a good spot from which to hitchhike. A car pulls over to offer me a ride before I even stick out my thumb. The trail continues to be challenging. Much like yesterday, I have a long ascent to the ridgeline, and then I bounce over many summits along the ridge. Plateaus high on the ridge are sometimes muddy, even swampy enough for bog bridges. Most of the summits have open areas with exposed bedrock, trimmed with straggly krummholtz, low shrubbery, and some blueberry bushes.

As the trail descends from an unnamed hill, I can see Dream Lake through the trees. The lake is 2,650 feet high and completely encircled by the forest. Near the perimeter a few boulders poke through the rippled surface of the lake. From my vantage point thirty yards above the water, it looks like one of the boulders is moving. I stop to get a better look, my mind trying to reconcile the bizarre sight of a boulder moving about in the water. I'm considering the plausibility of a manatee or a seal being in the mountains of Maine when the head of a moose rises from the water. I ease my way down to the lakeshore, and the moose either doesn't see me or is unperturbed by my presence. She continues her routine, dipping her head to the lake bottom to feed, allowing her body to float so she can rotate.

Moose feeding in Dream Lake, Maine.

I meet up with Ken and Marcia at Gentian Pond Shelter and hike with them the rest of the day. We would stay on a similar schedule for the remainder of the trail. I've spent more time with them than with any other thru-hikers, and they are outstanding company. Ken is unflappably genial. Marcia is the more driven of the two; she is definitely not just tagging along with her spouse. Marcia is a reader, and we spend hours discussing books.

The last four miles of our day are difficult, with steep climbs and descents. Trail builders have erected log ladders to help us up or down some of the many rock ledges. Late in the day we come to a sign posted on a tree:

WELCOME TO MAINE
The way life should be

We arrive at Carlo Col Shelter after 7:00 p.m. It is cold and nearly dark. I cook and eat in the shelter with my legs in my sleeping bag.

I plan for a short day, less than ten miles, because today I will traverse some of the most difficult terrain on the AT.

The morning is cold, below forty degrees, and windy as I head for the open summit of Goose Eye Mountain. I pass two southbound hikers and both have scraped knees. After Goose Eye Mountain, the trail descends to Mahoosuc Notch, a mile-long ravine reputed to be the hardest mile on the Appalachian Trail.

The notch is an alleyway between two steeply sloped mountain ridges, filled with boulders that have tumbled down from the mountainsides. The boulders are huge; many are as big as cars, some as big as trailers. They lay hodge-podge at different angles with gaps between them. The white blazes, almost entirely on rocks, just give a general idea of the intended path. Each chooses his own path, deciding when to go over or around, left or right, at every impasse.

At the start of the section, I collapse my trekking poles and tuck them into my pack. I'll use my arms as much as my legs, pulling myself up and dipping myself down. I enjoy navigating the obstacles and the uniqueness of the experience. It is more of a physical challenge than an aerobic challenge, and it is a time-consuming process. Hikers generally take fifty minutes to two hours to traverse the notch. I try to stay atop the boulders, and with the weight of my pack I can lunge three or four feet across the gaps between boulders. When the crevasse is too wide or the boulders too uneven, I descend into the rubble and pick my way through smaller rocks.

Sometimes white arrows are painted funneling all hikers through the same slot. A few times this is done to put hikers through a squeeze below a gap in the boulders. Most hikers need to take their packs off and push them through the tunnel ahead. I am able to keep my snug internal frame pack on through the tunnels, but once I nearly get stuck as I belly crawl. Inside the last of the tunnels I find a water bottle that had been dislodged from the pack of a hiker before me.

As soon as the trail exits the Mahoosuc Notch, another challenging mile of trail begins. The AT heads steeply up Mahoosuc Arm, gaining fifteen hundred feet of elevation in the next mile. The surface of the trail is almost entirely rock, like a sloppily poured concrete coating. The "sidewalk" is the core of the mountain, exposed by hikers wearing away the soil. There is soil, duff, and spruce trees on either side of the trail. Walking is difficult on this hard, sloped surface. I am taking my time, eliminating the challenge by choosing not to fight the mountain. I climb slowly and stop often.

There is a ray of sunlight through a break in the trees, and I lie on the slab of rock that has been warmed. I take out my fleece and use it as a pillow. My body enjoys the rest, but my mind is not tired enough to sleep. Further up the mountain I chase away a squirrel and sit on the log he vacated. He goes up a tree and complains. He comes back down onto the other end of the log to confront me. He makes tiny little lurches toward me with every obscenity he squeaks. I wonder if he will attack and what strategy he may have to overcome the size differential.

After the summit, I make a short descent to thirty-four hundred feet, where Speck Pond is nestled into a flat between the peaks of Mahoosuc Arm and Old Speck Mountain. The trail circles around the shoreline to Speck Pond Campsite and Shelter, where I will spend the night. The pond is large, larger than Dream Lake that I passed yesterday. My walk along half of its shoreline is longer than a quarter-mile. In Maine, it seems that "pond" or "lake" is an attribute ascribed at the discretion of the person naming the body of water.

Ken and Marcia are in the shelter, along with a southbound flip-flopper named Detour. This is an AMC-run campsite, and a caretaker has her semipermanent tent set up nearby. An Outward Bound group is tenting in the camp-site area. There is a fee for shelter use, but we all do work-for-stay. Detour and I are assigned the task of scouring the grounds for trash. I find nothing. Detour tags along behind me and confirms my findings. Ken and Marcia get the job of answering the Outward Bound group's questions about thru-hiking.

Usually I lay my head on a stuff sack filled with unused clothes. Tonight I am without a pillow because it is so cold that I wear everything to bed, including my rain jacket and pants, gloves, and my fleece cap.

I start my hike in the morning at the same time as Ken and Marcia, and we make the short but steep ascent up Old Speck Mountain together. The sky is blue, and large ponds, a deeper hue of blue, dot the expansive landscape visible from the rocky mountaintop. Ken and Marcia are on the trail below me, winding through the mix of stubby ever-greens and boulders. The speckled gray granite contrasts wonderfully with the deep green of the forest. It is a scene exemplary of Maine, the most beautiful state on the trail.

After a quick descent from Old Speck, I begin a long and arduous climb of West Baldpate. It is increasingly dif-ficult the higher I go. The trail leads directly uphill with no switchbacks, on a slope varying from fifteen to thirty-five de-grees, about the same slope range as the average residential roof. It is deeply rutted by erosion. Ruggedness can often be equated with unspoiled wilderness, but in this case, the dif-ficulty is due to the poor trail routing and the trail's popu-larity. Thousands of hikers use this section of trail every year, pounding away at the firmament that holds the soil in place. Initially, the path would have been difficult due to the steep-ness, but the terrain would have been smoother and cov-ered by soil, like the land on either side of the trail. Water from rainfall and melting snow channel into this cleared, slightly depressed path, streaming away loose soil. Rock and deadfall lie scattered on the trail, in a snapshot of their slow-motion tumble down the mountain. Tree roots exposed by soil loss form a ledge one foot, two feet, sometimes three feet high. At times soil is washed away below the roots, leaving them suspended like thick trip wires.

From Baldpate's West Peak, I look ahead to the East Peak, which is slightly higher. The top of East Baldpate is a head of stone, rounded if viewed from afar. Trees grow in a ring down from the peak, like the remnants of hair on a balding man. The trail is a visible scar across the saddle between the summits. The clearing atop East Peak, which looked like a smooth mound of stone from a mile away, is full of lumps, cracks, and ledges. Puddles of dirt and pebbles gather inside the irregularities, in which ground-hugging plants take hold. Knee-high trees, some of which may be over a hundred years old, are scattered about taking lonely stands on the weather-beaten mountaintop.

The East Peak of Baldpate.

The AT down the north face of East Baldpate is dangerously steep. Bedrock bulges out from the ground in mounded slabs ten to thirty feet long. Some of the slabs are sloped downward at an angle of forty-five degrees or more, and often are tilted to one side. Even though some of the angles are too steep for me to stand on, I find that I can walk down them if I am gutsy enough to scurry down without stopping. Some of the surfaces end with a drop-off, so this technique is not always an option. I am not too proud to sit and scoot down the rock on my behind; it is better than doing so involuntarily. Mostly, hikers skirt along the edge of the down-sloping bedrock, gaining footholds in the soil at the fringes and grabbing trailside trees to keep from slipping. The trees look abused and wobble at the roots like loose teeth.

Caution is on my mind. I've heard of two people who have been injured in Maine, ending their attempts to thru-hike. In Gorham I received an e-mail from No-Hear-Um, whom I last saw in Virginia before he had jumped up to Katahdin and started hiking south. Now, he is off the trail. He had lost too much weight on his journey; he felt weak and took too many falls on the precarious trail in this state. He decided to end his hike rather than risk getting injured.

The trail levels, and it looks like I should pass the last few miles of the day in relative safety. The most innocuous-looking branch lies across the trail, not more than an inch in diameter, and not more than a few inches off the ground. Stepping over, surely I've lifted my foot high enough to clear, but the branch lurches up to catch my toe. This is a problem, because the foot now caught on the branch is the one I was counting on having in front of me. I lurch forward with my torso horizontal to the ground. My pack has more momentum than my body. It is a slave to gravity and wants to dive into the ground, uncaring that my face will go with it. My free leg is hopping, frantically trying to do the work of two legs, and my arms are trying to keep up by pumping away at my trekking poles. Finally, my foot breaks free and I am spared.

East B Hill Road is a road with little traffic, but a truck comes along just as I reach it, and I get a ride into the town of Andover. I stop to eat at the diner. Ken and Marcia have arrived, and we eat dinner together. A wall of the diner is adorned with pictures of hikers who have completed the pancake challenge. If you can eat three pancakes, you get them for free. It doesn't sound like much of a challenge unless you see the photographs. Each pancake is as big as the plate, and about an inch thick. After dinner, Marcia, Ken, and I visit the grocer across the street. We will make our own pancakes in the morning.

All trail towns tempt me to describe them as "quaint," but Andover seems most deserving of the adjective. The town is centered on the intersection of Main Street and the road on which I arrive. On each side of Main Street there are only a handful of buildings. The largest, a pretty three-story building with white siding, is Andover Guest House. The house has bed and breakfast quality rooms for travelers and a special bunkroom for hikers. This is the cleanest hiker accommodation I've stayed in, thanks to the fastidious owner, "Ladyinnkeeper." "Packs and shoes stay outside," she says. She delivers her statements in bursts, like she is paying for air time, but any time she has saved is lost by me pausing to absorb the flood of words.

In the morning Ladyinnkeeper drives me back to the trail. She will pick me up today at another road crossing ten trail miles from here, and I will return to the guest house for another night's stay. Ten miles is a short day, and I don't have to cook or set up camp. It's just a walk in the woods.

The first six miles are easy, and then there is the moderately difficult ascent and descent of Moody Mountain. I struggle a bit on the climb. I've learned that as I tire my form gets sloppy, which makes matters worse. I tend to get duck-footed and let my weight drag. I can perform more efficiently if I keep my feet aligned with the trail, take shorter strides, and lean a bit forward when going uphill. If there is any science to my claims, it is coincidental; they are based only on feel. If I make a particularly steep step, I may plant both trekking poles and pull with my arms. Most of the time I avoid "ski-poling" and plant only one at a time. If I am on clear and level ground, I will pick up my poles and carry them by their balance point (near the center), one in each hand. My hike has made me a believer in trekking poles. They have saved me from a number of falls.

Back in Andover, I speak with Juli on the phone. The temperature in Florida is ninety-three degrees. In the morning, the temperature in Andover is thirty-eight degrees. Ken and Marcia also stayed at the guest house last night, so for the second consecutive morning, we make ourselves a pancake breakfast.

Continuing north, my hike starts with a long climb to the summit of Old Blue Mountain. The stunted pines, which cap nearly every mountain in Maine, are particularly dense and green on Old Blue. I've found a perfect chair-height lump of granite where I sit and write until Ken and Marcia come along. I hike with them, and we pass the miles talking. The trail stays fairly high on the ridge after Old Blue, and the weather is wonderful.

I reach State Road 17. Nearby there is a pull-off occupied by a handful of cars. Their owners are looking out to the mountain range and to a sprawling blue lake with an island of trees in the center. From there I hitch a ride into Rangeley, a small resort town, and stay at Gull Pond Hostel.

"Hello, Awol," Crossroads says as he steps out of the bunkroom to greet me.

I last saw Crossroads in the Shenandoah National Park. He wrote a register entry in New York saying he left the trail to return to his job. Now I eagerly listen as he tells the rest of the story. He worked only for one week before deciding it was more important for him to finish the trail. He quit, went up to Katahdin and has been hiking south. He'll have to find a new job when he finishes. Crossroads seems very happy, and I'm happy for him.

I update him on my progress, telling him of my sprained ankle and my struggles with the heat in New York and rain in Vermont.

"Geez, I thought none of that would bother you," he says.

"Why would you think that?" I answer.

"You were such a machine back when we met in North Carolina. I thought you were some military type, like a sergeant."

My recollection is of Crossroads powering up Standing Indian Mountain. He is younger than I am; he was hiking faster and was on a more ambitious schedule. At the time we first met, I was mired in doubt about my ability to thru-hike. We all perceive that the other guy has it easier than we do; we all assume that others know our inner doubts.

Bob, the owner of Gull Pond Hostel, takes me and Crossroads to the trailhead in the morning. He drives cautiously, explaining the hazards of driving roads through the woods where there is a moose population. Bob hit a sixteen-hundred-pound moose a couple of years ago. It came through his windshield, fractured his eye socket, and broke his hand. Four drivers have been killed this year in collisions with moose in Maine.

Crossroads and I part ways after our brief reunion. He will go south, and I head north. A short way up the trail, I find trail magic. Bottles of Gatorade are perched on rocks about fifty feet apart. I take one with me to have later with my lunch. I will return to Rangeley tonight from State Road 4, thirteen miles from where I started this morning.

The AT since Gorham has been as challenging as the trail anywhere. I feel sluggish and worn down. The trail is a bit easier today, as if it is cooperating with my lesser capabilities. The elevation goes no higher than twenty-seven hundred feet. I never get above tree line, and I stay submerged within a forest of spruce and birch. There are a few ponds and stretches of level walking along their shorelines. I do not see another hiker until returning to town.

I hitch back to Rangeley, having finished my hike early in the afternoon. I have time to mill about the downtown area. Rangeley is a resort town, similar to Gorham, with hotels and restaurants dominating Main Street. There is a full-sized grocery store, so I wander the aisles marveling at the abundance. I buy a package of cookies and a Coke and sit on a bench out front, blissfully eating away. Down the street at the laundromat, I use the bathroom to change into a fleece jacket and my rain pants so I can launder everything else. Everything else is just a fraction of a load. Ken and Marcia show up, as their clothes are nearing the end of the wash cycle. I sit with them in the laundromat, and among the smell of soap and the sound of tumbling clothes, we catch up on each other's days. I eat dinner with Ken and Marcia and then visit the Rangeley Inn, where they are staying. An enormous moose head adorns the lobby.

Bob again gives me a morning ride to the trailhead, this time at the intersection of the AT with State Road 4 where I ended my hike yesterday. The air is chilly, and there is a hazy cover of fog. Most of the first six miles of my day are uphill, since the trail is leading to the summit of Saddleback Mountain.

As I approach, I see that the peak is open and rocky, much like the Baldpates. Wind has blown away the fog. I eagerly rush to the top of the mountain because the guidebook says that Katahdin can be seen from the summit of Saddleback. I can see fog settled in pockets in the valleys, but it does not prevent me from seeing distant peaks. Dozens of mountains are visible. The Horn, the next mountain over which the AT passes, is only a mile away, and I can see trees and a rocky top. The more distant mountains lose detail and take on a bluish tint. The mountains furthest on the horizon are gray and blend with the color of the vanishing sky. I don't know where to look for Katahdin; it could be on either side of the Horn, depending on the bend of the trail. What would distinguish it from other peaks? Faraway mountains look uniform, like waves on the ocean. For a moment, I fool myself into thinking that Katahdin is one distinctive peak on the horizon, but I have no means to confirm my guess.

Katahdin is still more than two hundred trail miles away, which may make it about one hundred miles by line of sight. Nevertheless, I repeat my search from the summit of the Horn. I cannot even relocate the distant mountain that I thought looked most distinctive from Saddleback. The descent from the Horn is steep and time-consuming for me to traverse. The ascents of my day have been much less bothersome than the descents. Walking uphill is more strenuous, but it is a positive, constructive sort of strain. I imagine it strengthens my muscles and improves my aerobic capacity. It's hard to put a positive spin on the strain of walking downhill. My knees are jarred and my toes are crammed into the front of my shoes. It is mentally stressful because if I was to take a fall, I would slide, flip, or tumble before coming to a stop.

Saddleback Junior is the third significant mountain of the day. After I toil up and over this mountain, I am happy to transition to a stretch of fairly low and level land. There are streams to cross. These streams usually must be forded, but the recent dry weather has made it possible for me to pick my way across by jumping rock to rock.

I come to what looks like an overgrown logging road, and I scan the area briefly before locating the trail that continues on the far side of the road. The trail soon becomes challenging, wiggling through dense woods and then leading up a steep slope. There is a stream cascading down to my right and woods on my left; this looks like the path I should be on, but it is unusually sandy. My feet slide back in the sand, so I reach forward to grab whatever handholds I can find. I have to throw aside some dead branches. My feet dig trenches in the sand, uncovering a deteriorated log ladder. I wish it had been replaced by another ladder, rather than covered by sand. The work of climbing through this drains my energy. At the top of the dirt-covered path, I see another road-width path, curving at a nice grade up the hill. Trees alongside the "road" are marked with white blazes. For the past half mile, I should have been on that nicely graded road; instead, I was struggling, bushwhacking through an earlier routing of the AT that had been intentionally covered with debris by the builders of the new path.

After I cross the road, I see a stream off the trail to my left. The stream is moving slowly, bending around a flat piece of ground. The gap between the trail and the stream narrows as the trail begins to incline up the mountain. I look over to the stream, also on an incline now, lively and cascading over rocks. It is late in the day, and I begin to feel cold, even with the effort of hiking uphill. I am tired and it is apparent that I will not reach the next shelter today, so I consider looking for a place to tarp. The AT diverges from Perham Stream, into steep terrain with heavy underbrush. The flat that I passed a quarter of a mile ago comes to mind, and I backtrack to set up camp at that location.

The only clearing large enough for a tarp is on the other side of the stream. The stream is too wide to jump, so I make fruitless sorties up and down it looking for a narrowing or an opportunity to rock-hop. Not wanting to waste too much time, I simply step through the stream, wetting my feet. My tarp site is cozy, softened by fallen leaves. The stream trickles past, and the bank beside me is vivid green with moss. Moose tracks and droppings indicate that my site may be on their path to water. If one were to pass through in the night, I wonder if it would trample my tarp, either failing to see it or mistaking it for a bush.

After setting up my tarp, I drag a stone to the area just in front and use it as a seat while I prepare and eat my dinner. I am pleased with having such an ideal solo campsite. I leave the stove running after my meal is prepared and use it to ignite a few pieces of paper trash. Then I supplement the burning paper with twigs and leaves until I have a modest campfire. The sky is darkening and the temperature drops. I feel a chill on my back, but my face, my hands, and my knees are warmed by the fire.

Tarping last night and the coldness of this morning remind me of my first night on the trail, of earthy pleasures of traveling through the woods that I now tend to take for granted. I start the day invigorated. The trail goes up and down at a more even grade, so it doesn't feel like the day is much work, even with a good amount of elevation gain and loss.

I run out of water. Streams have been abundant in Maine, so I had not been paying close attention to my water supply. I pass a group of day hikers on the way up Crocker Mountain and ask about water in this section of trail. They are locals, who know the area well. They say I will pass no more streams before reaching the town of Stratton seven miles away, and they quickly add that they will give me some of their water. Each of them pours a cupful from his bottle into mine, and one of them gives me a handful of apple slices.

I reach the trailhead at State Road 27 at the same time as yet another day hiker. He offers me a ride into the appealing, tiny town of Stratton. My last workplace had more employees than Stratton has residents. There is a post office, a diner, a small grocery store, and a couple of motels. I stay in a motel that has six rooms. The White Wolf Inn next door has no vacancies because it is "overwhelmed" by about a dozen hikers.

Most of the hikers are in the rustic White Wolf Restaurant. Ken and Marcia are having pie to celebrate Marcia's birthday. There are more than a handful of thru-hikers, and section hiker 81 is here. 81 started hiking north from Springer Mountain twenty-two years ago, in 1981. Hence the trail name. He uses whatever vacation time he can manage, usually two weeks or less each summer, to piece together a hike of the entire Appalachian Trail. He will stop at Monson, Maine, this year and finish the trail in 2004.

Ever since the two-week period of rain that plagued me through Vermont, I have had good luck with the weather. It has rained, but I have been dodging it. I took a zero in Gorham on a wet day. It rained just after I snuck into the town of Andover. It rains hard overnight in Stratton. It is still raining in the morning. That is okay; I need to wait for the post office to open so I can retrieve my mail drop, and I need to write another newspaper article. I have breakfast at the diner and supplement my supplies at the grocer. I sit in White Wolf Restaurant to write, and by the time I am finished I am ready for lunch.

I return to the trail, planning to hike five miles out to the first shelter. It is a good chunk of trail to tackle in a short day since there is a nineteen-hundred-foot climb. Skies are overcast, and the trail is still damp from the morning rain. I am the first to arrive at Horns Pond Shelters at 5:30 p.m. Nearly as soon as I take my pack off, I feel the temperature drop. It will be a cold night. There are two spacious shelters. Each can hold about nine hikers, but only three more hikers arrive after I do: Ken, Marcia, and Crash Test Dummy. We all use the same shelter, thinking it will be best to share our warmth. Crash Test Dummy is hiking south. He started in Quebec and is hiking a route known as the Eastern Continental Trail that encompasses the AT and a handful of other trails. The southern terminus of the ECT is in Key West.[39]

I take time in the morning to plan out the rest of my hike. I should make it to the base of Katahdin easily by September 16, hiking less than twenty miles every day. It is comforting to have a relatively easy schedule ahead of me.

North from Horns Pond Shelters, I begin the ascent of Bigelow Mountain. The sky is wonderfully clear, allowing me to see my surroundings in such detail that I feel as though my vision has improved. The trail bends to the left and curls

---

39   On January 9, 2005, in Florida, well over a year after completing my hike, I drove across the southern part of the state, just above Lake Okeechobee. There was little traffic on two-lane Highway 98, miles from any town. I stopped in the middle of the road to talk to a hiker walking alongside it. In a lifetime of living in Florida, I had never seen a backpacker while driving. I asked if he was on the Florida Trail. He said yes and added that the Florida Trail is part of the Eastern Continental Trail, which he had started in Canada two years ago. Finally, recognition kicked in for both of us. It was Crash Test Dummy.

snakelike up the steep mountain. Through an opening in the dense but stunted spruce, I have a view back down to the saddle where I started the morning. Scanning carefully, I find the green roofs of the twin shelters and Horns Pond. It looks as if it is further below me than behind; my progress has been more upward than northward.

I continue uphill until the trees end and all that is before me is the rocky pinnacle. The sun is directly behind the peak, like it is impaled on the apex. The steepness of the final fifty yards is accentuated by the beams radiating down from up high. The rocky scene looks like an overexposed black and white photograph. Atop the mountain, color is restored. Alpine vegetation has already been singed by the cold and is deep reddish brown and orange. Ahead, I can see the second summit of this same mountain, which is called Avery Peak. The saddle between the peaks is dense with evergreens. Below, to the west, Flagstaff Lake is expansive and brilliant blue.

Avery Peak. Flagstaff Lake is to the left.

The trail descends all the way to Flagstaff Lake and passes briefly along its beachy shoreline. Down below timberline, the deciduous trees have started dropping red and yellow leaves. I cross Long Falls Dam Road, briefly stopping to sit on the pavement where "2000 mi." is painted in footlong white letters. The trail skirts West Carry Pond, and there is a shelter near the shore where I stop for the night. Ken, Marcia, and section hiker 81 also stay in the shelter.

I hike out from West Carry Pond Shelter with 81. The trail is very easy. I plan to reach the town of Caratunk today. It is fourteen miles away, just beyond the Kennebec River. My guidebook lists no elevation higher than the elevation of the shelter, so it looks to be an easy day. The trail meanders a little, crosses a few streams, and follows the shoreline of East Carry Pond. 81 and I catch up with Ken and Marcia, and we all stop for lunch at Pierce Pond Lean-to. Pierce Pond Stream flows out from Pierce Pond for three miles before emptying into the Kennebec River. The AT parallels the course of the stream.

The Kennebec is about seventy yards wide, for the moment slow moving. A bed of rocks, only slightly submerged, extends from the woods thirty feet into the river. There is a delta of rock where Pierce Pond Stream merges into the river. Sparkling clear water from the stream bubbles over the rocks. The river is the widest crossed by the AT without a bridge. Despite its width, the river looks shallow and tame enough to ford, but I have heard a number of warnings against fording. There is a dam upriver that releases on no set schedule, so the river could rise unpredictably. Two couples in canoes whisk by. Their canoes are in the deepest part of the river, closer to the far shore, and the speed of their canoes shows that the river is more powerful than it looks. In 1985 a hiker drowned trying to ford the river. Since then, a ferry service has been provided.

Ken, Marcia, and the Kennebec ferryman.

We wait about an hour before the ferry, a man with a canoe, arrives. He can take two hikers at a time, and Ken and Marcia go first. Suddenly, the current of the river strengthens, evident by deep ripples midstream. I take my camera and walk out as far as I can on the bed of rocks to get their picture as the canoe pulls away. The tide rises rapidly, moving three inches up the rock I am standing on and nearing my feet. By the time I return twenty feet to my pack, which I thought was on the shore, water has caught up to me and soaks the bottom of my pack.

Across the river, the trail crosses U.S. 201, a road parallel to the river. I turn right on 201 and travel a short way to Main Street of Caratunk, Maine. These are two of the four paved roads in Caratunk, a town with a population of about one hundred. I will stay the night at the Caratunk House, a large home with a hiker hostel built into the loft of a barn. Paul, the owner, is out front grilling hamburgers on the carpetlike lawn. The hostel is extremely comfortable, but my stay is brief. In the morning, I head north again after a hearty breakfast of eggs, French toast, coffee, juice, bananas, cantaloupe, and blueberry muffins.

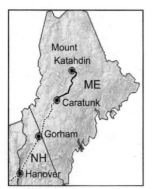

14
Caratunk to
Katahdin

Section hiker 81 is on his way up Moxie Bald when I join him. From the stony flank of the mountain, we have views to other hills and to ponds below. The views are similar to those I had from Bigelow Mountain two days ago, yet the elevation is little more than half as high. There will not be another mountain anywhere close to four thousand feet until I reach Katahdin. 81 and I hike together to Moxie Bald Lean-to, two miles from the summit. Walking is pleasant on slightly sloped inclines, with open views to the ponds of Maine. The walk is not strenuous and we have breath to spare, so we talk the rest of the way to the shelter.

We are like-minded in our views about economics, and I find it easy to converse openly with him. My part of the conversation drifts into the financial implications of my hiking now, in midcareer. Before hiking, I hadn't really articulated my fiscal malaise. Talking it through with 81 helps me to sort out my own thoughts on the subject. My frustration over money matters contributed to my decision to take an extended hike. That rationale may seem convoluted since there is absolutely no financial upside to months of unemployment. But I had my reasons.

The period from 2000 to the time I started hiking in 2003 was difficult. The stock market bubble was deflating. The attacks on September 11, 2001, sent stocks even lower, gas prices higher, and made the future more uncertain than ever. Juli worked as a consultant in 2001. Since she had no employer to withhold taxes, I took additional withholding from my paycheck. It wasn't enough, and we were staggered when we filed our taxes at year's end. We owed an additional thirteen thousand dollars. The amount was unbelievable. We weren't rich. We had spent six child-raising years living off a single income, and we had hoped that Juli's return to work would allow us to put more money aside. The tax bill erased our savings; it was heartbreaking.

Taxes are by far the largest single expense in my life—more than cars or my house—at least double the expense of anything else. I'd spill my tax woes on others from whom I'd get no sympathy. They'd react as if it was my own fault. "You must earn a lot of money." Or, "You should have a big mortgage, find more deductions, learn about tax-free investments, have more withheld, etc." The first argument, "you earn too much," implies that striving for financial security is a sin worthy of punishment. The second set of suggestions reek of manipulation. I detest tax perks and penalties designed by the government to engineer our lives.

I succumbed to the least distasteful means of easing my tax burden. In 2002 I increased my 401K contribution and had even more money withheld for federal tax. On top of my tax woes, my twelve-year-old truck broke down, and I purchased a new vehicle using a loan against my 401K. I repaid the loan through yet another payroll deduction. Social Security, Medicare, and insurance were taken away from the remainder of my salary. For the *year*, my take-home pay was a mere 22 percent of my gross pay.

I was doing little better than breaking even; the compensation wasn't enough to keep me motivated. If I had been bringing home more, maybe I would've had a harder time walking away from my paycheck. As it was, it seemed feasible to go without a job for a while, to seek other rewards, to take ownership of my own time.

❊ ❊ ❊

There is one other hiker at the Moxie Bald Lean-to, a previous thru-hiker named Dawn. She is filling in a small section of trail that she missed during her thru-hike. 81 and I undertake building a campfire. The ground is damp, and deadwood has been picked over by earlier shelter visitors. 81 has an abundance of matches, and we have a candle and strips of bark from plentiful birch trees. We get the fire to flame up, but it dies back down. I collect more birch bark, but again we do no more than torch the most flammable pieces. Dawn makes fun of us. We are two so-called outdoorsmen, with four thousand miles of backpacking between us, and we can't start a fire. Now that our pride is on the line, we scour far and wide to round up dry twigs. I also sacrifice a lump of toilet paper, slipping it into the pit while Dawn is not looking.

At twilight I walk down to Bald Mountain Pond, the water source for the shelter. The surface of the pond is flat and smooth, except for protruding boulders and reeds near the shoreline. I sit on a boulder with my water filter, hose dangling into the water, and pump water into my bottle. Back at the shelter I lie awake in my bag, perfectly content, whiffing the smoke from our sputtering fire. I can see the nearly full moon between the dark silhouettes of spruce trees, and its rippled reflection on the pond.

"Y'all missed it," 81 says (he's from Georgia). He was the first one awake and saw a moose near the shelter. I get up and go hunting with my camera, but the moose is gone.

I have eighteen miles to go before reaching Monson, the last trail town before Katahdin. The trail is nearly devoid of elevation gain and loss, but not without challenges. Thick tree roots lie like pythons across the trail. There are rocks to traverse. There are streams to cross: the Bald Mountain Stream, the Marble Brook, and the Piscataquis River. Some of them intersect with the trail in multiple places. None of the streams are bridged, but I am able to rock-hop across most of them. A larger variety of trees grow in this low-lying stretch of the trail. I walk through colorful stands of birch and maple trees.

In Monson, I find the largest group of northbound thru-hikers that I have seen since Gorham, including Ken and Marcia, Kiwi, Dreamwalker, Chief, and Jan Liteshoe. I met Chief and Jan back at Caratunk; Kiwi and Dreamwalker are new to me. All of us are electrified with the prospect of finishing the trail. It is all but over; 114 miles is like an afterthought in the scale of our journey.

Monson is about the size of Stratton, but there are no motels and no shops catering to tourists. Both restaurants on Main Street are closed. I visit the general store. It is no larger than a convenience store and peddles everything from food to clothes, drugs, cattle feed, and socket wrenches. Outside there is a pay phone, where I stand calling home at twilight. The sky is a brilliant purple, in its transition from blue to black, dark enough for the moon and stars to shine brightly in contrast. Trees and rooftops form a jagged horizon.

I stay at Shaw's Boarding House. Hungry Hiker is here; he is a young man I last saw in Virginia. He now has a head full of curly red hair and seems to have grown six inches taller. He finished his thru-hike over a week ago, with time to spare before his flight back to Israel, so he hiked south, back through the 100-Mile Wilderness. Hungry Hiker is a voracious eater. Pat Shaw's breakfast choices are "1-around," "2-around," "3-around," and so forth. Hungry Hiker has the 4-around, which means four blueberry pancakes, four eggs, four sausage links, four slices of ham, and four pieces of bacon, along with hash browns, coffee, and juice. Meals are served family style; all of us come to the table together. Ten hikers sit at one long table in the eat-in kitchen, and five more take seats at an overflow table on the porch. Hungry Hiker had Shaw's big breakfast yesterday, and he advises me to get only the 3-around. It is bad advice because it leaves me feeling hungry. Fortunately, Pat brings out a plate full of doughnuts. My typical trail breakfast is three packets of instant oatmeal and hot chocolate. Shaw's breakfast is far better. With meals like this, I've been able to maintain the same weight (about 160) since the middle of the AT.

Keith Shaw Jr., the son of the owners, will give Kiwi and me a ride back to the trail. Kiwi is a nimble sixty-one-year-old thru-hiker from New Zealand. He and his hiking partner, Dreamwalker, say their farewells. Kiwi needs to conclude his hike before his six-month visa expires, and Dreamwalker is staying in town a few extra days to meet family. For most of their hike, they had hiked in a group of four gentlemen roughly the same age, and the group was dubbed "The Four Geezers." Along the way, two fell behind. Dreamwalker and Kiwi hiked together all the way to Monson, but now have to part ways, a week away from finishing.

While we are loading the truck, a man from the house next door begins a bike ride with his two kids. The younger child is on a bike with training wheels; the older one is a girl about ten years old, similar in age to my oldest daughter. As they pull onto the road, the young one is having difficulty and falls behind. Dad looks back to see what is wrong and veers slightly toward his daughter. The daughter overreacts and jackknifes her front tire. She puts her hand out to catch herself, and the bike's handlebar falls across her arm, breaking her forearm near her petite wrist. She gets up confused and scared, holding her limp arm and calling for her father, "Dad, Dad…DAD!"

The event is troubling. I wish I could have done something; I wish kids never got hurt. They seem too tender to have to deal with pain. I take solace in believing that her initial shock and worry was the worst of it. By tonight, she'll be home eating ice cream and having friends sign her cast.

Keith Shaw drops us off at the trailhead, and we enter the 100-Mile Wilderness. From here to the base of Katahdin there is little access to civilization. The trail will cross a few logging roads, but hitches from these are improbable. A group of three young southbound hikers stop to greet me and Kiwi.

"Congratulations," they say. It is common for southbound hikers to congratulate us on the completion of our thru-hike, even now, far from Katahdin. One of the hikers looks familiar. It is Peter, the first thru-hiker I met on my journey. Back in Georgia he was a pale and timid kid; now he has filled out. He is bearded, with shaggier hair and much more confidence. We both recognize each other from a single two-minute trail passing 137 days ago. He flip-flopped and will finish his hike southbound. Just from the brief glimpse I have of his demeanor, I like the impact the trail has made on Peter.

Kiwi and I exchange equally uncertain plans for the remainder of our hike. I have a pretty good idea of where I will be each day, and I'm sure Kiwi does as well. Hiker etiquette necessitates vagueness in how you divulge your plans. If you find the new acquaintance disagreeable, you can deviate from your actual plan without effrontery. If you change plans for other reasons, you won't unintentionally offend hikers you really aren't trying to avoid.

In our walking and talking, the beauty of the scenery has not escaped me. There are still ponds, rocky summits, streams, and a variety of trees and brush. I linger at Little Wilson Falls. The falls cascade over a stepped rock wall with such uniform geometry that it looks man-made. I take a side trail to get better photo angles. By now I have concluded that Kiwi is in no way offensive—actually, he is very likable, and his pace is well matched to my own. Still, I think of my photo shoot as an opportunity for us to gracefully go our separate ways.

The next section of my walk is tiring. There is small elevation gain and loss, but little completely level ground. Continual change from uphill to downhill—roller coastering—is often more exasperating than extended climbs or descents. I push on without pause, wondering why I haven't caught up to Kiwi. I imagine the old guy ambling along while I struggle. When I arrive at Long Pond Stream Lean-to, Kiwi is there resting comfortably, looking as though he might be staying. I have my sights set on the Cloud Pond Lean-to four miles further. After a short break, I put my pack back on and notice that Kiwi does too. It occurs to me that Kiwi's vagueness of plan had a purpose I had not foreseen. I believe he did not pin himself to a specific schedule so that we might tacitly adapt to each other's plan. Kiwi has hiked with one or more partners for over two thousand miles; it is as natural for him to have a partner as it is for me to be alone.

The remainder of our day is all uphill, with a steep climb up Barren Mountain. Halfway through the climb, we pick our way up through a rockslide, culminating in a rocky ledge. We stand on house-sized boulders that elevate us above the trees, from where we have dazzling views of the Maine countryside. There are the omnipresent ponds and the gentle contour of low hills carpeted with dense green trees.

Kiwi on the Barren Ledges.

After our nineteen miles of hiking are complete, we still have a half-mile side trail to walk before reaching the lean-to. We arrive as the sky begins to darken. The sun sets about six minutes sooner each day as the season transitions from summer to fall. At 7:20 p.m. it is dark. Cloud Pond Lean-to is yet another in Maine that is paired with a pond.

The moon is illuminating the shelter when I wake up near midnight. Kiwi has a headlamp on and is watching the mice. His pack is hung about a foot from his food bag. The mice drop from the rafters onto the pack and leap from the pack over to the food.

In the morning, Kiwi finds that he has suffered only minor loss of food to the mice. Overnight the temperature fell into the thirties, making for a chilly morning, but shortly into my hiking day I am able to pare down to my shorts and T-shirt. It is excellent hiking weather, and I rarely break a sweat. Hiking in the 100-Mile Wilderness is easier than the hiking in southern Maine, but it is no cakewalk. Short but precipitous ascents and descents continue. I pause when the downhill trail leads into what looks like a rockslide, similar to the rockslide we ascended at the end of the day yesterday. Climbing down will be much more treacherous. The bike accident comes to mind, causing me to think how vulnerable people are and how unfortunate it would be to get hurt here, so close to the end of my hike.

I'm frustrated with the trail at the moment. There seems to be no reason for it to be so precarious. I wish the AT would wind down the mountainside on switchbacks. I'm taking this obstacle personally, as if it was put here with the intent to trip me up. I'd like to hurl every expletive I know at the trail at this moment. Kiwi comes up behind me and says, in his genteel New Zealand accent, "It's quite steep here, isn't it?" His statement is so understated it makes me laugh. After working our way down the mountain, I stop to take a long break and regroup. I encourage Kiwi to continue on, and I spend time writing.

Late in the afternoon I reach the Pleasant River. It is the widest river since the Kennebec, and there is no ferry.

It is twenty-five yards across, but studded with enough rock to give me hope of crossing without getting wet. I progress stepping from rock to rock, easily at first, then having to make longer jumps. I come to an impasse tantalizingly close to the far shore. I backtrack and then try to advance picking rocks a bit more upriver. Again, I am thwarted just fifteen feet from the north shore.

I return all the way to the shore where I started, change into my rubber clog camp shoes, and begin to wade across. The water is numbingly cold, and my ankles immediately start to ache with the curious pain induced by cold. The clear water in the deepest part of the river is deeper than I expected. It is up to my knees and is threatening the hem of my shorts. I'd like to hurry across, but the push of the water is surprisingly strong. I try to spear my trekking poles into the river bed for support, but the current slaps them away as soon as they touch the surface. The power of the river nearly dislodges one of my clogs. I wiggle my foot back into place and shuffle the rest of the way across the river.

Awol rock-hopping the Pleasant River.

On the north bank, I quickly put socks and shoes on my wet, blue feet. Beyond the Pleasant River the trail is smooth and takes a gradual upslope. I walk alone in the quiet woods and ponder the difficulties of my day. I think myself unfit for this hike, being so susceptible to cold and being discombobulated by the rockslide descent earlier. I want to give myself no credit for hiking two thousand miles; I am just the beneficiary of favorable conditions. The "cold" weather, as I perceive it now, is mild for Maine at this time of year, and I have been fortunate to have little rain to deal with since leaving Vermont.

My arrival makes for a full house at the Carl Newhall Lean-to. Kiwi is here, along with some weekend hikers, and I am surprised and pleased to see Biscuit once again. Her boyfriend, whom she has dubbed Grasshopper, has joined her for a week of hiking. A huge campfire is raging in front of the shelter, and the weekend hikers are throwing all of their trash, flammable or not, into the fire.

In the morning I wake to see Biscuit picking shriveled lumps of plastic and foil from the pit. Kiwi has already left, and Biscuit and Grasshopper leave before I am packed. The lean-to is located partway up the south face of White Cap Mountain. Immediately leaving the shelter, the AT steeply resumes the ascent of the mountain. It is a rocky and challenging walk, and I catch up with Grasshopper and Biscuit sooner than I expect. Grasshopper is standing with his hands on his hips, panting for breath. Biscuit is ahead of him, looking back over her shoulder, as if waiting for him to continue hiking. They are not talking, and neither says anything as I pass. I assume they may have been arguing, or that Biscuit was impatient with having to go at a slower pace. It would be difficult for any visitor to keep up with a thru-hiker at this stage.

I am moving a bit faster today, eager to get my first look at Mount Katahdin. My anticipation builds as I can see the trail peaking the crest ahead. At the top, I am disappointed to find that it is a secondary summit. The trail descends again before heading up the major summit of White Cap Mountain. Near the top, the incline of the trail lessens and bends to my right to make a more gradual, teasing approach to the top. I am not sure if my bearing is east or north, or if Katahdin is east, west, or north of White Cap. About the only place I know I can rule out spotting Katahdin is directly behind me. I am above timberline, scanning everywhere I can see and craning my head to peer over the shoulder of the mountain that I am on at this moment. My pace has quickened, as if Katahdin might sneak away if I don't rush to get a glimpse. I see some distant peaks, and I give each a good look, not knowing how "the Big K" will appear from this distance. Nothing stands out. I reach the peak of White Cap and see that the trail curves left and descends on a gradual side-hill course. I now have a clear view to my left, and there it is! Mount Katahdin stands out as a bulking, unambiguous monolith even when viewed seventy-two trail miles from its summit.

Content already with my day, I ease down to Logan Brook Lean-to on the north face of White Cap and take a lengthy lunch break. From there, I meander down to East Branch Lean-to, where I catch up with Kiwi once again. We are relaxed, put at ease by the sight of Katahdin. We really have made it. There are minor hills to climb, but they get progressively lower, diminishing like attenuating waves—the last ripples of the mountain range.

Kiwi and I are feeling hunger after three long days, and we talk about the food we enjoy "back home." Fish and chips is the most popular meal in New Zealand. I crave volume—all-you-can-eat-buffet food cooked three hours ago in five-gallon trays and warmed by heat lamps. I want to go to a place that has a dessert bar where patrons cut their own servings from a slab of cake, and I can come along and scoop up all the crumbs and oodles of leftover icing.

We stop at Cooper Brook Falls Lean-to. Cooper Brook Falls cascades into a wide pool of water in front of the shelter. A section hiker named David is also staying in the lean-to. He will be ending his hike sooner than planned and gives me a day's worth of food. I cook freeze-dried spaghetti.

Biscuit and Grasshopper come in around midnight, walking under the light of the full moon. Biscuit is quick to apologize for their reticence earlier in the day. It is September 11, and they had decided to observe the day with silence.

I cannot get back to sleep. I recall events of my thru-hike. I think about the conclusion of the trip, what it might feel like to finish, and what I'll do when I get back home. I dismiss some of the anxiety I had in Gorham over the lack of change effected by my trip. The radical break from routine that I made in coming on this adventure unloaded the attic of my mind. Everything that I had stored away, out of habit, I've taken out and reexamined. I've yet to rearrange, toss things out, and repack. But most important, I should not treat this journey simply as an agent for change. It is an experience in and of itself. I am unequivocally pleased doing this.

I am the first to leave in the morning. Less than a mile from the lean-to I see a mother bear with two nearly grown cubs. One cub climbs a tree, but he seems too heavy to get very high or hang on for long. Realizing the tactic is doing him little good, he jumps down and runs away.

The trail is level and smooth, and I speed along, all the way to Antlers Campsite. I read the guidebook mileage and

I'm able to determine that my pace is nearly four miles per hour. Just beyond the campsite, I find a rock the size of a bench and sit for a break. The forest looks ancient. Bark on the trees has accumulated moss and has deep fissures, akin to the age-spotting and wrinkling of aged humans. The added texture gives the trees character with no loss of vitality. They look like survivors, resilient and deeply rooted.

I dawdle, waiting for Kiwi. Now I am the one who enjoys having a hiking partner. I plan to end my day at a hostel called Whitehouse Landing. When I last spoke with Kiwi, he had not yet decided if he would stop there. Kiwi arrives, and we hike together to Pemadumcook Lake, where we get our second look at Mount Katahdin. The lake is shallow near this shore; large boulders protrude from the lake, far out into the water. Above the water, there is a band of dark green—the trees on the far shore—and then there is the ghostly lump of Katahdin, the only land visible above the trees. The color of the mountain is dulled by distance, but the timberline is distinct. The rocks atop the mountain give it the appearance of being capped by snow.

Two miles later, we reach the mile-long side trail to the hostel. Kiwi has decided to come along. At the end of the trail, we reach a boat dock on the extensive shoreline of Pemadumcook Lake, the same lake from which we had the earlier view of Katahdin. Whitehouse Landing is on the other side of the lake. There is an air horn on the boat dock; we give it a blast and Bill, the owner of the hostel, comes to ferry us across in a motorboat. Whitehouse Landing is a complex with multiple cabins alongside the bunkroom where we stay. The modest main building serves as the office, lodge, camp store, and dining area. A lazy hound dog is a fixture on the porch. Kiwi and I are the only guests tonight. Bill tells us that his place is also an ice fishing outpost in the winter.

There is no electricity or public phone, but there are propane-heated showers and battery-powered lights.

Bill cooks us one-pound hamburgers for dinner. "Would you like cheese on that?"

"Of course." The hamburger is a mess to eat, but it is delicious. For dessert, I have a New England whoopie pie. It is made with two bun-shaped pieces of chocolate cake and creamy frosting sandwiched between. It is as large as the hamburger.

At sunset Kiwi and I take the canoe out on the lake. We row far enough out on the choppy lake to get another view of Katahdin's peak. The sky on the western horizon is pink with the last traces of sun, and it transitions upward through shades of mauve, purple, and blue. Directly overhead, the sky is deep blue; panning down to the east, the hue darkens and stars are already visible. Darkness comes early and fast, too hurried, like a drawn curtain. My hike is nearly over.

In the morning, Bill gives Kiwi and me a boat ride back to the trail, and we hike on together. The AT takes a crabwise route to Katahdin, winding around lakes and ponds, which gives us views of the mountain from different angles. Nesuntabunt Mountain is the only climb of the day. It is an unusually twisting, disorienting climb. We stop for lunch on top, where we have a "side" view of Katahdin. The postcard view of Katahdin, which I arbitrarily deem to be the "front," shows the mountain broadside, with a barely discernible center summit and symmetrical summits on the shoulders that are nearly as high. From Nesuntabunt, Katahdin looks narrower and taller.

When we return to the trail, I am in front.

"Where are you going?" Kiwi asks.

"This is the trail, isn't it?" I answer.

"Yes, but you are going back the way we came."

"Are you sure?"

"Quite sure."

I feel certain about my choice, but there really is no way to be sure. Both paths seem to lead away from Katahdin. Since we are at the top of a mountain, both ways go downhill. I reluctantly follow Kiwi's direction since he seems more certain than I am. It takes me more than a quarter of a mile to be convinced of our direction, but he is right.

After descending Nesuntabunt, the trail levels and runs parallel to a gorge. A wide stream flows in the center of the gorge ten to thirty feet below us as the land undulates and the stream maintains its gradual downhill course. The coming of fall is increasingly evident; we crunch through fallen leaves, and the maple trees, still holding on to their red and yellow leaves, stand out like torches. Along with Kiwi, Ken, and Marcia, I set up my tarp next to Rainbow Lake. Loons on the lake make calls that sound as if they are blown from a flute. This will be my last night on the trail.

Way back in Hiawassee, I had cut eighty-five pages of mileage data loose from my guidebook. I keep the most current page in a Ziploc bag and tuck it in my pants pocket. I start the day by paring down to the last sheet. My goal is to get to the base of Katahdin and then hitch out to the town of Millinocket, where I'll wait for my family before hiking the final five miles of trail.

I leave camp and hike alone, quickly reaching Rainbow Ledges, a rocky cliff from where I get one last look at Katahdin before the trail submerges into the woods for the next six miles. Abol Bridge marks the end of the 100-Mile Wilderness. From the bridge, I pause to take in the new perspective of Katahdin. This is the postcard view, the unobstructed front, the broadside view of the mountain. I can see every crag and ridge, all the way down to where the mountain merges with the humble flat of trees before it.

There is a camp store near the bridge. I stop in to get my fill of food before tackling the remainder of the day. I see a newspaper with an update on Hurricane Isabel, an Atlantic storm that Juli had told me about when I was in Monson. Five days ago, the storm was a latent threat far out in the Caribbean. The storm is more worrisome now since it has yet to turn northerly. Like most Atlantic storms, it is potentially a threat to the entire East Coast, which could affect my home in Florida, my family's flight to Maine, or the weather here when I climb Katahdin two days from now. Ken, Marcia, and Kiwi arrive at the store while I am loitering, and we all proceed into Baxter State Park together.

There is a sign-up sheet at the park entry to ration the limited camping and shelter space within the park. A large sign is above the sign-up sheet so it will not escape our attention. Kiwi and I get our picture taken in front of the sign, conferring our own meaning upon the notice that reads, "Important: A.T. Thru-Hikers."

The trail is scenic within the park, for much of the way running parallel to the Penobscot River, the same river I crossed on the Abol Bridge. But my excitement wanes. The trail alongside the river is deeply rutted and rocky. My feet feel bruised, and I have seven more miles to walk, on top of fourteen that I've walked already. Our circuitous route through the park is actually taking us further away from Mount Katahdin. It looked so close from the bridge. The trail turns away from the Penobscot and follows a tributary upstream. The stream that we now follow, the Nesowadnehunk, is a wide stream cascading over massive boulders. I no longer appreciate the scenery; I just want my day to end. The threat of Hurricane Isabel weighs on me, and worries darken my mood.[40]

---

40   Isabel made landfall in North Carolina on September 18. None of my concerns materialized. "*When I look back on all the worries, I remember the story of the old man who said on his deathbed that he had a lot of trouble in his life, most of which never happened.*"—Winston Churchill

We come to a spot where a huge slab of bedrock slopes from our shoreline out into the stream, funneling the water into a cascade near the far side. Kiwi and I walk out and sit on the slab, essentially in midstream of this thirty-foot-wide creek. Other hikers are sliding with the cascade down the rock face, splashing into a pool of water below. Kiwi gives me half of a honeybun he purchased back at the Abol Bridge camp store, trying to cheer me up. Kiwi has been a great hiking partner, always positive, considerate, and sharing. I part with Kiwi at Katahdin Stream Campground. He will stay here tonight and conclude his hike tomorrow. He promises to look me up in Millinocket.

Luckily for me, Bob and Gloria Nicholson are descending from Katahdin just as I arrive, and they offer me a ride to town. They are from Maine and have driven out to hike up the mountain today. Their son thru-hiked in 2000.[41] They give me a tour of the town of Millinocket, which is more spread out than most trail towns. I stay at the AT Lodge, a bunkroom on Main Street.

I call Juli and we discuss our plans for her arrival in two days. She tells me that if it looks like the weather will change for the worse, I should go ahead and hike Katahdin by myself. I have been fortunate to have had excellent weather over the past week, and for the moment, it looks as if favorable weather will continue. Also, my day was exhausting. In the eight days since leaving Caratunk, I have averaged over eighteen miles per day. I am ready for two days of rest.

On my first day in Millinocket, I do laundry and eat well, like I've always done in town while on this hike. I visit the grocery store, but I really don't need any supplies. My last day on Mount Katahdin will be a day hike. I have no plans to make, and I miss the responsibility. I meet Kiwi at the

41   Bob "Now or Never" would go on to thru-hike himself in 2004.

Appalachian Trail Café just as he arrives in town. We sit for dinner (Kiwi orders fish and chips), and he tells me of his climb up Katahdin in perfect weather. Palpable excitement makes my retired friend seem like a schoolboy.

I spend my second day milling about town, waiting impatiently. The weather is overcast, and there are intermittent showers. I worry that I have missed the opportunity to end my hike on a clear day. Kiwi has headed home, but Ken and Marcia are still in town when my family arrives, and I am happy that they get to meet them. My youngest daughter, Lynn, is five years old, Rene is eight, and Jessie is nine. Juli's brothers have also made the trip. Mark is older than Juli, and Mike is two years younger.

Juli, Jessie, and Mike will hike the last five miles of the trail with me. We are awake and on the road before sunrise, making the twenty-mile drive to Baxter State Park. Nearing the park, the strip of road cuts a channel through the trees. A bear runs across the road. We can see Katahdin, perfectly centered in the swath cleared of trees. The side of the peak to our right is tinted gold with sunlight. The top of the mountain is the first piece of land in the United States touched by the morning sun.

At Katahdin Stream Campground, the weather is ideal, cloudless and about fifty degrees. We start at 7:15 a.m. The trail is densely wooded, "like a jungle," Jessie says. The footpath is moderately inclined uphill, somewhat smooth with only scattered rocks. Birch trees have dropped a coating of brown and yellow leaves on the trail. We cross Katahdin Stream and Falls on a footbridge. After a couple of miles, Jessie begins to tire, which is troubling because the most difficult climbing is still ahead. Mike volunteers to turn back, but Jessie is not yet ready to give up.

As we progress, the trail gets steeper, and the boulders get larger. One section reminds me of Mahoosuc Notch;

there are huge boulders gathered in a depression, mixed in with trees. We pick our way through and move higher. Jessie perks up with the change of terrain. She likes using her hands and wriggling through the rocks. Once above timberline, we feel a brisk, cold wind. I can see an un-bounded view of the Maine wilderness. Boulders are steep and precarious, especially with the wind. Rebar handholds are implanted into a few of them. Jessie hugs tight to the mountain when the wind gusts. Again, we stop to assess the wisdom of continuing with her. She's never done anything like this before. Getting down may be as difficult as going up. We are progressing very slowly. Most of the other hikers headed to the top of Katahdin via the AT started earlier or have already passed us. We proceed. Jessie is game, and there are three of us to help her. Someone nearly always has a hand on her in this stretch, supporting her from below or pulling from above. There is a solid mile of hand-over-hand climbing.

Juli, Jessie, and Awol headed up Katahdin.

Thru-hiking has been more of a challenge than I expected. Always, there were exhausting climbs and bone-jarring descents. The amount of elevation gain and loss on the AT is equivalent to climbing up and down Mount Everest sixteen times. The terrain was a greater impediment than I would have anticipated. Slippery roots and foot-bruising rocks slowed me more than any other factor. Rain, cold weather, and hot days would compound obstacles and make work of the easiest days. Countless days I struggled into camp with burning feet, aching knees, and soaking wet clothes. I won't miss stuffing blistered feet into stiff, muddy trail shoes.

But the pleasure and contentment I felt on the trail far outweighed the adversity. Even on the most exasperating days, I never considered quitting. The most uncertainty I had about continuing was when I had injuries: a sore knee, an infected foot, and a sprained ankle. Those injuries tested my resolve, but ultimately reinforced my desire to continue. Possibly it was a motivational advantage for me to be attempting a thru-hike in my particular circumstance: not young, not single, not retired, and not rich. If I left the trail, I couldn't try again next year. It was a one-shot deal. I am lucky to have experienced it all—the awe of seeing spectacular landscapes, the excitement of encounters with wildlife, and the invigoration of a physical lifestyle. It was always a treat to descend into one of the tiny towns the trail goes through, to get cleaned up, and emerge replenished.

Beyond the worst of the bouldering on Katahdin, we see a summit ahead, a pointed mound of rock piercing the unclouded blue sky. The trail follows a ridge up to this summit, a ridge like the edge of a pyramid, studded with boulders. The views are fantastic. I take photos from atop a boulder, thinking how the view before me is perfectly composed. Then I move forward fifty yards and have the same thought again. Hikers tend to speak of the mountain for its symbolic value as an endpoint of the Appalachian Trail, and not enough is said about the mountain's autonomous appeal. Mount Katahdin is the most picturesque mountain on the trail. It presents itself wonderfully from a distance. The views from the trail on the mountain itself are enthrallingly diverse. The landscape before me now is beautiful in its simplicity, grandeur, and immutability. It will be equally beautiful in the winter and in the summer. It will look the same next year and one hundred years from now.

The trail up Hunt Spur. Mike and Jessie are in the foreground.

For me, hiking up this mountain seems nearly effort-less. Perhaps it is because I am traveling at the pace of my group, the distracting beauty, or the excitement of finishing. On reaching the peak of our pyramid, we see that it is only the shoulder of the mountain. There is a nearly level expanse before us, with entirely new terrain, similar to a glacial plateau. This feature of Katahdin is called the tableland. The surface is peppered with rocks, but they are almost uniformly flat, low to the ground, and spotted with olive-green lichen. Alpine shrubbery coats the ground where rocks do not protrude. The shrubbery is as dense and as tight to the ground as grass, but it has a rusty brown color.

Mike, Juli, and Jessie crossing Katahdin tableland.

We see hikers who passed us earlier in the day, now on their way down. We yell congratulations over the howl of the wind. I recognize Dutch, Chief, and Dreamwalker. They are cheerful, talkative, and emotional. More than one of the hikers has red, watery eyes from a tearfully joyful summit. So much has happened over the past 2,172 miles. I have come through fourteen states, seen twenty-one bears, lost eight toenails, and gone through six pairs of shoes.

The work is behind us. The trail across the table-land is an easy walk, gently uphill. I'm proud of Jessie for climbing the mountain with me. Nearing the peak, the wind dies down. There are a hundred yards of trail up one last mound of rock to the mile-high summit. Hikers are taking celebratory photos behind the simple wood sign on top with a backdrop of blue skies: "KATAHDIN—Northern terminus of the Appalachian Trail." Even though the end has been on my mind for the past few weeks, finishing seems abrupt. This is it: 146 days of unforgettable scenery, seemingly endless miles of trail, rain, pain, and friendships. It's over.

There are no more miles to walk.

Epilogue

Awol at the end of his thru-hike, September 17, 2003.

Upon my return from the trail, friends, coworkers, and even an occasional stranger would stop to talk. "That was quite an accomplishment. Not many people do that—you must be proud." I was often uncomfortable, at a loss for how to respond. This was nice to hear, and it is considerate of people to congratulate me. But pride is not at the forefront of my feelings about my hike. I do not think of it as an accomplishment. I feel fortunate for what I have experienced.

My daughters, especially my youngest, missed me. Being away from home for long stretches cannot be a way of life.

Still, it is important for parents to continue to live their own lives. We can't sit by and say we've already made our decisions, done our striving, and dish out opinions on the doings of our children. Words alone lack authority, and we risk making them surrogates for the life we'd like to lead. We can better relate to the budding aspirations of our children if we follow dreams of our own.

I missed the trail increasingly over the first few months I was back home, and then the feeling matured to a combination of fondness, loss, nostalgia, and longing. Some moments on the trail were awe-inspiring. Many days were full of picturesque moments: the path lined with blue wildflowers, areas overrun by blooming pink rhododendron and white mountain laurel, the beckoning trail weaving through trees and boulders, the smell of the firs, exposed summits showing limitless horizon of mountains, rolling fields of hay and corn with an old barn in the backdrop. My mind is saturated with these memories. They return to my consciousness unsummoned, while I'm driving or sitting at my desk.

In 2004 I returned to the AT to hike from Erwin to Damascus during the week of Trail Days. The trail was still very familiar; I could tell when it was about to bend, go up, or go down. I would spot a rock where I had sat to take a break—one rock out of millions spread over 2,172 miles. At the same time I felt removed, like my hike that ended less than a year earlier was in the distant past. I felt a tinge of loneliness, unlike anything I felt during my thru-hike. I stayed at Overmountain Shelter. It was empty when I arrived. I could nearly hear the voices, ghosts of the previous year, buzzing with excitement over what we had learned, how far we had come, and what lay ahead. I thought of what I would have been doing during my thru-hike—writing my journal, reviewing photos, reading the guidebook so I'd know what to look for in the next few days. And I was sad that I no longer had to do those things. The whole timeline of my adventure came back to me: initially being intrigued with the idea, reading about it, taking practice hikes, trepidation of the start, excitement of being under way, even fondness for the drudgery of the middle ground, anticipation of heading into heralded locations, and contentment of travel when I knew the end was at hand. I had done it, written about it, and now it is history.

Of course pining for the past is part of life, not uniquely an AT experience. But the strength of that emotion— evoked when I moved away from my childhood home and again upon finishing college—I had not felt for years. Those were transitional events during emotionally sensitive adolescence. Now I am grown up, hardened, and yet still affected. There is redemption in sadness. It tells me that for nearly five months in 2003, I lived life with the open, raw, refreshing outlook of the young.

The payoff, though difficult to quantify, is much greater than I expected. I have no regrets about having gone; it was the right thing to do. I think about it every day. Sometimes I can hardly believe it happened. I just quit, and I was on a monumental trip. I didn't suffer financial ruin, my wife didn't leave me, the world didn't stop spinning. I do think of how regrettable it would have been had I ignored the pull that I felt to hike the trail. A wealth of memories could have been lost before they had even occurred if I had dismissed, as a whim, my inkling to hike. It is disturbing how tenuous our potential is due to our fervent defense of the comfortable norm.

As a result of my hike, I am much more inclined to *do* things. I will have fewer "should have dones," even if it means incurring some "wish I hadn'ts." I have changed in smaller ways, too. I am friendlier and more patient. I worry less about money. I can get by with less. It is as pleasing to get rid of old stuff as it is to get new stuff. Excess is a burden, even when you are not carrying it on your back.

And in a way, I do feel proud. I feel proud of the positive influence I've had on my circle of friends. One friend took a month's leave from her job to sail as a crew member on a replica of Columbus's ship *Nina*.

She told me, "It [your hike] made me feel like it was okay, like I was getting permission to go. I had the impression that things like this are irresponsible. But then, when I saw someone like you who is responsible do it, I felt okay. It is not unreasonable or selfish; it is healthy."

When she asked her boss for a leave, he said he had read about a guy who had to quit his job to hike the AT. Her boss thought it would be a great adventure for her and that she wouldn't have to quit her job to go.

Another woman took up long morning walks and got more fit than she had been in years. Yet another friend ran a half marathon. He said I inspired him to pursue an extraordinary personal quest.

Now I am more comfortable talking with people about my experience. When they say, "I would love to do something like that," I know how to respond.

"You can."

Afterword

Since writing *AWOL on the Appalachian Trail*, I've received a number of messages from readers who tell me that they've been inspired to hike the AT. Clearly these readers have not paid attention to what I've written. The book is replete with tales of misery: a sprained ankle, lost toenails, blisters, and a longer list of minor inconveniences. Often I've thought that if I could change anything about the book, it would be to present a more upbeat perspective on the hike. With this updated edition of *AWOL on the Appalachian Trail*, I had the opportunity to change it, but I have not. Instead, I've chosen to believe that readers, far from being inattentive, do perccive the underrepresented truth that hiking the AT was an overwhelmingly positive experience.

For readers who are not to be deterred, here are the questions that I've most often been asked:

What gear did you use?

A complete list of my gear is on the Web site www.AwolOn-TheTrail.com. The list should be considered notional because new and better choices are now available, although I still hike some every year and take essentially the same gear. At the time of my thru-hike, having a cell phone on the trail was anathema. I carried one at the start of my hike, hardly got any use from it, and sent it home after a few weeks. Cell phones are becoming standard gear because reception is increasing and pay phones are dwindling. Smart phones have become multipurpose tools that can also serve as a GPS, compass, and journal. Learn to use your gear before leaving, because you won't want to carry manuals. Or make more use of your smart phone by loading it with manuals.

Electronic devices, such as your camera, phone, and watch, are worthy of special attention. If your watch or phone has an alarm, be sure it is off before settling into a shelter or other common sleeping area. Take the best camera that you can afford and are willing to carry. Learn how to shoot the types of pictures that you will take on the trail: close-ups of flowers; wildlife in dense, low-light woods where a flash will have a spotlight effect; hikers sitting around a campfire. Know how to use the camera's timer or remote to take a photo of yourself alone at a scenic overlook. Take a minitripod and learn techniques for propping and stabilizing your camera.

What does it cost?

In 2003, five thousand dollars would be a good baseline. Most hikers will spend more on the gear and town stops to make the trip comfortable, and some frugal hikers will get by on less.

Opportunity cost—the income that you won't earn while hiking—is the largest expense of thru-hiking. Hiking is as cheap as any vacation that you can take. Virtually every night's stay can be free, and there's enough food left in hiker boxes to eat for free. No one does this, though, as the pull of a hot shower, soft bed, and "real" food is strong. A reasonable plan might be to factor in the cost of a hotel or hostel stay and a few restaurant meals every week. A thru-hike will last fifteen to thirty weeks.

The big three gear items—pack, tent, and sleeping bag—can all be had for less than two hundred dollars each. All the gear that I started with added up to about a thousand dollars. However, I purchased an equal amount of gear that I tested and chose not to take, and I bought more gear along the way.

What's the hardest part of the trail?
I have little doubt that with similar weather conditions and hiker fitness, slowest progress would be made through the White Mountains and southern Maine. Here the trail has its steepest ascents and descents, along with rugged, rocky terrain.

But conditions are not always the same, so the hardest part of a thru-hike is not easily predictable. The struggle to get in trail shape can outweigh initial enthusiasm. Dealing with bad weather, sickness, or injury can make any part of the trail a challenge. Emotional challenges are no less real. For some, the novelty of walking through the woods, mostly alone, without modern conveniences, is a novelty that wears off. The hardest part of thru-hiking can be dealing with loneliness, missing life as it was back home, or the temptation to jump into new endeavors.

For me, trudging through central Virginia was difficult. Reaching Virginia was a nice landmark, but then it seemed like work to register further progress. There was a rainy spell, and I had to take time off to nurse an infected blister. A too-brief visit from my family gave me a taste of what I was missing.

What's your favorite part of the trail?
I most enjoyed my time on the trail in Maine. There were many treeless summits from which I could see a seemingly endless forest generously dotted with ponds. The trail through the White Mountains is similar but more austere, with fewer bodies of water. The section of trail from Roan Mountain through Hump Mountain was memorable for its grassy balds. The trail in and near Grayson Highlands is unique and remarkable.

Did you ever feel like quitting?
No. There's a subtle distinction between hardship and amusement, and I more often assumed the latter. My age was an asset. I was old enough to realize the limits of my time, and I was in no rush to abandon an experience for which I might not have another opportunity. I always saw the trying moments as a component of the endeavor; they never defined it. I wanted the difficulties to end, not my hike. The times when continuing my hike was questionable due to injury strengthened my desire to finish.

Where you ever bored?
Yes. In part, that is the purpose of doing a hike. I keep myself too busy. As I said in chapter 5, hiking was a "forced simpli-fication of my life." We are in an era when the demand for our attention is exploding. TV, e-mail, and the Internet had blossomed before my hike, and in the short time since I've finished, smart phones, Facebook, and Twitter have been

added to the roster. There is a danger that we can confuse being busy with being entertained and being relaxed with being bored. When hiking, we don't just leave behind the customary distractions; we have to escape from our addiction to them. It can be a challenge to form new habits and to draw from within.

Would you do it again?
Yes. This is a reversal of the opinion that I held near the end of my hike, and I admit that I may have succumbed to selective recall. There is much to do on the AT. You cannot see it all in a single trip, and a repeat hike can be a substantially different experience.

What would you do differently?
Take more pictures. Experiment more with different hiking patterns and foods. See new spots, be more attentive. Take better care of my feet. I'd like to plan less and let every day take shape on a whim.

How did the experience change you?
My thoughts on this are unchanged from the epilogue, in which I cited patience, less concern over money, and a greater inclination to do things. I'll add that I did not seek these changes. Change is inevitable on such unique and prolonged endeavors, with one caveat: the journey is no cure-all. Loading it with expectations will increase the odds of a premature end. Issues festering at home will follow hikers onto the trail. If you are broke to begin with, you will be more broke upon your return. When setting out, I wanted a break from my routine; I wanted adventure. I received that, and more.

Did you plan to write a book?

No. I had written biweekly newspaper articles, and I was diligent about writing daily journal entries, but these formats were limiting. I had latent thoughts, things more worthy of discussing, that I could better explore in book format.

What are you doing now?

Since the days of my hike, I had harbored ideas about how a guidebook might be improved. In 2008 I acted on those ideas, and the result is *The A.T. Guide: A Handbook for Hiking the Appalachian Trail.* Development and maintenance of the guidebook consumes too much of my time, but it keeps me in touch with the AT community.

I was rehired to do the same software engineering job that I left. At times I feel stuck, in that I used my quota of time off during my prime working years. At times I feel less tethered, reassured in knowing that I can leave if I choose. I've done it before.

Acknowledgements

Thanks to all the hikers who were on the trail in 2003 who shared and defined my thru-hike experience. Many of my companions reviewed drafts of this book and refreshed my memory of the events. There are too many to list here; I hope I have fairly represented you in the book. Thanks to the ATC, all the other volunteer organizations, and the volunteers who—literally—make the trail.

During my hike I received help from numerous people, most notably Dan and Wilma Kesecker, who put me up while I recovered from injury. Dave Martinage (Arrow, Georgia-Maine 2002) helped with advice, encouragement, food, rides, and a place to stay. Richard Stowell (Bluejay Lafey) gave much-needed help when Juli visited. The Witchers were generous hosts. I appreciate all of the accommodations, often at significant discounts and many times for free, that I received. I am thankful to everyone, especially my co-workers, who gave me feedback, support, and encouragement while I was on the trail.

I thank ZipDrive and Leif, TrailJournals.com webmasters, for providing me with a means of organizing and posting my journal. I owe thanks to Suzy Leonard from the *Florida Today* newspaper for trusting me to report from the trail.

I am grateful for editorial input from John LaChance, Mike Perez, and my sister, Dee Bowman. Steve Wheeler created all the maps that appear in this book, helped with formatting the photographs, and collaborated with me on the cover design.

Thanks, Dad and Mom, for supporting me in every way possible, and Chris, who was with me in many of my early backpacking trips, and for insights into thru-hiking that helped me make the decision to go.

I thank my children, Jessie, Rene, and Lynn, for understanding my absence and for making me want to be a better person.

Last and most importantly, thanks to Juli for agreeing to the adventure, supporting me while I was hiking, and for doing the job of two parents. Juli influenced the content of this book more than any other person. She proofread and provided opinions on every aspect of the book.

About the Author

David Miller is a software engineer and writer. His book *The A.T. Guide*, which is updated annually, is considered a leading guidebook for those wishing to hike the Appalachian Trail. The author, his wife, and their three children reside in Titusville, Florida.